The Poetics of Plot

Theory and History of Literature
Edited by Wlad Godzich and Jochen Schulte-Sasse

Volume 1. Tzvetan Todorov *Introduction to Poetics*

Volume 2. Hans Robert Jauss *Toward an Aesthetic of Reception*

Volume 3. Hans Robert Jauss
Aesthetic Experience and Literary Hermeneutics

Volume 4. Peter Bürger *Theory of the Avant-Garde*

Volume 5. Vladimir Propp *Theory and History of Folklore*

Volume 6. Edited by Jonathan Arac, Wlad Godzich,
and Wallace Martin
The Yale Critics: Deconstruction in America

Volume 7. Paul de Man *Blindness and Insight:*
Essays in the Rhetoric of Contemporary Criticism
2nd ed., rev.

Volume 8. Mikhail Bakhtin *Problems of Dostoevsky's Poetics*

Volume 9. Erich Auerbach
Scenes from the Drama of European Literature

Volume 10. Jean-François Lyotard
The Postmodern Condition: A Report on Knowledge

Volume 11. Edited by John Fekete *The Structural Allegory:*
Reconstructive Encounters with the New French Thought

Volume 12. Ross Chambers *Story and Situation: Narrative Seduction and*
the Power of Fiction

Volume 13. Tzvetan Todorov *Mikhail Bakhtin: The Dialogical Principle*

Volume 14. Georges Bataille, *Visions of Excess: Selected Writings,*
1927-1939

Volume 15. Peter Szondi *On Textual Understanding and Other Essays*

Volume 16. Jacques Attali *Noise*

Volume 17. Michel de Certeau *Heterologies*

Volume 18. Thomas G. Pavel *The Poetics of Plot: The Case of English*
Renaissance Drama

The Poetics
of Plot
The Case of English
Renaissance Drama

Thomas G. Pavel
Foreword by Wlad Godzich

Theory and History of Literature, Volume 18

University of Minnesota Press, Minneapolis

This book has been published with the help of a grant from the Canadian Federation for the Humanities, using funds provided by the Social Sciences and Humanities Research Council of Canada.

Published by the University of Minnesota Press,
2037 University Avenue Southeast, Minneapolis MN 55414
Printed in the United States of America

Library of Congress Cataloging in Publication Data

Pavel, Thomas G., 1941-
    The poetics of plot.
    (Theory and history of literature; v. 18)
    Bibliography: p.
    Includes index.
    1. English drama—Early modern and Elizabethan, 1500-1600—History and criticism. 2. English drama—17th century—History and criticism. 3. Plots (Drama, novel, etc.) 4. English drama (Tragedy)—History and criticism.
I. Title. II. Series.
PR658.P6P38 1985   821'.309'24   84-15663
ISBN 0-8166-1374-5
ISBN 0-8166-1375-3 (pbk.)

Contents

Foreword *Wlad Godzich* vii

Preface xxiii

Chapter One   Introduction 3

Chapter Two   Plot-Grammar: Marlowe's *Tamburlaine I* 25

Chapter Three Semantic Considerations: Narrative Domains 43

Chapter Four   Marlowe — An Exercise in Inconstancy 54

Chapter Five   Two Revenge Tragedies: *The Spanish Tragedy* and *Arden of Feversham* 85

Chapter Six   *King Lear* 99

Chapter Seven *Move*-Grammars and Styles of Plot 115

Appendix   A Few Considerations on the Formalism of *Move*-Grammars 131

Notes 139

References 153

Index 163

Foreword
Where the Action Is
Wlad Godzich

He hadde a cote of crystendome . . .
Ac it was moled in many places with many sondri plottes,
Of pruyde here a plotte, and þere a plotte of vnboxome
     speche.

Piers Plowman

E puor' si muove!

Galileo

In his introduction to *The Poetics of Plot*, Thomas Pavel characterizes his study as a quantitative contribution to the field of formal narrative analysis. Quite rightly he observes that "more often than not, recent plot analysis has operated on relatively simple literary artifacts, such as folktales, short stories, or small poems." By contrast, his study "attempts to demonstrate the fruitfulness of formal analysis when applied to more sophisticated literary products," namely, several well-known English Renaissance plays. The claim is quantitative because it suggests that there is but a difference in degree of sophistication between a Russian wonder-tale of the type analyzed by Vladimir Propp and *King Lear*, the object of Pavel's last chapter; and, speaking strictly from the perspective of formal narrative analysis, there is merit to this view. But, as happens whenever a well-delimited subject is studied with rigor and thoroughness, Pavel's results, implicit and explicit, go well beyond quantitative considerations to address and inform such broad concerns of literary theory and cultural criticism as the role of linguistics in literary studies, the nature and function of agency in plot advancement and in history, and the relation of plot patterns to dominant epistemes. Pavel's clarity of style and lucidity of exposition are such as to require no paraphrase, but the issues that he raises deserve attention.

I

Disciplinary specialization has become so common among us that we accept readily the present division of labor among those who deal with language. In this respect, Thomas Pavel is an anomaly: he is a trained linguist with a background in the philosophy of language; he has written fiction in the form of the philosophical tale,[1] as well as that of modernistic *écriture*;[2] and he is the author of several studies in the field of literature.[3] Such a broad spectrum of activities leads him to cast a different glance upon what many of us take as a given in the present organization of knowledge, and this perspective is reflected in his critical practice, which implies a new set of relations between linguistics and literary studies.

Although interest in matters of language and of verbal art is as old as civilization itself, the institutionalized forms of this interest, which we call linguistics and literary studies, emerged more or less contemporaneously in the second half of the eighteenth century. They did not emerge in a vacuum however, but against the backdrop of another institutional practice that was directly concerned with language: rhetoric. It would have seemed that a modus vivendi could be arrived at between the three disciplines. Linguistics was but a fledgling endeavor then, and it was specifically concerned with the historical aspect of language.[4] Rhetoric was concerned with the social force of language: the study of the effects it could achieve and the means by which it could accomplish them.[5] Literary studies, primarily focused on matters of taste and literary history, were less concerned with the questions of power that rhetoric inevitably encounters than with the constitution of a distinct cultural tradition conceived of as the historical heritage of a nation. Given the historical nature of their respective concerns and the fact that both were more interested in integrative community functions than in polemical tactics, there developed an affinity between literary studies and linguistics, perhaps most evident in ancient and medieval studies, but actually inherent to the great philological project of the nineteenth century. Such a project could be carried out as long as inquiry into language, on the part of the linguists, was primarily concerned with the expressive qualities of specific languages and the determination of hierarchies between them by means of historical derivation and kinship. It also required that literary studies be focused upon the elaboration of so-called national traits and that such traits be shown to be evident in the work of the "great geniuses" of the literature, as well as in the almost unconscious folk productions of the speakers of the language,[6] although, in both instances, these traits would be offset by other features, of "universal" dimension. Both of these concerns were quite alien to rhetoric, and the latter found itself increasingly isolated and eventually eliminated from the school curricula in which it had prominently figured since the establishment of Greek presence in Sicily. However, linguistics and literary studies cannot be said to have shared the spoils of rhetoric since their relation to the older practice had been one of studied indifference. Their respective social functions had been different and did not require them to compete directly with rhetoric, whose social function was clearly in decline. Yet, rhetoric's passing created a vacuum—the study of the social sphere of language—that would prove to be a pitfall to both linguistics and literary studies, and it would come to haunt the relationship of the two younger disciplines.

The positivistic moment in literary studies, when it took hold in the nineteenth century, did so against the background assumption of a broadly shared general culture that did not need to make explicit many of the mechanisms of the actual functioning of literary works and was therefore much more at home examining the role played by individuals in the manipulation of linguistic resources and other cultural codes of the time. When the process of cultural production and reproduction functions optimally for a given social aggregate, considerations of style and individual expression will prevail over considerations of coding and code formation within this aggregate. The aesthetics of genius that is concomitant to positivism did not prevail because of some putative philosophical superiority, but because there obtained a social base for such an aesthetics that was precisely the broad sharing of these cultural codes. The crisis would come when these codes would no longer enjoy widespread social recognition, and it would require that a linguistic type of attention be paid to the functioning of literary writing.

Societies such as those of Spain and even France, in which social stratification was well established and deeply entrenched, would remain positivistic in their literary studies until modernization would begin to affect them, something that did not happen until the late fifties and early sixties in France, which saw then the advent of structuralism, and which began happening in Spain only in the late seventies. But the very same process struck Germany, Russia, England, and the United States much earlier, and in each instance, it led to the emergence of linguistic approaches to literature: the so-called morphological school in Wilhelmine and Weimar Germany, the Formalists in revolutionary Russia, and the New Criticism in the English-speaking countries.

The case of the Formalists is perhaps the most telling one. The very identification of defamiliarization as the fundamental mechanism of literary writing signifies two things of a rather different order: (1) such a mechanism or device can be effective only if there are shared cultural communicative codes between author and audience; (2) something puzzling must have been emerging, inasmuch as the focus of the inquiry was no longer on the individual's manipulation of the codes but on the actual mechanical functioning of the device. This suggests that the process of literary constitution had become at once very obvious and yet very mysterious. It was obvious in its actual workings: it may be unorthodox to say so, but anyone who has read a great deal of Formalist analysis cannot fail to be struck by how commonsensical and easy it really is. It was mysterious because it was beyond the powers of understanding and elucidation of many readers. Why? One reason is that many readers did not have the cultural background and training necessary to understand what they were reading. Accounts of Russian Formalism are written for students of literary theory; they therefore tend to focus on the issues debated between the Formalists and their opponents, all of them part of the intelligentsia, and they generally neglect to remind us of the fact that the Formalists, no less than their opponents on the Left, elaborated their concepts and analytical tools at the time of a vast increase in the literate population of Russia and the Soviet Union. Many of these newly literate individuals were the first in their families to achieve literacy, and they clearly had but vague knowledge at best of the codes of literary constitution that had been elaborated for a social class quite distinct from their own. They were in need of analytical approaches to the actual functioning of literary texts, much as the G.I. Bill of Rights-supported students in the United States were. Whether consciously or not, the Formalists, like their later counterparts among the American New Critics, began to provide such approaches, relying upon the demonstrated descriptive power of linguistics to do so.[7]

A rhetorical analysis, attentive to matters of manipulation, effect, and power, would have been appropriate—though it remains to be seen to what extent the scope of rhetoric is limited to a single cultural sphere—but instead, in a gesture that was to be repeated in all the other instances, linguistics was called upon. What was it that linguistics could offer? Most prominently, a scientific aura: a set of respectable and verifiable procedures that did not depend upon the idiosyncratic qualities of their performer for their successful execution. In other words, linguistics bracketed away the subject of the linguistic enterprise to focus exclusively upon the object. There lies the vaunted objectivity of linguistics, which appealed so much to the literary scholars of the first decade of the Soviet Union, who were faced with an increasingly heterogeneous population of readers. To be sure, there were some voices, most notably those of the Bakhtin circle,[8] that were raised in opposition to such a reductionist move, but they were a minority. The very same process was to take place in French structuralism some forty years later.

The paradigmatic moment in the French case is the one in which Roland Barthes launched his highly successful revisionist version of Saussurean semiology. Ferdinand de Saussure, it will be recalled, was far too prudent to make inordinate territorial claims on behalf of the science of linguistics that he was then codifying. He therefore assigned to something that he called "semiology" all the questions of social functioning that would remain outside of linguistics. In effect, Saussure was making semiology the heir to the abandoned tradition of rhetoric, this being most evident in his summary definition of semiology as a branch of social psychology. However, whereas rhetoric was based upon the notion of the proper, in the dual sense of the appropriate and of that which characteristically belongs to something—that is, it was still beholden to a problematics of mimesis—semiology would be based upon notions of difference and displacement, thus disrupting the mimetic ordering,[9] and, as the modifier "social" in front of psychology suggests, it would be resolutely sociohistorical in its concerns. Barthes, as is well known, radically reversed this vision. Basing his views upon the empirical observation that, at the time of his writing, linguistics alone among the possible semiological enterprises seemed to have undergone any genuine development, Barthes claimed that henceforth all further semiological studies would have to conform to the linguistic model of inquiry.[10] This act of revision, seemingly dictated by the unequal development of semiological studies, appears innocent enough, and the immediate gain is quite obvious: the analytical procedures of linguistics, many of its terminological coinages, its notational conventions, and indeed some of its theoretical orientations, were taken over wholesale, not only by semiology but by nonsemiological structuralist approaches, frequently with little consideration or even awareness of the problems that arise in connection with the transposition of terms and procedures generated within one field of inquiry to another. Linguists did attempt to sound some warnings but, by and large, they went unheeded, and, paradoxically enough, what was taken by many literary scholars as evidence of a great and fruitful rapprochement between linguistics and their own discipline, was seen by many linguists as the confirmation of the existence of an unbridgeable chasm between these two disciplines.

Barthes's revisionism had greater consequences still. It well-nigh obliterated the sociopsychological dimension of semiology, since, in the reversal of determination between linguistics and semiology, the dimension of the sociopsychological lost its theoretical raison d'être. Given Barthes's personal social and psychological interests, and given the structure of the problematic thus occulted, this dimension would reemerge both in Barthes and in semiotics but in a form that one is tempted to describe as pathological. The famous problematics of desire, pleasure, and the subject, which is so important to the later Barthes, could be seen as the return of this repressed dimension in a guise determined by its repression: the problematics of the individual subject without any social dimension.

It is, of course, precisely in this realm of the subject, of desire, of pleasure, and of language's centrality, that structuralism proved most vulnerable to the critiques of the various poststructuralisms. Despite their considerable differences, the strictures of Derrida, Foucault, Lacan, de Man, Lyotard, and Deleuze, to cite but some of the most prominent, all display an extraordinary awareness of linguistic operations at a level that exceeds both the formal approaches of linguistics and the more hermeneutical practices of literary studies, and indeed their arguments rely heavily upon rhetorical operations in their own constitution. In the light of the devastating power of these critiques, there are many among literary scholars who have come to think that linguistics has little if any contribution to make to literary studies.[11] Such a view is just as wrongheaded, in my judgment, as the one that claimed linguistics as a model for literary studies. For one thing, it betrays more ignorance about what has been going on in linguistics than anyone who deals with verbal artifacts ought to be comfortable with.

The structuralist view of linguistics was surprisingly selective and far from up-to-date in its awareness of ongoing linguistic research. The references in structuralism to Saussure, Trubetzkoy, Jakobson, the Prague School, Hjelmslev, and Benvéniste, were striking in their omission of the work of Anglo-American linguists. In some respects, the situation paralleled a similar omission of Anglo-American philosophy. Although the emergence of structuralism is contemporaneous with the relatively short-lived hegemony of the Chomskyan version of transformational generative grammar, references to the latter are very rare in structuralist studies, and rarer still are attempts to use its procedures in literary analysis.[12] Not that I wish to urge the adoption of such a course presently. Rather, I wish to point out that the course of evolution in the field of linguistics since the heydays of, let us say, Chomsky's *Aspects of Syntax*, shows some rather remarkable convergences with the evolution and present positions of literary studies, in spite of rather different points of departure and orientation.

The chief difference between the structural linguistics upon which structuralism rested and the Anglo-American linguistics that gave rise to Chomskyan linguistics is to be found in their tackling of the question of where the linguistic operations described in their theories take place. Characteristically, the Continental tradition is silent upon this score, being content with the description of the operations,[13] and thus it progressively gives rise in its descriptions to a notion of language as an entity endowed with the ability to function as an autotelic agent. By contrast, the Anglo-American schools draw upon their own philosophical tradition and locate these operations in the mind—a philosopheme that, conceived of in the form of the Cartesian Cogito and its subsequent avatars, has been subject to harrowing critique in Continental thought, but in its Anglo-American version continues to enjoy considerable status. My purpose is not to consider, let alone resolve, this curious happenstance of comparative cultural history, but to point out the consequences for linguistics and for theories of language.

A familiar argument for the existence of the mind is "that if you hear a bang and see a flash, you don't *hear* or *see* the simultaneity because you don't see the bang or hear the flash: so, it is argued, there must be something else, besides sight and hearing, that takes in the seeing and the hearing."[14] This something else is the mind. When Chomsky began to formulate his theory of language, he began by noting the extraordinary creative capacity that we, as humans, possess, which allows us to make up sentences that are understood by our interlocutors even though these are sentences that neither we as speakers or they as hearers may have ever heard uttered before.

Imitation of a mechanical nature and conditioning could not provide the explanation for this ability, Chomsky concluded, and he proceeded to take this ability to create new but grammatical sentences as evidence of an innate linguistic competence.

This notion of competence has to be understood in relation to two other notions—and not just one as is generally assumed. The one that is usually acknowledged, not least by Chomsky himself, even though he has proven unable so far to indicate its mode of articulation to competence, is the notion of performance, which designates the realm of the actual realizations of sentences. The second, which is more important for what concerns us here, is the notion of general intelligence. Chomsky means competence to differ from a general intelligence by which we would acquire our linguistic ability. He argues that there is a specialized module of the mind—which itself consists, in this view, of a large set of such modules—that deals with language. Each module is quite distinct from the others and there is no transfer from one module to another.[15] Hence the human linguistic capability must be innate and is not subject to learning since learning would presuppose the mediation of an intermediate module. Such mediation is presupposed in the notion of general intelligence, which obviously accommodates itself better to theories of language acquisition.

The argument may seem abstruse, but much is at stake here, and it does not appear to admit of empirical resolution, given the highly idealized form that competence takes in Chomsky's descriptions of it. Yet the very program of linguistic inquiry is at stake here. As J. Margolis puts it in his very apposite discussion of these issues:

In effect, if reference, speech acts contexts, nonlinguistic factors of experience and behavior, social practices, and semantic and pragmatic aspects of linguistic use essentially affect the development of the grammar of a natural language—if the "surface" and "deep" features of a language cannot be systematically sorted to insure the independence of innate generative rules, or if the syntactic dimension of language cannot be insured as a measure of autonomy relative to aspects of language clearly dependent on contingent learning, or if the systems of competence and performance cannot be independently sorted—then, in Chomsky's view, "language is a chaos." Of course, it would not be chaos, in the sense that it would remain subject to empirical analysis. But it would entail that the mind could not be a network of modular, genetically programmed competences of the sort Chomsky envisages; it would entail the work of innate general intelligence— and hence, of the social contingencies of language acquisition.[16]

Margolis goes on to examine the consequences of such a finding. To begin with, reliance upon the mind as the locus of a "psychologically internalized system capable of generating *all* the cognitively pertinent behavior of human agents" (ibid.) is no longer possible. This would shatter the scientific aura of linguistics, for the notion of competence —and its antecedents in linguistics—had permitted the discipline to function as if it were the science specific to something that was akin to an organ of the body: the language-making mechanism. The abandonment of such a view would require a redefinition of linguistics and its status as a discipline.

First and foremost, linguistics would have to give up reliance upon notions of causality that it imported from the physical sciences when it saw itself as their counterpart, and, with such an abandonment, it would have to give up its pretension to the discovery of laws, or of rules that would have the force of laws. Linguistics would rejoin the realm of the humanities then, and recognize that the regularities that it uncovers are not amenable to elevation to the status of causal laws but that they constitute what Margolis felicitously calls "covering institutions":

Institutions—practices, traditions, and the like—seem to have the peculiar property, first of all, that unlike causal laws, they are themselves the result of causal forces; second, that they afford sufficient regularity, within given social and historical contexts, so that particular behavior and work can be causally explained by reference to them.[17]

What is remarkable about this view is that, although it originated in a radically different philosophical tradition and from a very different set of initial concerns, it corresponds to some of the most advanced views on language that have emerged in literary studies as a result of poststructuralist critiques. Indeed, Margolis's final summation about language is, if anything, more explicit than some of the poststructuralist statements on this subject:

Language appears to be *sui generis*; essential to the actual aptitudes of human beings; irreducible to physical processes; inexplicable solely infrapsychologically; real only as embedded in the practices of an historical society; identifiable consensually or only in terms that presuppose consensual practices linking observer and observed; inseparable as far as meaning is concerned from the changing, novel, nonlinguistic experience of a people; incapable of being formulated as a closed system of rules; subject always to the need for improvisational interpretation and, therefore, subject also to the ineliminable psychological indeterminacies regarding intention and action.[18]

Within this perspective language is no longer an object, abstract to boot, that offers itself up passively for knowledge to the linguist, but is the complex interplay between institutionalized practices and individualized tactical decisions. It resembles far more the realm that the literary scholar has come to recognize as the field of his or her activity: a world of constituted discourses, whose institutionalization requires sociohistorical inquiry, and a set of practices that requires an inquiry into the realm of two complex and still little understood practices: writing and reading. In other words, for the emerging linguistics as well as for literary scholarship, the field of inquiry is praxical.

The dimension of the praxical poses many problems of analysis. No clear or unassailable claim has been made to its study. In the realm of language it involves the interplay of discourses. But it is also in literary studies that one finds one of the oldest approaches to this realm: it is that part of poetics that Aristotle assigned to the study of the imitation of action, that is, to the representation of praxis that we call plot. A study of plot, such as the one that Thomas Pavel undertakes in this book, is then doubly interesting: it addresses the problematic area that we have seen emerge at the nexus of linguistics and literary studies, and it addresses that area in its most strategic location. If, from now on, linguistic phenomena, including literary ones, must be seen as practices that are deployed against a background of "covering institutions," then praxical approaches, among which studies of plot occupy a venerable place, can claim a certain degree of priority. The study of plot is then not only a relatively specialized subject matter within the sphere of poetics that is called "narratology," but is also that part of literary studies that is relevant to the understanding of praxis. Pavel's approach, which unites his interest in literary texts with his expertise in linguistic analysis, leads him to clarify these issues and to shed light on an historical phenomenon of importance: the fate of plot in literature.

II

Our attitude toward plot today is rather ambiguous: on the one hand, studies of plot enjoy a new status in literary scholarship and appear to increase in number and in degree of sophistication; on the other hand, as readers, and particularly as specialist readers, we tend to be wary of discussions of plot and, unless they are couched in the terminology devised by plot analysts, we dismiss them as paraphrase. This attitude is consistent with our evaluation of literary texts and films: we are more likely to valorize those that defy plot summation and we associate the products of mass culture, best-sellers of the

Robert Ludlum type, for example, or television crime shows, with plot development. The divide that Fredric Jameson found to be characteristic of modernist ideology[19] appears to operate here as well: little or no plot in the works of high culture, plot in those of mass culture, and the uneasy mediation of literary scholarship, which, though a decidedly high-culture activity, studies plot in both the artifacts of low culture and in those of *past* high culture, in the attempt to effect a reconciliation between the two poles of present Western culture.

In our value system, plot ranks low. We do recognize that it is important to the activity of reading, but at a relatively unsophisticated level: school children write plot summaries for their first book-report assignments, but, as they progress, we expect them to go beyond this elementary level of narrative and to consider the intricacies of characterization and point of view, as well as to engage in a rudimentary form of exegesis. In other words, we treat plot as too obvious for critical discussion, and we do so primarily because it seems to be the element of narrative that least contributes to art.

The apparent artlessness of plot may explain why literary criticism has tended to disdain it, as well as why those folklorists who view the object of their studies as artless tales value it. As is well known, it is among folklorists that modern plot studies began. Since there exists a considerable literature on this subject,[20] there is no need to review the emergence and the evolution of this field, save to note a few of its most salient features.

The decisive step in plot studies was taken when folklorists realized that their attempt to determine the provenance and the mode of transmission of the tales they study could not be carried out by means of a simple characterization of the content of these tales; it required an analysis of the structure of the tales, and such an analysis could be performed only if the basic unit of composition could be identified and specified. In a work whose Russian title, *Poetika sjužetov*,[21] is similar to Pavel's, Aleksandr N. Veselovskij proposed plot be considered as a structured series of motifs. The study of plot would then consist in determining the number and nature of motifs and the manner of their possible combination. Veselovskij further thought that there were certain types of plot that could be described as interrelating in more complex works.

Veselovskij's approach was fundamentally substantialist in that it was based upon actually occurring segments of narrative. Typically a motif may be: a dragon kidnaps the daughter of the tsar; another motif may be: a witch steals a child. Vladimir Propp's well-known critique of this approach consisted in pointing out that such a conception of the fundamental unit remained much too beholden to the texts it immediately analyzed and that, as a result, it lacked any genuine power of generalization.[22] Propp recognized that Veselovskij's motifs could be understood in two complementary respects: they all represented an action and they all had to contribute to the completion of the tale, whereas their other features could be considered text-specific variants. Propp combined these two aspects in his definition of function, the name that he gave to the basic unit: "A function is an action by some character or characters, defined from the point of view of its signification for the course of the action in the tale considered as a whole (p. 19)." Contrarily to Veselovskij, Propp believed that his minimal units did not admit of free combination but that, within a given genre, they were limited in number and had to follow a rigorous order of appearance, determined by the teleology of the story.

Subsequent plot research has taken issue with this last stipulation, arguing, among other things, that Propp's morphological structure was really based upon a single tale, and urging a return to an Aarne and Thompson-type of motif analysis.[23] But this is to condemn the whole of the Proppian enterprise for the failure of one of its elements. The syntactic claims of Propp's theory ought not to blind us to the fact that by taking Veselovskij's substantialist notion of the motif and freeing it of its substance, he has given us access at a theoretical level to the notion of action. For Propp, it does not matter who performs an action, by what means, and for what reason. What matters is the action itself and the role that it plays in the story. Narratologists have not always separated these two aspects and have therefore concluded, too hastily, that shortcomings in one area affect the other. They have, as a result, encountered problems, chiefly with respect to the question of temporality in their models, the dimensions of which have not been apparent to them.

One of the areas in which we do not disparage plot quite as much as in those that I discussed earlier is the area of experience. We acknowledge that plot, or, perhaps better, emplotment, is essential to the articulation of experience. Experience as a series of discrete events gains meaning and endows these events with signification only in the course of a reflection that relates these events through a "process of exclusion, stress, and subordination . . . carried out in the interest of constituting a story of a particular kind."[24] But although acknowledging the necessity of such emplotting, we distrust its results since, as Hayden White puts it, it does lead to a story of a particular kind;

and we fear that the requirements of storytelling may prevail over what we would like to think of as the truth of the experience. It is disturbing enough to have a historian tell us that the accounts of the past produced by his colleagues are subject to a poetics of composition that may well determine their form without having to face the possibility that the same is true in everyday life. Yet, that is precisely the step that Peter Brooks, and others in his wake, have taken in reading Freud's case histories as narratives. Narrative ordering, far from being secondary to the events that it supposedly orders, may in some instances be the very determinant of what constitutes an event.[25] Such a finding infinitely problematizes the relationship between the two dimensions of narrative that the Russian Formalists called *fabula* and *sjužet*, that is, story and plot. This had led a distinguished narratologist like Gérard Genette to put the usefulness of the distinction into question and to call for a new sort of realism in discussions of narrative, one in which it will be acknowledged that actions do not exist independently of their representation.[26] Peter Brooks, on the other hand, less disturbed by the inability to maintain distinctions that motivates Genette than by the empirical observation that plot does matter, has sought to inquire into the psychological motivations of plot and has built a critical apparatus around the desire for plot.[27]

Brooks's approach produces very fruitful readings of important nineteenth- and twentieth-century texts, but at the same time it exemplifies the problematic position of plot studies and narratological research presently. In elevating desire to the central position of his narratological conception, Brooks attempts to resolve a problem that has hovered in the background of this discussion: what is it that propels plot and story forward? The failure to answer, and most frequently to consider, this question has been the greatest shortcoming of this branch of literary scholarship to date. Most of the models of narrative that have been proposed turned out to have been surprisingly static. A more interesting attempt has been the formulation of a model of options in the action, as in Claude Brémond's work.[28] Both types of models have not been praxical, however. To some extent this is part of the Proppian legacy in which the perspective upon the plot was anchored in the locus of its completion, thus reducing everything to the timelessness of that moment. Brooks's great merit is to have drawn attention to this failure and to have attempted to resolve it. His solution however is not without problems. To rely upon desire is indeed to identify one of the great reservoirs of energy that twentieth-century theory has uncovered, but it is to project outside of plot and story the power of the propulsion. The temporal perspective remains that of someone looking back, and even though Brooks's analyses follow the movement of the text, they do so from this perspective. A purely praxical approach requires a very strong conception of the immanence of decisions and of the interplay of the institutionalized with the possible. It requires a dialectical relationship between imposed patterns and optional ones.

Furthermore, Brooks's decision to locate the propulsion in a psychological category endows this entity with a form of ahistoricity that is belied by his selection of texts, something that Brooks does not entirely ignore. Unless one is to historicize desire—a distinct possibility, although presently of rather difficult undertaking—one has to explain why stories emphasizing plot thrive at some times and do not at others. The fragmentation of plot in the most recent fiction is a point in fact, and even though Brooks does show that it depends for its own forward movement upon the readers' knowledge of more traditional plot elements, it is nonetheless the case that plot recedes in this fiction to let such elements as the articulation of linguistic codes take over the task of forward propulsion.

What Brooks's exemplary gambit points to is what plot analysis and narratology in general have been all about—the problem of agency—and furthermore the problematic aspect of his approach makes clear that the problem of agency is a historical one. This is a matter of considerable philosophical and historical weight, and it pervades all of Western culture. It is therefore not surprising that it ought to manifest itself in plot analysis. In fact, as we saw earlier, this may be one of its strategic locations.

The problem of agency arises in modern times from the partial nature of the secularization that was carried out by Enlightenment philosophy. For the Scholastics, agency was one of the attributes of God; and the world, and everything in it, moved insofar as he exercised his divine will. Human will could rise in opposition to the divine will as part of its own freedom, but it did not have any agential power as such to determine the course of the affairs of the world. The Enlightenment encounters the problem of agency because the secularization that carries out consists in bracketing away the divine instance and to let loose all that which had previously been an attribute of God. Although some of these attributes could function autonomously, others, and most notably agency, proved far more problematic. Diverse philosophical and, given the implications of this problem, political solutions were proposed, ranging from the consensus of free consciousnesses in Kant to the slave-master dialectic in

Hegel, the class struggle in Marx, and the will to power in Nietzsche — to cite but the better known. The inability to identify a viable social agent of change haunts the thought of Adorno, and the search for a capable agent in the light of the apparent reluctance of the Western proletariats to fulfill that role has marshalled the forces of thinkers on the Left, while the Right has either referred to the mysterious, because apparently unknowable, laws of the market or to the even more mystical Invisible Hand. It is thus not only in the theory of plot that some sort of aporia has been reached.

The failure here has been one of historical analysis, both with respect to the emergence of the problematic philosopheme of agency and to the sociohistorical circumstances of its problematization. With respect to the first, we need to recognize that the Enlightenment gesture that loosened the philosophical problem of agency upon us was resolutely ahistorical in that it did not inquire into the attribution of agency to God in the first instance. A complete historical reconstruction is beyond the scope of these pages, but it would need touch upon the role of Plotinus in the thought of the Fathers of the Church, and beyond, to the Aristotelian distinction between *dynamis*, *energeia*, and *entelecheia*. In Heidegger's summary definition these must be understood as follows:

Force, the capacity to be gathered in itself and prepared to work effects, to be in a position to do something, is what the Greeks (above all, Aristotle) denoted as *dynamis*. But power is every bit as much being empowered, in the sense of the process of dominance, the being-at-work of force, in Greek, *energeia*. Power is will as willing out beyond itself, precisely in that way to come to itself, to find and assert itself in the circumscribed simplicity of its essence, in Greek, *entelecheia*.[29]

But Beyond these lies the unresolved problematics of being and change, in the doctrine of a Heraclitus, for example. For our purposes here, what we need retain is that the problem ought not to be put in terms of who or what is the agent of action or the purport of action, but, as Propp dimly recognized, that there is action inasmuch as there is change, whether this be located in a Heideggerian problematic of the nonidentity of being or some other philosophical framework.

Such a primacy of action justifies the attention that plot studies devote to their subject. By the same token, this very primacy ought to permit us to dispose of one of the problems that has agitated the field: the question of whether temporality or causality plays the determinant role in the articulation of actions. I would like to suggest that the ontological primacy of action renders this question moot and that one has to turn it around and see whether the articulation of action is not what gives us both our sense of temporality and of causality. Some evidence of a linguistic nature could be adduced here: there are languages in which the representation of action is wholly mediated, in the absence of a tense system, through a system of aspectuals that distinguish stages of becoming in the accomplishment of an action without recourse to any notion of temporality or causality whatsoever. This suggests that immanent studies are called for and that they ought to take the form of descriptive grammars.

This is precisely what Thomas Pavel has to offer us in these pages. Unlike his predecessors in this branch of poetics, he never loses sight of the action and of its transformative power. Adopting the conceptual apparatus and the notational conventions of transformational generative grammar, he makes *Move* the basic element of his grammar and proceeds to generate his terms from it, as well as to describe the modes of articulation of moves. His is a treatment that recognizes that plot is a covering institution in our culture and that it imposes, like any institution, restrictions on mobility. He repertories possible moves at a specific point in time and in a specific cultural milieu: the English Renaissance. The grammar that he puts forward in these pages, the reader will rapidly discover, is accompanied by a praxical approach that determines its function in specific texts.

Pavel's selection of his texts serves to further elucidate the question of the historicity of plots and of their roles in the epistemes of their day. In one of the first texts that he analyzes, Pavel comes across the puzzling figure of Marlowe's Tamburlaine. Literary criticism has not been kind to this figure, whom it has contrasted with Faust. Whereas the latter's striving has been presented to us as an instance of the human existential predicament, Tamburlaine's apparent lust for power has been described in decidedly negative psychological and philosophical terms. But what if Tamburlaine were nothing but the rediscovery of agency as an autonomous force? His lack of a moral dimension would precisely correspond to the amorality of the world flux and be free of any pathos. Marlowe may well have represented at the beginning of our modernity the loosening away of what had until then been an attribute of God. It took philosophers some additional two hundred years before they came upon the problem, and by then the inquiry into agency in fiction had moved to the psychological sphere, save in the emergent popular literature of action and adventure. By starting with Tamburlaine, Pavel begins with his subject in its naked form.

The editors of this series gratefully acknowledge the assistance of the Graduate School of the University of Minnesota in the furtherance of their work.

Preface

Fifteen years ago, it was still possible to write that "Plot has no strong place in the pantheon of acceptable literary terms" (Dipple 1970, p. 1). Today, an assertion of this kind would be unthinkable. The last two decades have witnessed an unprecedented development of formal narrative analysis as one of the strongest branches of poetics. Rival theories have blossomed, new concepts and methods have been created, and a good many analyses proposed.

Still, more often than not, recent plot-analysis has operated on relatively simple literary artifacts, such as folktales, short stories, or small poems. The present study attempts to demonstrate the fruitfulness of formal analysis when applied to more sophisticated literary products.

Dramatic texts were the most obvious choice: more elaborate than folktales or short stories, dramatic plots are, by virtue of genre constraints, easier to analyze than the plot-structure of complex novels. They can thus provide for an intermediary stage between the texts that attracted the attention of classical structuralism, and the plots of more intricate narratives, probably still beyond our analytical means.

My personal interest in the theater of the late sixteenth and early seventeenth century played a role in the selection of the texts, which was also determined by the desire to examine a set of plays chronologically close to one another, but diverse enough to allow for typological statements. I included most of Marlowe's tragedies, hoping to gain some insight into a single writer's strategies of plot construction.

The purpose of this essay is both theoretical and analytic. Trying to reduce the formalism to a minimum and to make my prose as readable as I could, I spread out the theoretical remarks through the entire book, mixing them with text-analyses. I also attempted to engage a dialogue with more traditional criticism, comparing my results, whenever possible, to those of other writers on the topic. Since, in order to avoid digressions, I concentrated references to other critics in the notes, I would like to call these to the attention of the unhurried reader.

The first chapter examines some of the epistemological problems raised by the use of formal models in poetics and succinctly presents the model employed in this essay. The functioning of the syntactic component of the proposed grammar is made explicit in the second chapter, with the first part of Marlowe's *Tamburlaine* used as an example. The third chapter investigates the structure of the semantic component, again employing *Tamburlaine I* to illustrate the theoretical proposals. These are tested and refined in the next three chapters, where several additional English Renaissance tragedies are closely examined. The last chapter of the book explores the relation between the stylistic properties of plot and the new grammar.

The Canada Council and the Social Science and Humanities Research Council of Canada supported the research leading to this book through several grants. I completed the last version of the manuscript during the tenure of a Killam Research Fellowship granted by the Canada Council. The Canadian Federation for the Humanities assisted the publication of the manuscript through a generous subsidy. Professors Morton Bloomfield, Claude Bremond, Matei Calinescu, A. J. Greimas, Harry Levin, Krystyna Pomorska, Gerald Prince, Moshe Ron, Shlomith Rimmon-Kenan, Eugene Vance, Teun A. Van Dijk, and Douglas C. Walker read the manuscript wholly or in part, and offered encouragements and valuable suggestions. I feel especially indebted to Professor Ellen Schauber and the anonymous reader B (the Canadian Federation for the Humanities), whose penetrating remarks and criticisms were of considerable benefit. I wish to express my gratitude to Wlad Godzich and Lindsay Waters for their interest in my work and their kind advice during the preparation of the last version. For a most patient and careful handling of a difficult manuscript, my warm thanks go to the copyeditor Virginia Hans.

The Poetics of Plot

Chapter One
Introduction

Literary criticism makes use of two distinct kinds of evaluation. One involves the explicit estimation of the literary value of a text. The other deals with questions like "Is this text a novel?" "Is this character the villain?" or "Is the conclusion of this play satisfactory?" It is sometimes assumed that while value questions are difficult to answer, solutions to the latter queries are widely known. During the process of canon constitution and revision, interminable attempts are made to decide whether a given literary work is good or not, with a definite answer resisting discovery for centuries. Racine's *Athalie*, for example, was poorly received by its contemporaries, highly praised by Voltaire, then less highly spoken of by the same Voltaire, etc. But no critic asked whether or not Athalie is the villain in the play. The answer was always taken to be yes.

Such properties as the literary genre to which a given work belongs, the role of a given character in the plot, or the nature of the denouement can be called "structural regularities"; they are the object of poetics (Todorov 1968; Culler 1975). One possible attitude toward structural regularities consists in seeing them as an unconstrained field of relationships, brought to light within the framework of the theoretical description. Under this attitude, the description may obey certain general requirements such as the need for consistency, exhaustiveness, and simplicity, but the results it offers are no more than

a (possibly elaborate) structural description. Now, structural descriptions vary greatly as to the theoretical equipment presupposed in the
analytic criteria. Thus, one may distinguish between *well-constrained*
and *programmatic* structural descriptions.

Well-constrained structural descriptions start with an explicit set
of theoretical and methodological assumptions. One of the major
interests of classical linguistic structuralism has been how to constrain
in an optimal fashion the assumptions underlying the description. In
contrast, programmatic structural descriptions replace the theoretical
and methodological constraints with a general statement of purpose.
The analysis itself proceeds with a minimal structural orientation.
While in a well-constrained description the detailed precepts of his
methodology virtually compel the analyst to make one decision over
another, programmatic descriptions resemble the free exploration of
a field with the purpose of finding structural properties. The lack of
constraints is explicitly or implicitly attributed to the state of the
field. Programmatic structural descriptions are presented as pioneering work, to be followed by stricter regimentation.

Typical examples of programmatic structural descriptions are Lévi-
Strauss' well-known cycle *Mythologiques*, and Roman Jakobson's
stylistic analyses. The theoretical articulations of the *Mythologiques*
are kept to a minimum. Lévi-Strauss' description of South and North
American mythology is based on the central structuralist postulate:
myths, like most human activities, are language-like, rule-governed
behavior. Several additional hypotheses are mentioned as well: that
each myth is organized around a limited number of semantic oppositions, that myths relate to one another by means of these semantic
oppositions, that the oppositions tend to arrange themselves in pro-
portional clusters (e.g., *a* is to *b* as *c* is to *d*) etc. The weight of the
work consists in its descriptive endeavor, namely in a step-by-step
consideration of a large number of myths, the semantic schemes of
which are progressively uncovered. Lévi-Strauss' analyses have often
been criticized as unsatisfactory from a methodological point of view.
However, their main purpose and utility was less to provide for a
workable method and a well-constrained description than to prospect a
field and to suggest a series of problems. Similarly, Roman Jakobson's
seminal poetic analyses should not be judged according to severe
methodological constraints. The array of parallelisms and regularities
Jakobson finds in "Th'expence of spirit" (Jakobson and Jones 1970)
or "Les chats" (Jakobson and Lévi-Strauss 1962) are there to open
up a field and to lay down a program of work.

A structural description thus contains a series of findings related to the structure of the object or field under study. These findings should be more complete and systematic in a well-constrained description than in programmatic descriptions. But neither well-constrained nor programmatic structural descriptions provide a theoretical model of the way in which the object or the field is structured, although they can point to the possible construction of such a model. Indeed, the results of structural descriptions often prove crucial in the process of devising a model. Model construction belongs nevertheless to a different range of theoretical activities.

In the theory of language, explicit modeling most often takes the form of constructing (semi-) formal grammars. The term *grammar*, which here is opposed to *structural description*, has various uses. Consider the purely metaphoric acceptation, not so different from the metaphoric use of *anatomy*; thus, Burke's *Grammar of Motives*. There is in addition the traditional linguistic sense, meaning "book or treatise on a given language." More recently, theorists of language, notably Chomsky (1957), have developed a further sense of the term, under which the (generative) grammar of a given language is a system of rules capable of enumerating all and only the sentences of the language, and of assigning each sentence its correct structural description. Under a strong realist view, it is assumed that the speaker of a given language possesses the *competence* of producing and understanding new sentences of that language, generative grammar being an idealized and explicit representation of this competence.

Similarly, assuming with structuralist poetics that literature is a rule-governed institution, it can be submitted that the whole process of literary production and consumption depends on the ability shared by the writer and his public of more or less uniformly understanding structural regularities. This shared ability has been called literary competence.[1] An important task of poetics would be to provide for an adequate representation of this competence. But how high may the ambitions of a literary grammar be? What would it represent and against what kind of facts would the representation be checked?

II

The generative grammar of a natural language is a formal system that accounts for all and only the sentences belonging to the language in question. In order to increase its theoretical relevance, one can design the grammar in such a way as to provide, besides the list of correct sentences, a way of assigning to these sentences correct descriptions of their structural properties. A grammar of English, for instance, can do more than generate a sentence like "Freud psychoanalyzed Gradiva." It can incorporate a mechanism of representing various relationships within this sentence, parsing the sentence into its constituents, assigning each constituent a correct categorical label, indicating the syntactic functions of the constituents, etc. In other words, such a grammar will indicate as structural properties of the given sentence that *Freud* and *Gradiva* are noun phrases, that *psychoanalyzed Gradiva* is a verb phrase, that *Freud* is the subject of the sentence, while *Gradiva* is its object, etc. These structural properties are not facts belonging to the outside world. They are bits of implicit *knowledge* shared by the speakers/hearers of English. Accordingly, the grammar faces the task of representing implicit knowledge.

This is done by means of the assumption that sharing a language means sharing a certain number of rules. The speaker follows the rules or else he utters incorrect sentences. The hearer understands the sentences by virtue of the same rules. These rules can be construed in the fashion of Wittgenstein's language-games: in this case they would be normative rules, obligatory and accessible to the consciousness of the speakers and hearers. Normative rules are obligatory in two ways. First, they are constitutive: outside them, the language does not exist. Second, they are obligatory in the social sense. If the speaker does not appropriately apply the rules of his language, he is said to be mistaken. Scrupulous observance of the rules yields correct utterances of the language in question. Any violation is noticed and penalized, more or less severely, depending on the customs of the community. Moreover, speakers and hearers have a certain access to some of the normative rules they employ. Although the speakers of a language are not always clearly aware of all the rules they correctly follow, in many cases it is possible to bring them to the recognition of these rules. Exposure to grammatical education usually results in the sudden discovery that grammar has always been the subject of an extensive tacit knowledge. Thus, Monsieur Jourdain's pleasant recognition that he had always been speaking in prose.

In this context, one should distinguish between two types of tacit knowledge. First, there is the tacit understanding of a configuration independent of the information carried by its parts. One example is the grasping of an expression on a face. Michael Polanyi (1966) discusses at some length this kind of knowledge, from which he derives the principle that "we can know more than we can tell." A characteristic of such knowledge is that the person who possesses it does not have access to its explicit motivation, nor is he able to localize the symptoms of change in the configuration. In the example of physiognomic knowledge, the beholder does not know exactly what makes a phys-iognomy look puzzled or excited, nor is one able to locate on a face what happened when the expression of sorrow was replaced by an expression of resignation.

A second kind of tacit knowledge allows the subject both to identify and to locate violations, and, under certain conditions, to make his knowledge explicit. Rules governing normative behavior are known in this way. Presented with an ungrammatical sentence, the average speaker of educated English is capable of locating the mistake and even of explaining the rules that were violated, if the violations are not too complicated. Everyone, for example, knows where the mis-take lies in the sentence "The child cames home." As it will be shown later, more complex regularities can be situated beyond the speaker's actual or potential awareness. For the moment let me note that the difference between the two types of tacit knowledge can be related to the nature of explication. To find out why a human face looks puzzled, one needs information about muscular movements; the ex-planation would thus connect two distinct realms: physiological phe-nomena, and human feelings. The relation between the explanans and the explanandum is a relation of *emergence*. In the case of nor-mative knowledge, to point out that "The child cames home" has the wrong verbal ending means to merely clarify nonexplicit knowl-edge. The input and the output of the explanation belong to the same ontological level. The two cases seem thus to relate to the traditional distinction between *explanation* and *understanding*, the former being characteristic of the exact sciences, while the later is employed in so-cial, meaning-permeated sciences.[2]

To give a literary example, Jakobson's poetic analyses, which postulate subliminal patterning in poetry, appeal to inaccessible knowledge and to emergence. The reader of Baudelaire's "Les chats" may feel a vague impression of phonetic beauty and grammatical harmony. But this impression does not necessarily become more pre-cise with the unfolding of Jakobson and Lévi-Strauss' (1962) analysis of the poem. Many of Lévi-Strauss' myth descriptions are also meant to handle a level of facts irreversibly situated below conscious per-ception.[3]

Different writers have argued against overdescription of intuitively inaccessible effects in poetry. Thus, to Riffaterre (1960 and 1971), only perceptible patterning is of interest in the study of literary style. A pattern is considered perceptible if the reader detects its presence in the poem. Among the readers one can include the critic himself or herself, other critics writing on the poem under consideration, or any educated person. Out of different reactions to the poem, Riffaterre constructs what he calls the "average" reader's reaction, which signals the places where interesting stylistic effects are situated. These effects are then explained by the critic in his own metalanguage.

The average reader technique, meant to provide some sort of empirical constraint on the patterning proposed by critics, can be further refined through the introduction of sociohistorical variables. It is clear, for example, that the average spectator of Büchner's plays did not react in the same way when the texts were first written compared to a century later. German Expressionism, by developing some of Büchner's themes and techniques, changed the average depth of perception to that author's effects. As T. S. Eliot pointed out long ago, every new literary work retroactively changes the perception of the entire spectrum of literary history. But this does not necessarily contradict the hypothesis of an average, or ideal reader.[4]

In the practice of criticism the various properties discovered in literary texts can be divided into "basic" properties, such as plot, primary features of characters (e.g., "hero," "villain," "helper," etc.), general and uncontroversial statements (e.g., statements on human destiny in *Oedipus Rex*, the view of marriage in *Anna Karenina*, the role of past and heredity in *Ghosts*, etc.); versus more sophisticated properties, such as hypothetic features of the plot (cf. Empson's idea that in *The Spanish Tragedy* the killing of Andrea has been plotted by the Duke of Castille), elaborate traits of the characters (e.g., discussion of Hamlet's Oedipus complex), or advanced semantic interpretations (e.g., Gillet's 1940 existentialist reading of *Arden of Feversham*, some of Barthes' 1963 remarks on Racine, or S. Burkhardt's readings of Shakespeare's tragedies).

Of course, not all basic properties are uncontroversially established once and for all. Both modern practice and prerealist careless writing leave some of these undecided in the text. However, it is clearly one thing to appeal to the ideal reader or spectator in connection with an uncontroversial intuition, such as the reason why Othello killed his wife, and quite another thing to discuss higher-order insights, such as the view that in Racine's play, Athalie (the villain) is constantly pitied by an author who tries to diminish her guilt (Venesoen 1976). With respect to most basic structural properties, it can safely be assumed that the sociohistoric variations in their perception by the ideal reader or spectator do not constitute an insuperable difficulty for the analyst.

In relation to more elaborate insights, the ideal reader is however less reliable, as critics of this approach didn't fail to point out. It has often been argued that formalist-structuralist research cuts off linguistic-oriented description from literary interpretation, and that literature as an institutional fact deserves more than analyses limited to structural regularities. One of the most frequent criticisms leveled against structuralist poetics is that it does not supply the much-needed connection between description and interpretation.[5] Before going further, it may be appropriate to comment on this last distinction.

One is certainly correct in opposing atomistic practices and in deploring poverty of literary insight. It should, however, be pointed out that the distinction between description and interpretation is a relative one. There are different levels of description, as well as different levels of interpretation. What appears to be mere description at one level may function as daring interpretation at another. Leo Spitzer's reading of *Don Quixote* as a perspectivistic text (Spitzer 1948) may seem timidly descriptive to a critic used to, say, Unamuno's views on the *Quixote*. But when compared to purely philological work on proper names in Cervantes' oeuvre, or even to classifications of different stylistic registers in this novel, such as Hatzfeld (1927), Spitzer's paper on *Quixote*'s perspectivism appears to propose a strong interpretive hypothesis.

In addition, it must be kept in mind that poetics is not devoted to proposing illuminating interpretations of individual texts. The study of literature as a rule-governed institution cannot be achieved without examining general, trans-textual properties and conventions which, seen from the point of view of the individual work, may be perceived as merely descriptive. Such has always been the case of formal work on metrics. What a good treatise of metrics provides is a frame of reference within which the metrics of individual poems can be judged and appreciated. Among other things, it helps us categorize verses like

> Th'expence of spirit in a waste of shame
> Is lust in action, and till action, lust
> Is perjur'd, murdrous, blouddy full of blame
> (Shakespeare, Sonnet 129)

as iambic decasyllables, rather than as, say, alexandrines. At another level, one can listen to the second verse in the light of Jakobson's theory of rhythm as unfulfilled expectation (Jakobson 1960). The metric scheme of an iambic (en)decasyllable looks like:

$$\cup \,'\cup \,'\cup \,'\cup \,'\cup \,'(\cup)$$

while the pattern of accents in the second line above is:

$$\cup \,'\cup \,'\cup \,\cup \,\cup \,'\cup \,'$$

Moreover, although metrically the verse ends on the word *lust*, grammatically the verse continues immediately with the following line, in what prosodists call an enjambment. To point out these facts is not only to describe the quoted verses, but also to interpret them according to a theory of rhythm and meter. Such microinterpretive statements may play a role in the characterization of Shakespeare's poetic diction. It has been noted that Shakespeare's treatment of the (en)decasyllable became freer toward the end of the poet's career, and that the syntactic structure of a cue became the rule rather than the pleasant exception.[6] When compared to the microinterpretation of individual verses, this last statement would certainly satisfy more completely the literary critic interested in Shakespeare's metrics, even if to the critic dedicated to interpretation of individual works, it still may seem that formalist concern with diction is there only to distract critical attention from stronger interpretive statements.

Similarly, when a traditional plot-oriented critic, such as Bradley, claims that "Shakespeare's general plan . . . is to show one set of forces advancing, in secret or open opposition to the other, to some decisive success, and then driven downward to defeat by the reaction it provokes" (Bradley 1904, p. 42), and then discusses individual plots against the background of this general statement, he not only describes these plots, but also interprets them according to his theory. When later, New Criticism displaced the focus of critical attention, Cleanth Brooks (1947) showed how imagery of garment relates to *Macbeth*'s plot. But the new approach was not by necessity more interpretive than the former. Both Bradley's and Brooks' enterprises qualify as descriptive-interpretive, and the difference between them should simply be attributed to the field of interest of each theory.[7]

To come back to tacit knowledge, it may be the case that in the exploration of a rule-governed behavior, the theorist is pushed by the logic of his inquiry to state empirical regularities in an increasingly abstract and general way. The study of English grammar begins with a specification of easy rules that are accessible through introspection, for example, "The article precedes the noun." However, there comes a time when the linguist is tempted or required to formulate significant linguistic generalizations, and accordingly to state more abstract rules that do not correspond to simple, clear-cut intuitions of the speaker.

Extensively used by transformational generative grammarians, such abstract rules are different from mere normative rules in that they are more distant from the practical knowledge a speaker has of his language. While normative rules adhere closely to the operations the speaker performs and is aware of when he utters a sentence, abstract rules are parts of a system of representation or simulation of what the speaker produces.

To give a literary example, normative rules for folktales would have to include provisions for known regularities such as the fact that the folktale is simply a tale (rule of fictionalization), that the dragon is the villain, that to marry the king's daughter is an enviable goal, that the hero is bound to emerge finally as a victor, etc. There is little doubt that an average taleteller would agree with these statements. On the other hand, similar to abstract linguistic models, a recent study of the Romanian folktale *Sander Viteaz* (Fotino and Marcus 1975) shows that the tale can be generated by a context-free grammar containing the following abstract rules:

(1.1) $A \to \alpha B; B \to \beta C; C \to \gamma D \gamma; D \to \alpha \beta$

These rules are not accessibly known *as such* by the taleteller. Thus, they do not refer directly to normative knowledge. Can we construe them as related to a kind of emergent knowledge? Clearly not, if by this we understand a situation in which facts at some ontological level are related to a superior level in an intuitively unanalyzable way. Indeed, as Polanyi's example shows, between the expression read on a physiognomy and the muscular explanation of it, there is an epistemological discontinuity. In the case of the abstract rules, however, it is possible to trace them back to the accessible knowledge, out of which the abstraction process derived the rule. Thus, according to Marcus and Fotino, α represents "the help towards an action," β "the motive of an action," while γ is a sequence made up of "rivalry, slaying, return and victory." The folktale *Sandor Viteaz* consists of a series of events which can, through an elaborate analytic procedure, be reduced to the string:

(1.2) help for an action, motive for an action, rivalry, slaying, return, victory, help, and motive for an action.

At no moment during the analysis is the intuitive ground left behind. The help for action, for instance, refers, at the beginning of the story, to a series of events thanks to which the hero gets a magic sword and three faithful hounds. The motive for action is the meeting of a dragon who is just preparing to sacrifice the king's daughter, the rivalry refers to the combat between the hero and the dragon, with the outcome being the latter's slaying, and so on. Up to the formulation (1.2), Marcus and Fotino's analysis remains within the limits of accessible knowledge. The analysts then notice that if they assign

Greek letters to the elements of (1.2) as proposed above, the string (1.2) can be represented more abstractly as:

(1.3) (a) $\alpha \beta \gamma \gamma \alpha \beta$ (b) $\alpha \beta \gamma^2 \alpha \beta$

According to Marcus and Fotino, γ may appear again at the end of the string. Thus, the tale belongs to a formal language whose sentences have the general form $\alpha \beta \gamma^n \alpha \beta \gamma^n$. The formal grammar that generates this language is precisely (1.1).

Properly constructed, an abstract narrative grammar should generate only the correct narrative strings. The adequacy of such a grammar is evaluated by checking its output against narrative knowledge. Thus, although it is not certain that the taleteller *actually* performs the operations represented by the rules, the abstract grammar that contains them is related in principle to accessible narrative knowledge in two ways: first, the formalization has as its point of departure accessible knowledge; second, the output of the grammar is checked against narrative knowledge.

It must be noted also that abstract literary grammars are not *complete* in the sense that they do not account for "actual" literary texts, and in the sense that they do not cover all aspects of these texts. Indeed, it is unlikely that one can construct a device that will generate, say, all and only the correct tragedies, or all and only the correct literary texts. If the purpose of a grammar is to account for tacit knowledge, then it seems unlikely that one would ever be able to construct a single, complete formal grammar of a natural language.[8] There is little chance, for instance, of integrating all lexical knowledge into a syntactically based grammar otherwise than by *ad hoc* links. *A fortiori*, in the case of literary texts, the remarkable freedom prevailing in this field renders the task of constructing a single, complete grammar most unattainable. A complete grammar of literary *texts*, moreover, would have to account for all and only correct literary texts. Besides the difficulties inherent to the notion of literariness itself, notice that such a grammar would have to account for the correct text of all tragedies, including *Hamlet*. But this is an impossible task, since we simply do not possess the correct text of *Hamlet*, and no empirical verification of the grammar's output can be produced. Texts are too complex to be accounted for by a single grammar.[9] From a literary-grammatical point of view, literary monuments should rather be seen as the meeting place of several types of poetic regularities, from metric and stylistic ones, to narrative and semantic patterns. Each type of patterning can be described by a literary grammar, or a component thereof. It goes without saying, therefore, that narrative grammars are only one type of literary grammar, and that it is not their purpose to cover every regularity manifested in literature. It is clear also that since grammars aim at grasping the generality of a given type of patterning, they are primarily directed toward what is common to different literary objects. A grammar of plot, for instance, will not produce a finite number of already used plots, but an infinite number of plot-structures, of abstract objects embodying the regularities that plots respect. These abstract structures represent the infinite possibilities from which the writer "chooses" his plots before giving them a text. Accordingly, plot-grammar makes use of systematic idealization concerning some aspects of literary texts. As such, it differs from critical approaches that aim at grasping the specificity of texts. Idealization is the unavoidable method of any inquiry; the formalism used by poetic grammars only pushes the operation a bit further, rendering clear its scope and purpose. The reader should thus keep in mind that the analyses proposed here are less oriented toward promoting original readings of the plays examined than unveiling general properties of plot.

III

The plot-grammar to be presented in this work belongs to the already numerous class of recent structural analyses of stories.[10] It has been developed as an attempt to avoid the shortcomings of available models and to integrate the findings of structural analyses of plot within a more explicit grammar, tentatively linked to a plot-based semantics. While the grammar proposed here owes much to its predecessors, both in the general orientation and in the details of its functioning, it aims at improving the standards of narratological models in several areas. Thus, my inventory of categories is tributary to Greimas', Todorov's, and Bremond's models. Such notions as narrative program (Greimas), narrative embedding (Todorov), or narrative possibility (Bremond) have determined some of my theoretical choices, Prince's and Van Dijk's generative narrative grammars were a source of formal inspiration. Doležel's and Ryan's narrative semantics decisively influenced my attempts to relate the formal model of plot to a theory of narrative domains. At the same time, the present system has been designed to perform better than its competitors in three important areas, namely the explicitness of plot-advance, the role of characters and groups of characters, and the links between plot and its meaning.

In representing plot-advance, the available models disregard either the detailed links between actions, or the abstract narrative categories that confer meaning to each section of a plot. In Greimas' and Todorov's narrative grammars, stories are divided into major narrative sections (*Inverted Content* vs. *Posited Content* or *Troubled Universe* vs. *Reestablished Universe*), and narrative sequences are subjected to detailed classification. But neither model offers an explicit formulation of the step-by-step unfolding of the plot: categorial taxonomy lacks a syntax. Conversely, Bremond's (1973) and Rumelhart's (1977) models, being conceived as dependency grammars, indicate in detail the progress of action, but lack a battery of abstract categories that would help the interpretation of the plot.

With respect to characters, while Greimas and Bremond proposed comprehensive typologies of actants and roles, their models overlook the connection between actions and characters or groups of characters. Hendricks' (1977) suggestions have been most useful in filling this gap. My own solution, which rests on notions derived from game-theory, suggests that plots as strategic clashes cannot be reduced to sequences of anonymous actions; a proper understanding of plot includes knowledge of the person or group who performs an action, the reason for it, and its effect on the overall strategic configuration.

In addition, to understand a plot involves not only relating actions to one another and to the characters who perform them, but also to a group of general maxims that define the meaning of "raw" actions and give them a cultural and narrative status. To slap someone in the face can be a gentle blessing if it occurs during the confirmation ceremony, or a deadly insult if it happens in *Le Cid*. These kinds of narrative regularities have been discussed by Todorov (1968) and Pavel (1976a) in relation to plot, and by Doležel (1976b) and Ryan (forthcoming) in the context of narrative semantics. No explicit link between the articulation of plot and such regularities has been yet proposed.

I would like also to note that after a period of intensive research on the structure of plot, narratologists gradually turned their attention to the discursive aspects of narratives. While as defined by Todorov (1969) or Prince (1982) narratology includes both the poetics of plot and of its textual manifestation, some researchers (Bal 1977; Genette 1983) tend to restrict narratology to the textual study of narratives, thus eliminating on the one hand the abstract level of plot, on the other hand artifacts containing plots, but not centered around diegetic techniques: drama, film, narrative painting. Against this practice, I want first to argue that although discourse-narratology provides us with important conceptual tools and invaluable insights, there are areas where an abstract narrative structure independent of its discourse-manifestation is indispensable for an adequate representation of our literary knowledge: the poetics of plot, though situated beyond the scope of discourse-narratology, as understood by Genette (1983), still belongs to narratology in the broad sense.

Second, it must be added that tempting as it may seem, narratology cannot be limited to narrative, just as poetics does not study just poetry, metrics meter, and logic language. In fact, metrics makes sense only when meter is contrasted with rhythm, and of course poetics handles much more than poetry, logic is not limited to the study of language, nor is philosophy merely love of wisdom. The object of a discipline does not follow from its name. As the study of both story *and* discourse, narratology must feel free to examine plays, films, narrative music and painting: Thus, even though the objects of my grammar are *dramatic* plots and not those of folktales, short stories, or novels, I shall occasionally use the adjective *narrative* to refer to the action of a play. Expressions like *narrative domains, narrative syntax; narrative trees*, and so on should accordingly be understood as related to plot as a general structuring principle, common to drama and prose fiction.

Like its predecessors, the present grammar starts from the assumption that plot-structure is comparable to the syntactic structure of sentences. Imagine the set of possible plots as a language obeying tacit or explicit rules. The author composes a plot and the reader or spectator understands it by virtue of these rules. One is thus allowed to say that, ideally, the author and the spectator have internalized the same plot-grammar. Let us add that cases of misunderstanding can be due either to the lack of a common grammar, as was the case in eighteenth-century readings of Shakespeare's tragedies, or to a more radical rejection of the very idea of a commonly shared grammar, as happens in some modern trends striving toward complete unreadability.

The rules from which the commonly shared literary grammar is made up are probably mainly simple, accessible rules. However, several regularities are better expressed as complex, abstract rule systems. For both kinds of rules the empirical basis is formed by the literary intuitions of the reader, as sometimes expressed by literary criticism. It will be seen that in most cases the kind of intuitions used here are of the simple and widespread variety.

It has been shown elsewhere (Pavel 1976a) that a grammar which generates stories is subject to the same restrictions as grammars for natural-language sentences. Arguments similar to those proposed by

Chomsky (1956) against regular and context-free grammars can be constructed in order to show that typically narrative phenomena cannot be accounted for by these varieties of formal grammars. Consequently, the grammar adopted here belongs to the family of transformational generative grammars.

It should be nonetheless said from the outset that although the linguistic research of Chomsky and his followers has determined the orientation of my approach, between the rich, varied set of generative transformational theories and results, and the tentative plot-grammar herewith proposed, there are considerable differences. The level of development and formal sophistication of linguistic grammar appears yet to be beyond the reach of poetics and narratology: our field not only lacks the centuries of grammatical research that offered contemporary linguistics a sound basis for higher-level formalization, but also there is little in narratology to resemble the concerted effort of hundreds of linguists over three decades of intensive work. Thus, knowing too little about the formal properties of plot, one cannot but contemplate with an admiration not entirely free of envy such elaborated formal findings as the X-bar theory, the Specified Subject, Tensed-S, and Subjacency Conditions, or Chomsky's ability in developing philosophical arguments on the basis of linguistic evidence.[11] Besides, traditions within each field set powerful limits on new speculation. Although linguistics has long ago earned the reputation of an empirical discipline, which renders plausible Chomsky's case for unity of science, such a plea could not but be met with suspicion by literary scholars used to the informality of rhetorical and hermeneutic approaches.

For all these reasons, the plot-grammar advanced in this essay stresses primarily the elementary stages of the construction of a formalism. I tried to make sure that plot can indeed be represented as a hierarchical system of dependencies, and that theoretical categories play an interesting role in such representations—aspects that linguistic grammar has taken for granted since Aristotle. Hence my insistence on the base-component and my constant reference to elementary intuitions. This is also why the semantic considerations are limited to the interpretation of plot-structure and do not aim at offering comprehensive readings of the texts under analysis.

Plot-grammar consists, under this proposal, of a categorial vocabulary including an initial symbol indicating what kind of objects the grammar accounts for (enumerates), and two formally distinct kinds of rules: a set of context-free rules and a set of transformations.

Since there is no such thing as *the* correct plot-grammar, it is realistic to assume that for each grammar one may establish a certain inventory of categories according to the specific needs of that grammar, adapted to both its formal structure and to the range of intuitions it strives to account for. The grammar proposed here tries to grasp the phenomenon of plot-advance, the simple and obvious fact that plots link together actions performed by the characters. The categorial vocabulary used in the grammar contains the symbols *Move, Problem, Solution, Auxiliary, Tribulation*, and the prefixes *Pro-* and *Counter-*.

To better perceive the bare link between actions, the notion of *Move* is used as the central operational concept of the grammar. As in game-theory, a *Move* is the choice of an action among a number of alternatives, in a certain strategic situation and according to certain rules.[12] From this tentative definition, it follows that in this grammar the logic of the story is a progressive one. Accordingly, Bremond's (1966 and 1973) criticisms of the deterministic aspects of Propp's (1928) narrative model are assumed to be basically correct. Naturally, not every action of the characters constitutes a *Move*. The main criterion for an action to be considered as a *Move* is its impact on the overall strategic situation. An action is a *Move* if it either, directly or indirectly, brings about another *Move*, or if it ends the story.[13] The place of the notion of *Move* within the narrative grammar is approximately comparable to that of the *Sentence* in the syntax of natural languages. Complex sentences are made up of simple sentences hierarchically linked according to the rules of the grammar. Similarly, the abstract story, which is structured as a complex *Move*, is made up of several simple *Moves*, embedded one under another, according to the prescriptions of the narrative grammar.

To illustrate how the grammar works, let us examine Edgar's revenge in *King Lear*. Schematically, this section of the play consists in two main *Moves*: first, through the evil machination of Edmund, the natural son of Gloucester, his half-brother Edgar, Gloucester's legitimate heir, is banished from his father's castle. Second, Edgar finds the means to destroy Edmund and does so. Admittedly, this account considerably simplifies the action of the episode, which in the play is interconnected with other happenings; however, it will suffice for our present purposes.

Moves can be analyzed in two main components. Any such *Move* is called for by a *Problem* and represents an effort toward its *Solution*. The notions of *Problem* and *Solution* may be understood as abstract categories, covering a great number of concrete situations. The choice of these categories has been influenced by Maranda and

Köngäs (1971). In our example, at the beginning of the play Edmund's problem is how to overcome the disadvantages of his illegitimate status. His solution will include the stratagem resulting in Edgar's banishment. Represented as a plot-grammatical rule, this can be expressed as follows:

(1.4) *Move: Problem + Solution*, in which : means "is manifested by" and + means "is followed by." (The colon corresponds to the arrow found in transformational grammars.)

Similarly to the syntactic constituent trees used by linguists, I will represent the structure of plots as narrative trees, closely related to the rules of the plot-grammar. A rule like (1.4) will result in a tree like (1.5), in which the symbol appearing in the rule at the left of the column directly dominates the symbols that in the rule are situated at the right of the column. The narrative content of the *Problem* and *Solution* is represented as simple narrative sentences within brackets, which schematically describe the happenings in the story. By adding an indication about the character who initiates the *Move*, the first *Move* of the episode will look like tree (1.5).

(1.5)

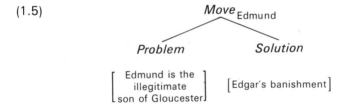

The tree means simply that to the *Problem* constitued by his own illegitimate status, Edmund brings a *Solution* consisting in Edgar's banishment. The *Move* "belongs" to Edmund, since the problem affects him and the solution is initiated by and principally favors him. The set of moves belonging to the same character will be labeled the *domain* of that character. Thus, tree (1.8) below opposes Edmund's domain to Edgar's.

Sometimes, in order to achieve their purposes, the actors who initiate a *Move* make use of auxiliary actors or circumstances. Thus Edmund takes advantage of Gloucester's credulity, which functions as an *Auxiliary* to Edgar's banishment. To include this possibility, rule (1.4) can be modified as follows:

(1.4') *Move: Problem + (Auxiliary) + Solution*, in which the parentheses indicate that the category inside them is optional.

Under this rule, the first *Move* of the episode will look like tree (1.6).

(1.6)

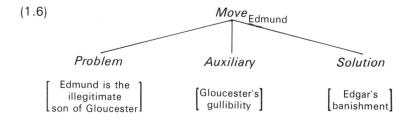

The second *Move* of the episode has a similar structure. Edgar's problem consists in having been banished and separated from his father. His solution, which requires the destruction of Edmund, will be significantly helped by the killing of Oswald and the subsequent finding of Goneril's letter to Edmund. The *Move* has the (simplified) structure of tree (1.7).

(1.7)

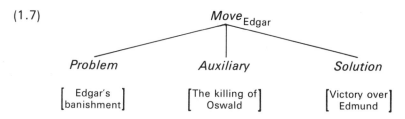

Notice that the *Problem* of tree (1.7) is entirely due to the *Move* of Edmond in tree (1.6); the content of this problem is the same as the solution in (1.6): Edgar's banishment. To represent the whole development within a single tree, one can embed (1.6) under the *Problem* of (1.7), with the purpose of indicating that Edmund's actions *cause* Edgar's *Problem*. See tree (1.8).

Although tree (1.8) is only a rudimentary representation of the episode, it shows clearly how the embedding of a *Move* under the *Problem* of another *Move* represents a chain of narrative causality. The tree reads upward from left to right: faced with the problem of his illegitimate status, Edmund, helped by Gloucester's gullibility, obtains Edgar's banishment. This in turn constitutes a problem for Edgar, who, . . . etc. A rule like:

(1.9) *Problem: Move*

accounts for the possibility of rewriting a *Problem* as a whole *Move*.[14] The symbols *Auxiliary* and *Solution* can dominate *Moves* as well:

(1.8)

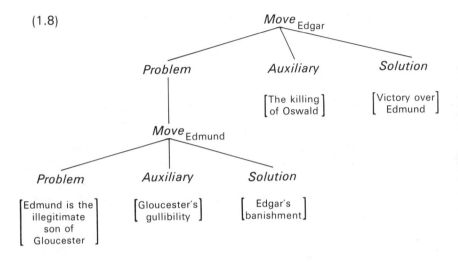

(1.10) *Auxiliary: Move*

(1.11) *Solution: Move*

An interesting property of the *Problems, Auxiliaries,* and *Solutions* is that in some cases they can be analyzed as sequences of these symbols, as in the following rules:

(1.12) *Problem: Problem$_1$ + Problem$_2$ + . . . + Problem$_n$*

(1.13) *Auxiliary: Auxiliary$_1$ + Auxiliary$_2$ + . . . + Auxiliary$_n$*

(1.14) *Solution: Solution$_1$ + Solution$_2$ + . . . + Solution$_n$*

In more intuitive terms, the main problem can sometimes be made up of a series of problems, each needing its own solution. Similarly, a solution may consist in several subsolutions or in several attempts to implement it. A more detailed discussion of the structure of the *Solution* can be found in the last chapter. The formalism will be commented on in the appendix.

As Bremond (1966 and 1973) has shown, any *Solution* goes through three stages, each consisting of a choice:

(1.15) *Solution*: [± considered]
[+ considered] : [± attempted]
[+ attempted] : [± success]

These stages being probably universal, they will be incorporated into the grammar under the name of *Bremond-stages* for *Solutions.*

The two prefixes *Pro-* and *Counter-* may be attached to the *Solution* according to the episode-generating rule:

(1.16) *Solution*: $(Pro\text{-}Solution + Counter\text{-}Solution)^n + (Solution)$

Pro-Solution events favor the implementation of the *Solution*, while *Counter-Solution* events work against it. If the *Solution* succeeds, the last symbol of (1.16) is selected. The parentheses indicate that the choice of the enclosed symbol is optional. The exponent n means that the sequence indexed by it may be repeated any finite number of times.

Rules (1.4′), (1.9), (1.10), (1.11), (1.12), (1.13), (1.14), (1.15), and (1.16) constitute the base component of the *Move*-grammar:

(1.4′) *Move*: *Problem* + (*Auxiliary*) + *Solution*

(1.9) *Problem*: *Move*

(1.10) *Auxiliary*: *Move*

(1.11) *Solution*: *Move*

(1.12) *Problem*: $Problem_1 + Problem_2 + \ldots + Problem_n$

(1.13) *Auxiliary*: $Auxiliary_1 + Auxiliary_2 + \ldots + Auxiliary_n$

(1.14) *Solution*: $Solution_1 + Solution_2 + \ldots + Solution_n$

(1.15) *Solution*: [± considered]
[+ considered] : [± attempted]
[+ attempted] : [± success]

(1.16) *Solution*: $(Pro\text{-}Solution + Counter\text{-}Solution)^n + (Solution)$

Rules (1.9) to (1.11) can be abstracted as:

(1.9′) X: *Move*, in which X $\neq$ *Move*

Rules (1.12) to (1.14) can be simplified as:

(1.12′): X : X^n, in which X $\neq$ *Move*

The narrative trees sketched throughout the present work will constantly refer to the rules. But similar to the situation in grammars of natural languages, the set of context-free rules is not sufficient for an elegant representation of narrative structures. Several narrative phenomena have to be represented through transformations.[15]

A transformation is basically a rule relating two classes of (narrative) trees. The domain of a transformation contains a class of trees satisfying certain structural conditions. The output of the transformation consists of a new class of trees, modified according to a certain structural change.[16] Since we do not yet possess sufficient knowledge about the more elementary articulations of plot-structure, the narrative transformations received only limited attention in this essay. During the analyses that follow, reference will be made to a few transformations, like the *Episode-Attachment Transformation*, which inserts relatively unconnected episodes into a narrative tree, and the *Solution-Generalization Transformation*, which allows the last Bremond-stage of the *Solution* of the highest *Move* to be generalized to the *Solutions* of lower *Moves*.

Among other things, transformations may account for the differences between the abstract order of events in the plot, which in my model is based on strategy, and the textual succession of presented events. Many narratives and dramas start *in medias res*, and later tell the earlier events more or less succinctly. Homer's epic poems, Racine's tragedies, are among the most obvious examples of texts that start late. To open a poem or a play long after the beginning of the conflict, means to present the reader or spectator with a strategic situation in which many, sometimes most of the *Moves* have already been performed, the load of *Problems* unveiled, and the final race for a stable *Solution* set in motion. The Transformation *In medias Res*, as it may be called, would thus search for a *Move* that takes place after a

(1.17)

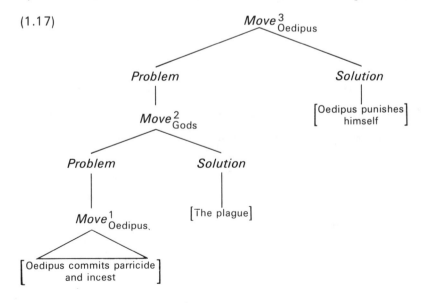

certain number of *Problems* have been presented, and a few provisional *Solutions* attempted. Let me take the example of tree (1.17).

Tree (1.17) schematically represents the *Move*-structure of *Oedipus Rex*. The text of the tragedy starts only after *Move*², that is after Oedipus' parricide and incest violate the order of things and are punished by the plague affecting Thebes. The transformation *In Media Res* will operate on events under *Move*¹, which will be brought to light *after* the *Solution* of *Move*², but before the *Solution* of *Move*³. Thus, it will attach *Move*¹ somewhere under the *Solution* of *Move*³. See tree (1.18).

(1.18)

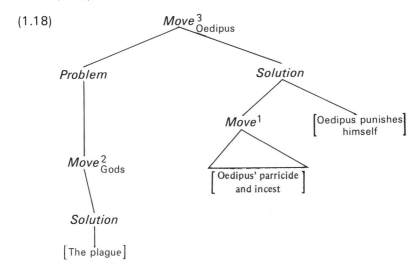

Tree (1.18) is closer to the unfolding of the text that tree (1.17); nonetheless we understand the strategic situation of *Oedipus Rex in spite of* and not *because of* the late discovery of *Move*¹. As soon as Oedipus' transgressions are learned, we project them back at their strategic place, as the violation of natural order that calls for the *Solution* of *Move*², the plague. Tree (1.18) represents the conflict as affected by the transformation *In Medias Res*, that is, as presented by the play, while tree (1.17) represents the conflict as understood by the spectator—and by the protagonists.

Finally, narrative trees end in narrative "leaves." These are bundles of *narrative propositions* in the sense of Todorov (1969), that is, abstract sentences made up of one (possibly modified) predicate and one or more actors. A narrative proposition makes sense only when considered together with the symbols that dominate it. A proposition like "Gloucester banishes Edgar" has a certain narrative function when it represents the *Solution* of the *Move* initiated by Edmund, and a different one when it is the *Problem* of a *Move* belonging to Edgar. Accordingly, it seems unlikely that there are predicates which simply by virtue of their semantic content fit naturally under *Problem* or *Solution* symbols. It is more probable that, depending on the specific narrative context, any narrative predicate may serve in a *Problem*-dominated branch as well as in *Auxiliary*- or *Solution*-dominated branches. However, once the *Problem*-creating predicate is chosen, not all predicates may provide the *Solution*. There are a limited number of acceptable solutions to a given problem. The banished Edgar has only a few choices for improving his condition. Semantic interpretation of narrative trees thus involves the examination of narrative predicates and propositions with respect to the context in which they appear. More detailed consideration of narrative semantics will be offered in chapter 3.

Chapter Two
Plot-Grammar:
Marlowe's *Tamburlaine I*

In this chapter I will present an analysis of *Tamburlaine*'s plot, explaining the fuctioning of the *Move*-grammar.

I

The first episode of the tragedy is designed to present succinctly the strategic state of affairs at the beginning of the action.

The tragedy begins "early," before any major event determining the course of the action occurs. The episode in question consists of an unsuccessful attempt by the weak king, Mycetes, to convince Tamburlaine to abandon his paramilitary activities within the boundaries of the Persian kingdom. Theridamas, the king's delegate, fails to persuade Tamburlaine, but is converted himself into an ally of Tamburlaine against the king.

The Theridamas episode can be represented as a two-stage operation: first, the attempt by Mycetes to neutralize Tamburlaine, and second, Tamburlaine's own success in converting Theridamas. These two incidents can be further decomposed into several elements, in accordance to the grammar previously outlined. Thus, Mycetes' *Move* is caused by what the king perceives as a violation of the established order, namely by Tamburlaine's hopes of becoming king of Asia and his ensuing robberies. Theridamas' mission is an attempt to reestablish the order. But from Tamburlaine's point of view, Theridamas' mission represents a violation. In Tamburlaine's domain the main rule is to fight for power. Theridamas' and Mycetes' attempts threaten Tamburlaine's purposeful actions. Thus, the seduction of Theridamas functions as a *Solution*. Since Theridamas' attempt was triggered by Mycetes' effort to put his domain in order, one can embed Mycetes' *Move* under the *Problem* of Tamburlaine's *Move*, showing that the state of affairs in Mycetes' domain constitutes a *Problem* in Tamburlaine's domain. In this example, the immediate reason of Tamburlaine's problem is the action that serves as a *Solution* in Mycetes' *Move*, namely Theridamas' mission. See tree (2.1).

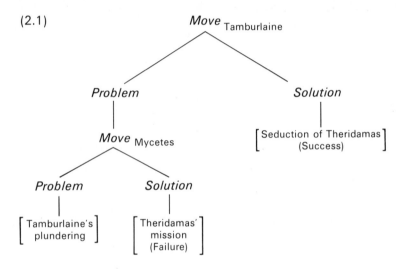

This structure is complex enough to provide an acceptable plot of a very simple play or a short story. Some of Boccaccio's tales are hardly more complex than this single-embedding tree. With enough suspense devices and secondary developments, the plot-structure of Theridamas' episode could have served as the frame for an entire tragedy. Plot-syntax is essentially flexible, and since a small episode possesses the same basic structure as a more complex plot, the difference between them lies less in the categories used than in the number of *Moves* and dilatory devices, and certainly the textual emphasis and editing.

In *Tamburlaine*, Theridamas' episode is of little consequence for the overall plot. Even before Theridamas reaches Tamburlaine's camp, Mycetes is overthrown. The episode stresses the political instability of the society in which Tamburlaine is expected to act and reveals the hero's charismatic powers. Usually, in both fairy tales and dramas, the first king to be shown is expected to play a major role in the plot, either as a donor and guardian of order, or as the main victim of disorder. But Mycetes is neither a powerful king nor an important victim. His anticlimactic dismissal gives the spectator an idea of the weakness of Tamburlaine's adversaries.

The deposed king has, however, a loyal army. His brother, Cosroe, the new king, must fight for his recently acquired crown. He decides to ally with Tamburlaine, whom he knows only from hearsay. They join forces against Mycetes, but after the former king is defeated, Tamburlaine turns against Cosroe and defeats him, thus becoming the king of Persia.

The whole episode serves the interests of Tamburlaine and will accordingly be represented as a *Move* belonging to Tamburlaine's domain. Obviously, Tamburlaine's problem consists in Cosroe's possessing the crown. In turn, Cosroe's victory over Mycetes belongs to Cosroe's domain and comes as a reaction to the reign of the weak Mycetes ("I see the state of Persia droop / And languish in my brother's government," says Cosroe to the noblemen, I. i, v. 155-56). Cosroe's seeking the friendship of Tamburlaine (II, i and iii) functions as the main *Auxiliary* to the plot against Mycetes. Carefully planned, Cosroe's conspiracy is actually performed, and its outcome is successful. As such, it fulfills all three Bremond-stages of the implementation of *Solutions*.

In order to understand the position of Therimadas' episode—*Moves* 1 and 2 of tree (2.2)—in relation to the victory over Cosroe, I shall distinguish between two kinds of narrative impact an event or a series of events may have on another event or series thereof. An event can be the core of the problem-producing situation that calls for a *Solution*. Thus, Cosroe's winning of the Persian crown is a *Problem*-creating event, at least in Tamburlaine's domian. The impact of this kind of event is immediately felt in the solution of the *Move*, and acts indirectly through the affected *Move* on the rest of the plot. It can be labeled *direct impact*. A less direct influence, which could be called *contingent impact*, makes itself felt when a given event, without precipitating a second event, still helps the second event to occur, either by providing the occasion for its occurrence, or by supplying the appropriate conditions for the second event.[17] In this case the first event is not dominated by the symbol *Problem* in the *Move* in which the second event appears as *Solution*.

Theridamas' episode influences Tamburlaine's destiny in two respects: first, it provides Tamburlaine with a faithful follower, second, it offers Tamburlaine the opportunity to exert his charisma on a well-known Persian character, giving him enough publicity to make possible his short-lived alliance with Cosroe, and implicitly granting him the status he needs to win the crown. Accordingly, Theridamas' episode functions as an *Auxiliary* in Tamburlaine's domain and can be attached immediately under the node *Move*$_{Tamburlaine}$. Thus, the overall structure of the two first acts of the play will look like tree (2.2).

(2.2)

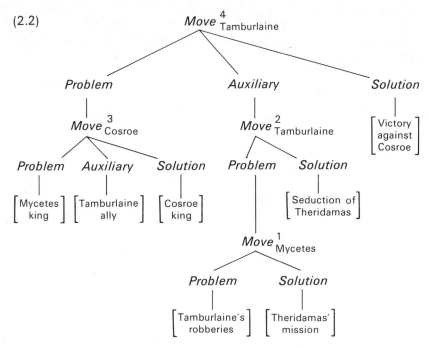

This structure is interesting from several points of view. The following comments have the double purpose of stressing some of the properties of tree (2.2) and of simultaneously familiarizing the reader with the details of the *Move*-grammar.

Move Numbering

This device indicates the logical (and sometimes, but not necessarily, chronological) order of the *Moves*, starting with the most deeply embedded, and very often the earliest, *Moves*. In many narrative structures, an uninterrupted action advancing corresponds to the progression from one *Move* to the next. In such "regular" narrative structures, each *Move* constitutes a problem triggering the next *Move*. Such narrative structures are typical of strong conflict stories, stories in which every *Move* is an answer to the problem created by the preceding *Move*. If, moreover, every other *Move* is performed by the same character or group of characters, the whole chain of *Moves* being evenly divided between only two groups of people, the structure can be called a *polemical configuration* (Pavel 1976a). During our analyses, we will find many such configurations, which form a favorite framework for epic and tragic writers. A classical example is the family story of the Atrids, in which Agamemnon orders the sacrifice of Iphigenia, a move that offends his wife's love for her daughter; this move requires a solution in Clytemnestra's domain, but the new move, namely Agamemnon's murder, sets a new problem for the survivors of Agamemnon's party, Electra and Orestes. Their solution is the killing of Clytemnestra. Here Aeschylus puts an end to the series of murders: the problem raised by the last crime will not be solved through another crime, but will be pardoned. Schematically, this story is represented by tree (2.3).

(2.3)

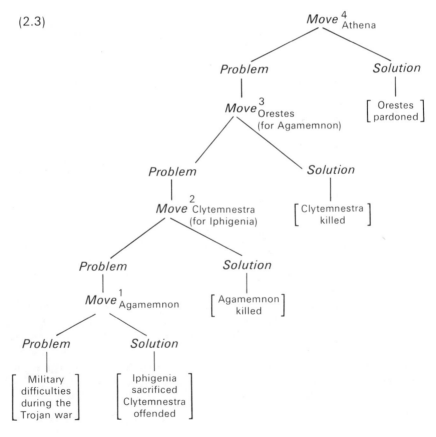

In Marlowe's *Tamburlaine*, the episode of Theridamas is (nontypically) a polemical configuration. Nontypically, because of the lack of duplication of action in at least one domain. One can, however, easily imagine how such a duplication would have looked. Suppose that, instead of being overthrown, Mycetes had sent a strong mission to Tamburlaine. Suppose then, that in a real or linguistic battle, Tamburlaine had overcome this new challenge; that as a consequence Mycetes, or even his rebellious brother Cosroe, would have continued the fight. Such a story would produce a usual Elizabethan chronicle play, based on chains of revenge. But nothing of this kind happens in *Tamburlaine*, where a typical dramatic feature is precisely the absence of well-structured polemical configurations. The pattern of *Move*-numbering in tree (2.2) shows, on the contrary, that the opening of the tragedy carefully avoids the usual chain of revenge scheme. *Move*^{2} is dominated by *Move*^{4}, and by the less dynamic abstract symbol *Auxiliary*. Notice also that both *Moves* 2 and 4 belong to Tamburlaine's domain.

Since the spectator expects the action of this historical play to follow the polemical configuration course, the quick disappearance of Mycetes and the conflict between Tamburlaine and Cosroe set an unanticipated mood of loosely bound actions. In contrast to the vagaries of the events, Tamburlaine's personality emerges as the only constant element of the first two acts.[18] Every action of both Mycetes and Cosroe is taken advantage of by Tamburlaine, so that at the end of act II, he is strongly in control, having asserted his charisma and his strategic qualities, in sixteenth-century words, his *virtue*.

Move Embedding

Another significant aspect of the narrative structure under study is the placement of the *Moves* under the abstract symbols *Problem, Auxiliary*, and *Solution*. I have just said that *Move*^{2} in tree (2.2) is dominated by the "less dynamic" symbol *Auxiliary*. This impressionistic statement can be rendered more explicit.

In early transformational grammar, dominance receives an intuitive grammatical interpretation. A node X dominates another node Y if the path between X and Y is uninterrupted and only descends. If a given node labeled X dominates the nodes Y, W, . . . , Z, then the string Y, W, . . . , Z *is an* X (Chomsky 1965). To give a simple example, in the tree (2.4) the node *Noun Phrase* dominates the nodes *Article* and *Noun* at one level, and at the next level, the nodes *The* and *boy*. According to the above agreement, this is interpreted as meaning that the sequence *Article Noun* is a *Noun Phrase*, and that *The boy* is a *Noun Phrase* as well. This also means that *boy* is a

(2.4)

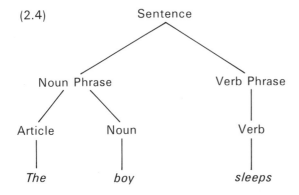

Noun, that the string *The Boy sleeps* is a *Sentence,* and so on. This is a most natural way of interpreting the grammatical relevance of labeled trees. However, as it stands, it cannot be applied to narrative trees. The reason is that narrative trees incorporate crucial information about the causal and logico-temporal order of the *Moves.* Although the numbering of the *Moves* does not necessarily refer to the temporal succession of the events, it is generally clear that the *Solution* of a *Move* takes place later than everything else dominated by the move, including, of course, the embedded *Moves* and all the events they contain. This constraint, which can be called the *Principle of Solution Postponement,* restricts the range of possible narrative trees for a given story.[19]

Under this principle, it becomes difficult to extend to narrative trees the "is a" method of interpreting the relation of dominance. The relationship of a *Move* to all symbols under it requires a more sophisticated interpretation. Indeed, the division of a *Move* into *Problem, Auxiliary,* and *Solution* is not a uniform one. Rather, the first two constituents are grouped together as the elements that *lead to* the *Solution.* The *Solution* is thus the *focus* of a *Move,* the event toward which the whole *Move* is oriented. Accordingly, the node *Move* has two ways of relating to the dominated nodes: on one hand it "opens" with everything that precedes the *Solution,* on the other hand it is "closed," or "cleared up" by the *Solution* itself. Thus, the interpretation of a *Move* will consist of two distinct aspects. Branches to the left of the *Solution* are said to *lead to* the uppermost *Move,* while the *Solution* itself *constitues* the *Move.*

Notice that often the spectator feels that certain events are less pertinent to a given *Move,* although they may somehow contribute to it. To account for this intuition, the two relations can be refined. One can thus introduce a distinction between *directly* and *indirectly leading to.* A node directly leads to a given *Move* if it is dominated by that *Move*, the path between the node and the *Move* being at the left of the path between the *Move* and its *Solution*, and between the node and the *Move* there are no other nodes labeled *Move*. In tree (2.2) the node *Mycetes king* directly leads to $Move^3_{Cosroe}$, while this last node directly leads to $Move^4_{Tamburlaine}$. A node indirectly leads to a given *Move*, if it leads to the *Move*, and if between the node and the *Move* there is another node labeled *Move*. In tree (2.2), the node *Mycetes king* indirectly leads to $Move^4$, because it is dominated by $Move^4$; because the path between $Move^4$ and the node *Mycetes king* is at the left of the path between $Move^4$ and its solution; and finally, because between $Move^4$ and *Mycetes king* there is another *Move*, namely $Move^3_{Cosroe}$. Similarly, the distinction applies to the *Solution* nodes. A *Solution* directly constitutes a *Move*, when there is no other *Move* between them; it indirectly constitutes a *Move*, when between them there are other nodes labeled *Move*. Tree (2.2) does not contain such a situation, but it is not difficult to imagine what such a tree would look like.

A further distinction involving the relation of *leading to* a *Move* differentiates between the more essential events that trigger the *Move* and the less essential ones. In the grammar proposed here, the events which make a *Solution* necessary, and which are thus the main elements in starting a *Move*, belong to the node labeled *Problem*. In contrast, events which simply help to implement the *Solution*, but which are not explicitly presented as the source of the entire *Move*, belong to the *Auxiliary* node. In tree (2.2), the contribution of node *Tamburlaine ally* to the constitution of $Move^3$ in Cosroe's domain is certainly less marked than that of the main *Problem*: the weakness of Mycetes. Accordingly, we must distinguish between *Problem*-leading to an event and *Auxiliary*-leading to it.

This last distinction is related to the difference between the *task* that faces a hero and his *ability* to perform it. Naturally, the elements that contribute to the hero's ability seem more instrumental to his victory than the events leading to the formation of the task. Despite its greater degree of indirectness, Theridamas' mission is felt as more directly relevant to Tamburlaine's accession than Mycetes' reign. However, the relevance of the *Auxiliary* elements is strongly stressed only when the course of the action leads to a final success in the performance of the task. Assume that Tamburlaine had been beaten by Cosroe and subsequently killed. Then the preeminence of Tamburlaine's *Auxiliaries* would have been certainly diminished. In contrast, the importance of the unaccomplished task itself would have greatly increased.

This last remark, if correct, throws an interesting light on the semantic interpretation of tragedy as opposed to that of comedy. If the failure of the hero in his attempt to perform the main task leads to a supplementary focusing on the task itself, its origin, the constraints related to it, etc., and if the success of the hero emphasizes the secondary means by which he achieved his performance, it is only natural, on one hand, that comedy traditionally deals with intricate strategy and that the helper plays such a crucial part in it, and, on the other hand, that tragedy scrutinizes in such detail the initial flaw. It is perhaps also the reason why tragedies like *Romeo and Juliet*, in which the final catastrophe is due less to some feature of the task than to a failure in the *Auxiliary* system, are usually considered to be less perfect than the tragedies with final downfall due to a flaw in the design of the task.

Chronology and Narrative Precedence

Syntactic trees benefit from a most natural way of ordering nodes from left to right, according to the correct succession of the constituents. In transformational generative grammar, however, a given sentence can be represented by a set of trees in a transformational derivation. Constituent trees that satisfactorily represent the grammatical relations in a sentence cannot, in most cases, represent as well the correct order of the constituents and, particularly, the correct order of the ultimate constituents, morphemes and words. A similar problem arises in narratology. All proposed varieties of narrative structures, our trees included, have at least an abstract narrative level, in which the order of the ultimate constituents (events) can be different from the chronological order.[20] It must be added that the temporal sequence is once again disrupted at the textual level, where a wide range of chronological figures diversify the presentation.

In tree (2.2) one can easily see that the order of the narrative elements mentioned at the bottom of the tree is *not* a chronological one. The most obvious discrepancy is situated at the left of the tree. Indeed, although in the play everything under $Move^1_{Mycetes}$ takes place before any of the events under $Move^3_{Cosroe}$, the order of the narrative branches is determined by the necessity of *first* introducing Cosroe's *Move*, as the immediate cause of Tamburlaine's worries, and only then Mycetes' actions, which contribute to Tamburlaine's victory as mere *Auxiliaries*. Tree (2.2) thus represents something that could be called *abstract narrative precedence*. This relation strives to represent the narrative role *Moves* play with respect to one another. Accordingly, it can make use of nonchronological ordering of the *Moves* from left to right.

Indeed, from a chronological point of view, the *Moves* are not compact entities. The *Solution* to a *Problem* can arrive long after its first appearance. Chronological order is thus a property of *individual events* rather than of entire *Moves*. As a consequence, it cannot be located at a very abstract level of plot-structure. If this view is correct, then the old dictum *post hoc, ergo propter hoc* works mostly for surface aspects of narrative structure. A more abstract analysis shows the relative independence of the logical narrative structure from the chronological order of events.

This important aspect of narrative structures deserves a brief comment. *Move*-grammar stresses the logical and causal succession of actions insisting on their reciprocal links and on their strategic role in the advance of plot. Thus, it accounts for intuitions more properly narratologic than Lévi-Strauss' achronic structure of myth (1963) or Greimas' semiotic square (1970). In contrast to these, a *Move*-structure can be easily traced back to common intuitions about plot. Compared with a highly abstract and nonintuitive representation of the Oedipus story, such as Lévi-Strauss' (1963), who finds in this myth an achronological opposition relating *over-* and *underestimation of kinship* and *affirmation*, and *denial of chthonian origin of man*, tree (1.17) in chapter 1 has the advantage of representing accessible knowledge about Sophocles' plot.

Moreover, in contrast to narratological studies relying solely on chronological considerations, *Move*-grammar offers a supplementary level of information, essential for a full understanding of plot. Those authors who acknowledge only the linear succession of events in discourse and their chronology miss an important narrative point. Textual succession, especially in modern novels, combines references to events, habits, feelings, projections, and remembrance. To simply group events according to their chronology means to neglect all these distinctions, which are relevant at the level of plot.

There are two ways of dealing with the noncoincidence between *Move*-structure and chronology. One can postulate the necessity of *chronological transformations*, which would have as an input the *Move*-structures and as an output some sort of narrative constituent trees in which the order of events would be the chronologically correct one. This option would be the best if the chronological properties of narrative structures were highly uniform. If such were the case, the chronological transformations would represent the regularities of the relationship between *Move*-structures and temporal succession of events. But, as Genette's and Bal's work suggests, the chronological order of narrative events is rather idiosyncratic, depending on literary trends and fashions, or on individual preferences and effect-searching. If so, then a preferable way of dealing with the temporal order is to consider it a property of individual narrative leaves (events). In a completely elaborated tree, the moment when a given action takes place should be indicated by a time index having a status comparable to that of narrative predicates.

If we assign the index t_0 to the first event of the story, and the indices t_1, t_2, t_3, . . . , t_{n-1}, t_n to the later events, we shall notice that in tree (2.2) the temporal order of the events does not coincide with the left-to-right order at the bottom of the tree. *Mycetes king* has the index t_0, *Tamburlaine ally* (of Cosroe) t_4, *Cosroe king* t_5, *Tamburlaine's robberies* t_1, *Theridamas' mission* t_2, *Seduction of Theridamas* t_3, and *Victory against Cosroe* t_6.

The assignment of time indices shows how the chronology of the two first acts of the play gives a kind of false priority to events that fill a rather unimportant place in the *Move*-structure. In spite of its chronological priority, Mycetes' reign is only a contingent element in the plot. The alliance between Tamburlaine and Cosroe (t_4) doesn't originate directly in the seduction of Theridamas (t_3) and leads only indirectly to Tamburlaine's victory over Cosroe (t_6). This is probably why the beginning of the tragedy looks slightly tortuous. The temporal order of the events gradually uncovers a divergent narrative flow.

Analyzing the succession of events as different from the *Move*-structure of the play is not sufficient for the explanation of all dramatic effects obtained through the manipulation of the story. Indeed, the stage succession of the incidents does not entirely match the temporal order. One can consequently distinguish between *time order* and *textual order*. The textual order provides the author with the opportunity of variously changing the focusing pattern of the play. It gives him more freedom for powerful stylistic effects. Other methods of changing the focus include choosing between direct stage presentation of an event and the narration of the event, the length of time devoted to a given event, and so on. These stylistic tools are well enough known. The point of mentioning them here is to suggest that they are only a part (albeit an important one) of a greater array of narrative and dramatic effects, and that in order to better understand the textual arrangement of a literary work, knowledge of the abstract *Move*- and chronological structures is necessary.

Consider, for example, the major divisions of a play. Many commentators have noticed that after act II in *Tamburlaine*, there is a certain pause, followed by a resumption of the play on quite different premises. This division is not chronologically based: nothing indicates a lapse of time between acts II and III. The partition of the play probably belongs to a more abstract *Move*-structure level. The perceivable effect results from the fact that "as early as the end of Act II the audience is convinced that no one can defeat him [Tamburlaine]" (Spence 1927). A narratologist could say that the hero has successfully passed the *qualifying test*, which could well be the conversion of Theridamas; that he has successfully attempted the *main test*, consisting of the victory over Cosroe; and that all he now needs is to pass the *consecrating test*.[21] We shall see later how the division of *Tamburlaine* can be explained at the level of *Move*-structure. For the time being I will argue that the division of the first two acts into scenes provides for a level of event-arrangement distinct from both the *Move*-structure and the chronological order. Here, based on tree (2.2), is a list of the scenes, the narrative content of each being specified in a separate column, followed by the indication of the *Move* it belongs to:

Scene I,i   Mycetes king (*Move*³);Tamburlaine's robberies (*Move*¹); Theridamas' mission (*Move*¹); Cosroe king (*Move*³).

Scene I,ii   Tamburlaine and Zenocrate; Theridamas: mission (*Move*¹); Conversion of Theridamas (*Move*²).

Scene II,i   Cosroe king (*Move*³); Tamburlaine ally of Cosroe (*Move*³).

Scene II,ii   Mycetes king (*Move*³).

Scene II,iii   Cosroe king (*Move*³).

Scene II,iv   Cosroe king (*Move*³); Tamburlaine ally (*Move*³).

Scene II,v   Tamburlaine king (*Move*⁴).

Scene II,vi   Cosroe king (*Move* 3 and 4).

Scene II,vii   Tamburlaine king (*Move*⁴).

The list of scenes shows that the text of the tragedy freely mixes episodes belonging to different *Moves*, stretches some incidents over several scenes, compresses other events, and introduces plot-elements that do not even belong to tree (2.2) as sketched above. Thus, one gains a detailed insight into Marlowe's dramatic techniques in the first part of *Tamburlaine*. The play opens with two long scenes (act I), each introducing several narrative themes. There follows a series of short scenes (act II), each dedicated to only one protagonist (and possibly to his allies). Thus, the rhythm is accelerating as the play progresses towards Mycetes' and Cosroe's downfalls. But the main element of surprise at the end of the dynastic fight is, after the victory of Cosroe, the sudden change in Tamburlaine's attitude, his quick decision to compete for the crown and the equally quick victory over Mycetes.

Notice also the simplicity of the chronological properties of events. One finds no temporal artifices like remembrance of forgotten things, late revelations of past events, or anticipations, other than those called for by the simplest kind of planning during the preparation of the actions. Differing from the temporally sophisticated plots of *Hamlet*, in which the murder of Hamlet's father remains a secret until the ghost reveals it, or of *Macbeth*, in which there is a cruelly ironical contrast between the prophecies of the witches and the actual outcome, *Tamburlaine* has a strong epical bias. Even the mild chronological disorder of the first two acts later disappears, making room for an unusually monotonous plot.

To sum up, the first two acts of *Tamburlaine* offer a good example of a complete action, that is, of an action in which every explicit or implicit (but distinct) problem receives a satisfactory solution. This statement does not take into consideration the short dialogue between Tamburlaine and Zenocrate in scene I,ii, but it can be argued that the sole function of this scene is to establish a bridgehead between the two initial acts and the rest of the tragedy.

The structure of the *Moves* is only moderately complex, due perhaps to the absence of strong devices, like chains of violations or polemical configurations. The main surprise of the *Move*-structure consists in the sudden discovery that Theridamas' episode is not an incident of little concern leading to the success of Cosroe's conspiracy, but rather that together with Cosroe's plot it prepares the striking accomplishment of Tamburlaine's accession to power.

The textual arrangement does not always back up the *Move*-structure. Some *Moves* are insisted upon at the textual level, while the importance of others decreases on stage. Thus, several scenic artifices stress the episode of Mycetes king much beyond its actual weight in the overall plot. In tree (2.2), Mycetes occupies the secondary position of a *Problem*-creating character in $Move^3$; his own $Move^1$ is a deeply imbedded one, leading only to an *Auxiliary* symbol. This accounts for the rather insignificant role of Mycetes in the plot. From the point of view of the reading or the performance-attending process,

Mycetes' position is, on the contrary, a privileged one. He is the first monarch in a play in which the crown is at stake; in the war against Cosroe, he is granted the honor of a confrontation with Tamburlaine himself. Also, Mycetes' character is more closely designed than any other in the first two acts, except Tamburlaine's.

There must thus be two distinct ways of stressing a given character, situation, or idea at the textual level: by means of a *plot-reinforcing emphasis*, or by a *counter-plot emphasis*. The insistence on Mycetes belongs to the latter category. On the contrary, Tamburlaine's place in the first two acts is promoted beyond its local narrative function through plot-reinforcing emphasis.

Indeed, Tamburlaine's role before becoming king is rather limited: a peripheral adversary of the Persian kingdom, he is far removed from decision-making activities; later, due to his reputation for being a good warrior and of possessing unusual charisma, he is promoted to a still secondary position as Cosroe's ally against Mycetes. Up to that moment, Tamburlaine's status in the plot is no greater than, say, that of Kent in *King Lear*. But, several cues, apparently contrary to the *Move*-structure, prepare us for the reverse of fortune at the end of the second act. First, the title of the play warns the spectator about the real weight of the character. Then, for a second-rate actor, the suddenness of his seduction of Theridamas is unusual. Even more unusual is the fact that in the battle between Cosroe and Mycetes, the coward king is confronted not by his actual rival, but by Tamburlaine. By then, even someone who does not know the title of the play begins to sense the outcome. But the strongest device used to emphasize Tamburlaine's preeminence over the other characters is language. From his first speeches, Tamburlaine makes it clear that he is addressing everybody else from a privileged vantage point. His poetic discourses hint, from the beginning, that he looks over the heads of his interlocutors.[22] Consequently, although according to the *Move*-structure alone, Tamburlaine's turning against Cosroe comes as a surprise, as does his capture of the Persian crown, the textual setting of the *Move*-structure is filled with hints, moderating the shock and making it intelligible when it finally occurs. These effects cannot be explained without positing an independent, well-structured level of plot. By providing a detailed account of plot as strategic development, *Move*-grammar renders possible a better understanding of textual arrangement as well.

II

Tamburlaine's success and the death of his adversaries having ended all conflicts, the continuation of the play becomes possible only if old friends become enemies, as had already happened to Cosroe and Tamburlaine, or if new enemies appear from outside. The first alternative would be anticlimactic: it would not only employ the same device twice in a row, but, more seriously, it would present Tamburlaine with a lesser challenge than the previous one. A freshly crowned king should be able to meet adversaries greater than his former opponents; hence the pleasant feeling of continuity experienced by the spectator at the gathering of Emperor Bajazeth of the Turks with his allies, kings, and pashas.[23] In Bajazeth's eyes, Tamburlaine represents a danger too unimportant to deserve more than a warning. But this warning being defied, the emperor must confront his turbulent neighbor. After an exchange of ritual insults,[24] the battle ensues, and following a brief combat, Bajazeth is defeated and taken prisoner. One can find here at least two explicit moves: Bajazeth's attempt to prevent Tamburlaine from achieving more power, and Tamburlaine's aggressive rejection of Bajazeth's supremacy.

One serious problem with a plot like that of *Tamburlaine* is how to create the illusion of action continuity despite the purely episodic nature of the play.[25] True, the increase in rank of Tamburlaine's adversaries serves as a device suggesting escalation. There are also Tamburlaine's own personality and his speeches, but a standard Elizabethan play cannot be based only upon these elements, and even a nonstandard play has to provide for more links between the episodes. This may explain why the rest of the play, chronologically dedicated mainly to the siege of Damascus and to the war against the Soldan of Egypt, Zenocrate's father, is interspersed with the fragments of a long coda to Bajazeth's defeat. Although they bear no relevance to the new wars of Tamburlaine, the scenes dedicated to Bajazeth's captivity, humiliation, and death give the last three acts some dramatic cohesiveness.

The new moves in acts IV and V relate to the first two acts in the loosest way. By now the spectator takes for granted that Tamburlaine's martial thrust will go on indefinitely, so there is no need for a specific link between the siege of Damascus and the previous moves. The fourth act starts bluntly with the news of the siege, for which there is no other justification than Tamburlaine's plans to conquer the world. Tamburlaine employs a warning system based on three tent colors, changing the message every morning. White means pardon for everybody, red entails death for those who bear arms, and black indicates a complete massacre. Only when the color displayed by the encircling army turns to black do the officials of Damascus realize the danger and send a group of virgins to Tamburlaine, hoping to make him change his mind. The virgins are handed down to the soldiers. Damascus is taken, and the entire population massacred. Soldan's army is defeated and Soldan himself taken prisoner and condemned to death; but at the last moment, wishing to please Zenocrate, Tamburlaine pardons the father of his bride and proceeds to a sumptuous wedding.[26]

A possible way of accounting for the discontinuity between the Bajazeth and Damascus episodes would be to represent the whole play as made up of a single highest *Move*, the *Solution* of which embeds all main episodes. The *Problem* triggering the highest *Move* is not of a local narrative nature. It could be equated with Tamburlaine's inextinguishable thirst for worldly domination.

Most *Problem*-creating narrative situations could be divided into two main categories: *violations of the accepted order*, and *lack*. *Violations* are active, external actions. Naturally, the person or group affected by a violation is different from the person or group that perpetrated it. Violations are thus prone to lead to group confrontations and to formation of polemical configurations.

Most often *lack* relates to situations when the origin of the action lies inside a character, often caused by desire (P. Brooks 1977 and 1984), but sometimes taking other forms, religious zeal, for example. (For a more detailed discussion of *lack* see Pavel, forthcoming.) The character who feels the lack is usually the one who undertakes its liquidation. Subsequent actions do not necessarily lead to chains of embedded structures, but can take the form of successive attempted solutions, each dominating one or more moves. There are certainly cases when, at the origin of the first violation in a series, one finds an attempt to liquidate a lack. Or, conversely, a violation or a series of violations can lead to a solution that proceeds by successive attempts. One can, however, separate those narrative structures in which the main force behind the development of the action is a lack (as in the plots of *Tamburlaine* or *Arden of Feversham*) from narrative structures in which the lack (if there is one) serves merely to set off the first in a series of violations that quickly become the main feature of the plot (as in *Oresteia* or *The Revenger's Tragedy*).

Assuming that the proposed distinction is correct, all episodes of the tragedy under consideration reduce to unsatisfactory attempts to liquidate the fundamental lack. Without going into the details of Damascus' and Soldan's episode, an overall structure of the play can be sketched that would account for the division of the tragedy into four distinct macroepisodes: the rise of Tamburlaine to power, Bajazeth's defeat, the siege of Damascus, and the war against Soldan. These macroepisodes would be attached directly to the uppermost *Solution*. Thus every macroepisode would appear as an independent attempt to appease Tamburlaine's thirst for power. See tree (2.5).

(2.5)

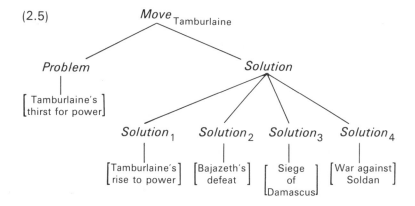

This representation of the plot points to the possibility of a second tragedy. Indeed, if the first three attempts to solve the main lack fail, why should the fourth attempt achieve success? Should we assume that the unprecedented show of generosity that ends the play is a sign of a power more confident in itself, perhaps even reaching its natural limits? But this would be a precarious assumption. Everything has been done to convince the spectator that there is no such thing as a natural limit for Tamburlaine's power; consequently, the end of the tragedy may be suspected of being only an interruption in the series of successive solutions to the global problem.

The previous analysis handles *Move*-structure as a syntactic object. This is, of course, peculiar. The *Move*-structure can be *compared* to the syntactic structure of a sentence, but it is not necessarily more closely related to it than is some other feature of a literary text. As a matter of fact, the categories employed here are strongly permeated by semantics, not unlike traditional grammatical categories themselves.

I must also note that the term *syntax* plays an important role in Todorov's (1968) poetics, as well as in Greimas' semiotics (Greimas and Courtés 1982). According to these authors, narrative syntax consists of a taxonomy of narrative propositions, divided into propositions about states of affairs, propositions about actions, and modal propositions. (See also Todorov's [1969] detailed classification of narrative propositions.) These distinctions are of considerable importance, as the above comments on narrative chronological analysis showed. Nonetheless, Greimas' system lacks an explicit grammar that would link together narrative propositions and narrative programs.

This situation may have something to do with the fact that Greimas' syntactic model is Tesnière's dependency grammar, which doesn't use categorial nodes and thus cannot explicitly represent more abstract grammatical knowledge. *Move*-grammar attempts to fill precisely this gap by accounting for the formal links between narrative events. If we use the metaphor of syntax for such links, *Move*-grammar provides for a stronger and more explicit syntax than Greimas'.

To justify the metaphorical use of syntax in relation to *Move*-structures, I can offer two more arguments:

First, *Move*-structures can be represented as labeled trees, a possibility that is also a characteristic of the syntactic structure of natural language. Second, and more important, syntactic structure has often been defined negatively, as the combinatory pattern of signs, "before" or "outside" any concrete semantic content. In both formal semiotics and most trends in linguistics, semantics is conceived as an additional component, bringing a palpable interpretation in terms of a dictionary plus a set of rules of interpretation, or in terms of a model structure. In any case, the syntactic framework appears as the most elementary abstract organization, independent of the dictionary or of any interpretation in a set of possible worlds. It seems to me unlikely that one could go much further in eliminating the concrete narrative content than the reduction of the plot to a hierarchical structure of moves. To obtain a specific plot from these empty trees, one needs at least a set of semantic elements that "fills" them with content.

In the next chapter, the kind of semantic devices needed for the description of *Tamburlaine* will be explored. It will be assumed that the semantic structures proposed operate on the syntactic basis offered by the *Move*-structure.

Chapter Three
Semantic Considerations:
Narrative Domains

In this chapter, I shall explore the semantic dimension of the plot-grammar outlined above. The following proposals are considerably indebted to the pioneering work of Todorov (1966, 1968, and 1969), and Greimas (1966 and 1970), as well as to the important contributions of Doležel (1976a, b, and c), Hendricks (1976 and 1977), and Ryan (forthcoming).

I

As we already have seen, in the system proposed herein the actions are not independent of the narrative context in which they occur. The *Move*-structures explicitly relate every narrative predicate to a certain categorial symbol (*Problem, Auxiliary, Solution*) and to a certain domain in which that predicate occurs. Thus the narrative proposition

(3.1) Tamburlaine seduces Theridamas (*Move*² in tree [2.2])

makes full sense only when read together with the symbol *Solution* above it and with the name that indexes the whole *Move* (in this case Tamburlaine). A narrative proposition functions by virtue of at least three elements: its linguistic meaning, its role inside a move, and the domain to which the move belongs.

The semantics of plot is intimately connected with the indexation of *Moves* by proper names of characters. A character or a group active enough to give his or her name to a *Move* can be labeled a "main" character or group in the narrative. If the name of the character or group appears as the index of a *Move* at least once by itself, it will be considered as a genuine "main" character or group. If, however, the name appears only in association with other names, it will be called an "associate main" character or group. In the analysis of *Tamburlaine* proposed in the preceding chapter, Cosroe, Mycetes, Tamburlaine, Bajazeth, etc., are main characters, since each of them has his name attached to at least one move. In later analyses we shall find examples of associate main characters. The remaining characters belong to the category of secondary characters. The intuitive basis of this classification is the feeling that in order to be considered as a main actor, a character must react distinctly to the general strategic state of affairs or to a specific action.

The set of *Moves* indexed by the same actor X form the *narrative domain* of X. Thus, a plot contains more than one narrative domain.[27] According to this purely syntactic definition, a narrative domain is a set of *Moves*. From a semantic point of view, however, one can define the domain of a given character X on a broader base than the set of *Moves* with which he is associated. Think of the progress of action-evaluation and decision-making that takes place every time an actor starts a *Move*. He must discover whether the state of affairs around him is satisfactory, or whether it has to be assessed as constituting a *Problem*. He must similarly evaluate the actions of other actors and decide, if necessary, how to react. He has to go through the Bremond-stages of *Solution*-binding. All this must be done in an intelligible way, so that the audience can follow the course of the action.

To perform these tasks, a character cannot invent at each step his reasons and way of reacting. Rather, he follows a system of maxims instructing him how to assess the strategic situation and how to react to it. Obviously, these maxims are not the same for each character, but some of them may be shared by many, if not all protagonists. Consider, for example, the unanimity reached by *Tamburlaine*'s characters concerning the desirability of an 'earthly crown' as opposed to the idiosyncratic maxims followed by Tamburlaine when dealing with his enemies (e.g., the rule of the three colors, so effectively applied to Damascus).

As a consequence, the meaning of a given evaluation or decision cannot be fully grasped outside the set of maxims that regulate the judgments and the actions of the characters. But since I defined the set of *Moves* indexed by the same name as constituting a narrative domain, the meaning of the actions in a domain is given by the set of maxims that are in force in that domain. We are, therefore, capable of defining both a syntactic and a semantic narrative domain: the domain of the character X is, from a syntactic point of view, the set of all *Moves* indexed X, and from a semantic point of view, the set of all maxims in force in the syntactic domain of X.

Domains are related to the problem of the so-called narrative modalities. Narratologists have often noticed that the predicates naming the actions in a story are modified by a group of operators which indicate that the actions are possible, likely, obligatory, known, unknown, etc. Attempts have been made to relate these operators to the ones employed in modal logic and its extensions, deontic, axiologic, and epistemic logic.

The specific point where the present proposal differs from other suggestions already present in the field is that according to this proposal, a plot is split into *more than one* narrative domain, and is accordingly divided into several distinct sets of propositions or maxims. The nature of these propositions is heterogeneous. Following Doležel's suggestion, I shall distinguish inside each domain the ontological, the epistemological, the axiological and the action propositions—summing up, respectively, what is the case in that domain, what is known in it, what is good/better/bad/worse, and what may/has to be done in that domain. Ryan's (forthcoming) attractive proposal contains a wider range of modalities and allows for a more differentiated account of narrative semantics. It came too late to be incorporated here in its entirety. Notice that I have omitted moral propositions, considering that some belong to the set of axiological propositions, while some others are included in the action-governing propositions.

An author or a literary trend, either deliberately or by simply following literary conventions, can endow some or all the narrative domains in a plot with the same sets of propositions in some or all four main categories. A work in which all narrative domains contain identical sets of propositions is *semantically homogeneous*. Further classification yields works ontologically homogeneous, epistemologically homogeneous, etc. In contrast to these, one can talk of *partitioned* works, either globally, or from a specific point of view. *Tamburlaine*, for example, looks like an ontologically homogeneous and axiologically partitioned work: this means that the various domains (belonging to the main actors) function under the same ontological assumptions, but obey different axiological principles. The possibility of partitioning the semantics of a literary text accounts for the various types of tensions and contradictions favored by recent criticism:

dialogic works, texts fighting against themselves make use of generous semantic partitions.

An important distinction should be made between maxims that govern the actions of the characters, such as

(3.2) Earthly power is the most desirable thing,

and more general statements, such as

(3.3) Power seekers succeed, power keepers fail,

which, rather than normatively directing the actors, represent general regularities in force in a certain domain or text. Often, these general regularities express higher-level hypotheses on the most probable course of action. Some authors call these regularities *conventions* in a somewhat improper sense, meaning that actions which conform to the regularity should not be explained by psychological reasons, but simply by reference to the regularity in question. A good example is Stoll's (1933) convention, which requires the good characters to believe the confabulations of the evil ones. No psychological explanation is needed for Othello's gullibility: he listens to Iago's slander by virtue of the convention. Todorov (1966) calls these regularities *Rules of Action*.

In order to understand a plot, it is necessary to grasp correctly the content of each semantic domain. However, it is not always obligatory to fully understand the *logical* properties of the sets of sentences included in each semantic domain. This remark is called for by a recent tendency toward making strong statements on the logic of the fictional propositions in particular literary works. It is not uncommon to find assertions on the adequacy of the LPC-T, S4, or S5 models for this or that particular literary text. My feeling is that the semantic efficacy of at least the majority of plots is due to the material content of the norms or laws involved rather than to their logical organization. True, very elementary logical properties are sometimes used for dramatic effect, but this is far removed from the formal complication implied by the choice of a modal logic system.

Following Von Wright (1963), Doležel (1976b) speaks of "anthropological" notions, as opposed to purely logical modal concepts: "Modal concepts have to be distinguished from 'anthropological concepts. . . . Anthropological concepts are used to express human abilities, attitudes, emotions, wants, hopes, etc. At the same time we have to bear in mind that . . . there exists a close association between the two sets of concepts. We can say that modal concepts represent the substratum of anthropological concepts, or, conversely, that anthropological concepts are manifestations of modal concepts" (p. 149). In the present work, I use the anthropological correspondents of modal concepts.

It should be made clear that the purpose of the following analyses is not to provide sophisticated interpretations of the texts examined. It will *not* be claimed, for instance, that *Tamburlaine* exposes the dangers of modern Promethean projects, their unavoidable demonism (Pavel 1983). The semantic considerations offered here are limited to those elements that make comprehension of the *plot* possible. The maxims and regularities involved in the semantic domains contribute to the intelligibility of *Moves*, by making clear the conditions under which *Problems* arise, *Auxiliaries* can be sought for, and *Solutions* devised. Since plot is only a part of a literary work, the overall meaning of the text could not be reduced to plot-semantics. The maxims and regularities that constitute semantic domains play, nonetheless, an important role in the construction of the overall meaning. Since semantic domains represent elementary intuitions about plot, they can be incorporated at a more advanced stage into critical readings and elaborated interpretations of the text. Conversely, as we shall see several times during the analyses of plays, a critical interpretation can be challenged if it neglects important elements of the *Move*-structure and semantic domains.

II

The semantic study of *Tamburlaine*'s domains includes, according to the discussion in the preceding paragraphs, the examination of the ontological, epistemological, axiological, and action-governing propositions.

There is no particular reason why we should assume that there are any ontological differences between the various domains of *Tamburlaine*. Ontologically homogeneous works seem indeed to be the most common kind, at least in premodern literature. For such works, the study of their ontology is significant only if it contrasts with either the one commonly accepted by the author's contemporaries, or if it is stimulatingly distant from the critic's own ontology. Now, although Marlowe is one of those authors whose ontological interests constitute a central part of their message, in *Tamburlaine I*, one is not compelled to assume a special ontology. All the poetic passages about the power of man, his closeness to God, and so forth, can be taken as mere metaphorical expressions.

Notice, however, that uniformity of perception is less taken for granted in many Renaissance plays. Think, for instance, of the numerous cases when a supernatural creature, ghost, elf, etc. is visible only to some actors. Hamlet's mother does not see or hear her husband's ghost, nor is anyone except Macbeth aware of Banquo's presence at the king's table. This shows that the actual knowledge available in different quarters may vary substantially. A certain actor or group of actors may have access to invaluable information denied to other groups. A plot that uses the contrast between well-informed actors and ignorant ones may be said to be *epistemically partitioned*. Effects of conspiracy, cunning, surprise, are possible only in epistemically partitioned plots. In *The Spanish Tragedy*, for instance, the characters are partitioned into groups possessing various pieces of crucially significant information. Balthazar and Lorenzo must keep Hieronimo from learning who the murderers of his son are, while Hieronimo, once in possession of their secret, has to plan the most impenetrable vengeance. In contrast, plots in which there is a free flow of information may be called *epistemically open*. In an epistemically open plot, all characters have access to the current information. No action is based on surprise, nor are there carefully kept secrets. *Tamburlaine* is a typical epistemically open play. No move is planned in secret with the purpose of catching the adversary off guard, not even the two-stage conquest of the crown by Tamburlaine. Indeed, the main actor could have laid plans to fight on Cosroe's side and then to turn against him in cold blood. Instead, he is presented as suddenly interested by the crown only after Cosroe's victory over Mycetes. The only moment in the play when something close to a secret plot occurs is Agydas' attempt to persuade Zenocrate into abandoning her conqueror. But the incident does not qualify as a move, and, moreover, as if drawn there by the very epistemic openness of the plot, Tamburlaine overhears everything.

At the axiological and action-governing levels, it is worthwhile noticing that all *Problems* and *Moves* are fully determined by decisions of the characters. No event is due to mere chance, luck, or coincidence. Plots in which this is the case are completely *internally motivated*. They exclude any intervention of what is traditionally called Providence, namely an outside, unnamed, invisible, volatile force, regulating the events independently of any of the parties present in the plot. The absence of Providence in this play eases the decision-making processes, since the actors of a completely internally motivated play need not pay heed to any risks other than those due to the expected course of action of rival characters.[28]

A remarkable unanimity on the maxims of power characterizes

the narrative domains of the play. Significantly, with the exception of the last *Move*, the nature of the *Problems* that bring about the *Moves* is always related to power. The characters are worried by the lack of power, which is the main stimulus for Tamburlaine's and Cosroe's actions, or by the threat of a growing outside power, which justifies Mycetes', Bajazeth's, and Soldan's *Moves*. These two basic power-*Problems* are dealt with by corresponding power-*Solutions*. The lack of power may be felt in a "reasonable" way. Thus, in Cosroe's apparently justified revolt against his feeble brother, the motives seem to be oriented toward the common good. Or, power may be sought for in a "demonic" way, the main stimulus being an irrepressible desire, such as Tamburlaine's thirst for power. Once the decision is taken to fight for power, be it "reasonable" or "demonic," there is no moral restraint on the ways to achieve one's aims. True, Cosroe's actions are less violent and repulsive than Tamburlaine's, nevertheless Cosroe as well is guilty of treason.

The other type of power-*Problem* is the defense of existing power against challenge. An important maxim of diagnosis requires authority to interpret as a threat *any* existing power outside the empire. Mycetes worries about Tamburlaine's successes as soon as they take place; Bajazeth takes the first steps against the new king of Persia as soon as Tamburlaine gives sign that he "presumes a bickering" with the Turkish emperor, etc.

To meet the challenges to his authority, every king and emperor in the play resorts to the same two-step procedure: first he warns the challenger to either restrain his activities or to submit entirely. Then, after the uniformly negative reaction of the opponent, he takes strong military action against his adversary. Tamburlaine's progress from bandit to king goes together with a change in strategy: after the third act he no longer attacks by surprise, but instead considerately warns his future victims of his intentions, in the same way as he, in his former days, was warned by Mycetes or Bajazeth.

The outcome of every conflict is regulated by a simple trans-domain maxim: every power seeker succeeds in his endeavors and every power keeper, except Tamburlaine, fails. It is easy to usurp power, but, if one is not Tamburlaine, impossible to secure it. This maxim accounts for Cosroe's and Tamburlaine's successes in the first two acts, as well as for Mycetes' and Bajazeth's failures.

The main difference between the various domains of the play consists in his treatment of the opponents. Tamburlaine is notoriously cruel to his unlucky enemies, while the only other victor in the play, Cosroe (but, presumably, every other potentate would act like Cosroe rather than like Tamburlaine) gives no sign of brutality.[29] Notice that in *Tamburlaine I* this aspect does not become a narratively significant one. No *Move* is caused here by the bad treatment of Tamburlaine's adversaries; nobody cares yet about Bajazeth being kept in a cage and starved. Seen from the point of view of its impact on the plot, Tamburlaine's viciousness is merely an ornamental device.[30]

If one adopts a *mythocentric* point of view and accordingly considers plot as the central element in a play, the importance of the semantic elements in the work will be recognized by their contribution to the advancement of the plot. Moral attributes of a given character, for instance, will be said to be central to a work only if they determine a significant move. Such cases can be called plot-significant attributes, or, more generally, *plot-significant semantic elements*. It is unlikely, however, that all semantic elements meant to impress the average reader or spectator are plot-significant. A large category of semantic effects is based on the mere showing of things. The *exemplary* function of literature is not limited to the manifestation of the consequences for the action of such and such (moral) attributes. Often, its purpose is equally well served by showing that such things could exist. True, in premodern literature, the main accent of a literary text most often falls on plot-significant elements. But unusual properties, the mere existence of which can become a subject of wonder, are also strongly focused upon.

Thus, even if it doesn't determine the shape of the plot, Tamburlaine's cruelty creates a semantic partition of the play into two "cells": Tamburlaine's domain vs. all other narrative domains. The latter display a remarkable uniformity, in spite of the potential differences between the main actors. But the play is calculated to concentrate on Tamburlaine. The other characters and their domains are simply the background against which the overwhelming hero is projected.

III

Semantic domains are sets of propositions that describe ontological configurations, give the relevant epistemological and axiological information, and list the maxims for action. One can think of each domain as possessing a *book* in which all this information is recorded. When a chapter in the book recording the true propositions and the rules of a certain field (say, the ontology) of the domain D_1 is identical with the corresponding chapter in the book of the domain D_2, the two domains D_1 and D_2 belong to the same division with respect to the field in question. If all chapters referring to a given field are identical, the play is *open* from the point of view of the field. A literary text in which all books of all domains are identical is an open work. (Whether such a work has ever been written or not is an empirical question: *Tamburlaine I* certainly gives a good idea of what such a text would look like.) Now, imagine that in the books of a play someone marked with *red* ink all sentences that bear relevance to the plot. The set of sentences thus marked is a subset of the set of sentences in the books; it can be called the *plot-relevant set* of sentences. All the distinctions sketched above apply as well to the plot-relevant sentences. Two chapters dealing with the same field in two different books can be identical in their plot relevant sentences, but are still different when one takes into account all the sentences. This is precisely the situation of *Tamburlaine I* regarding the maxims for action, as described above.

As for the substance of the chapters in the books belonging to different domains, one may mark with *blue* ink all the sentences on which the text seems to insist, regardless of their plot-relevance. The set of blue-marked sentences constitutes the *semantic focus* of the work. It is obviously unnecessary that the blue-marked and red-marked sentences be the same. Thus, in *Tamburlaine I* the cruelty of the hero toward his enemies belongs to the semantic focus of the play, without being plot-relevant. As for the size of the semantic focus, it can vary substantially from one literary text to another.

In *Tamburlaine I*, the number of maxims belonging to the plot-relevant set or to the semantic focus seems to be rather limited. Among those maxims one may count the following:

(3.2) Earthly power is the most desirable thing;

(3.4) The aim of gaining power justifies any action;

(3.5) Neighboring power is a threat to power;

(3.6) Kings and emperors warn their enemies before attacking;

(3.7) A defeated enemy can be dealt with in the cruelest fashion.

Add to this,

(3.3) Power seekers succeed, power keepers fail,

which is a more general regularity in the play.

Maxim (3.2) indicates the uniform nature of the problems leading to moves. Maxim (3.5) supplements (3.2), giving a maxim for the cases when the character already possesses a crown. Maxims (3.4) and (3.6) prescribe the kind of action to be taken once the problem has been identified and the strategic setting examined. The two maxims distinguish between the possessor of a crown and the adventurer who attempts to gain one. Being a king restricts the possible courses of action. They relate to (3.3), which in spite of its providential character, appears to be at least obscurely known by Cosroe and is firmly upheld by Tamburlaine. Much of the fascination the hero exerts on his bewildered interlocutors in the first two acts stems from his certitude that (3.3) is the case. As for (3.7), it is a sentence that belongs to the semantic focus of the play, without having any impact on the plot.

Maxims (3.2)−(3.7) function together with a set of more general regularities concerning plots and their understanding. Such is

(3.8)   When a given state is the most desirable for some actor, then, if the actor is not in this state, his problem will involve how to reach it.

The above proposition stipulates that the main purpose of characters in fiction is to reach optimum states. Together with (3.9), it constitutes the basis of the classical theory of action.

(3.9)   If a given actor's obtaining the optimum state leads to another actor's being prevented from obtaining *his* optimum state, the first actor is said to violate the second's interests.

The last two propositions provide the missing link between maxims (3.2-7) and the more concrete narrative sentences of *Tamburlaine I*.

For other details of the play, it may be useful to add a maxim for making allies, as well as two propositions related to courtship.

(3.10)   In the process of fighting for power, any alliance is allowed. No previous alliance is to be respected if it goes against the purpose of gaining power.

(3.11)   The main hero of the play must be in love.

(3.12)   His affection for his beloved extends to her family.

Maxim (3.10) allows for the alliance between Cosroe and Tamburlaine, as well as for the parallel "treasons" of Cosroe toward Mycetes and of Tamburlaine toward Cosroe. Maxim (3.11) is an omnipresent rule, especially in the tradition of chivalric literature. Its role in *Tamburlaine I* is less central than in romance or in some other

Elizabethan plays. It merely provides for a useful relief of the martial tension of the play and has an indirect impact upon the plot by means of (3.12), which makes the denouement possible, since Tamburlaine gives priority to maxim (3.12) over (3.7) and suspends his usual cruelty.[31]

Chapter Four
Marlowe—An Exercise in Inconstancy

I

The second part of *Tamburlaine* differs considerably from the first.[32] Instead of a coherent, if monotonous plot, one finds a play divided into episodes ill related among themselves. A simple group of semantic regularities is replaced by a more complex semantic component. The splendid poetic spell is still there, but its flamboyance cannot conceal the structural problems of the play.

Superficially, the plot of *Tamburlaine II* resembles that of the first part. In both plays the first scenes open with a secondary episode, leading, next, to a major confrontation between Tamburlaine and the Turks, after which a siege against a powerful city ends in a complete massacre of the population. Both plays conclude with a strong episode contradicting the previously assumed conventions and containing a main existential event. The initial episodes are the conflict between Mycetes and Cosroe in the first part and that between the Turks and the Christians in the second. Tamburlaine confronts first Bajazeth and later, in the second part, his avengers. The besieged cities are, respectively, Damascus and Babylon. Tamburlaine's magnanimity toward Soldan contrasts with his usual ferocity in the same way in which his weakness when confronted with disease and death contrasts with his previous invincibility. The main existential events concluding the tragedies are marriage and death.[33]

A Proppian analysis could thus find in both plays the following sequence of functions:

(4.1)   Secondary conflict – Main confrontation – Victory-Siege
          – Change – Existential event.

Such an analysis would however miss the complex hierarchical relations between the events as they are determined by the competition
among the different domains of the play. As represented by the
Move-grammar, a plot is not a sequence of events (not even a sequence of abstract events), but rather a hierarchy of relations involving events, narrative categories, and narrative domains. To better
grasp the structural richness of *Move*-grammar when compared to a
linear Proppian analysis like (4.1), the reader is referred back to tree
(2.5), which represents the action of *Tamburlaine I*.

    In the second part of the tragedy, the conflict between Turks and
Christians contains several *Moves* which, while representing a fight
between two opposite camps, do not qualify as a polemical configuration. The Turks, led by Orcanes, king of Natolia, cannot wage war on
two distant fronts – in Europe against Sigismund, king of Hungary, and
in Asia against Tamburlaine. They conclude a truce with the Christians
in order to be secure in confronting Tamburlaine's forces. For the
Christians, however, the truce is only an auxiliary move in their effort
to cope with the problem of the Turks' presence in Europe. They see
nothing wrong with breaking it, for, as a companion of Sigismund expresses it, "with such infidels / In whom no faith nor true religion
rests, / We are not bound to those accomplishments / The holy laws
of Christendom enjoin" (II, i, v. 33-36). Christian treason constitutes
a new challenge to the Turks, the successful solution of which is the
victory over Sigismund's troops and the death of Sigismund.

    Notice how peripheral is Tamburlaine's presence in this episode.
In the second part of the tragedy the hero loses the quality of omnipresence he enjoyed during the first part.[34] This loss has a definite
impact on the epistemic laws of the play. Moreover, Tamburlaine is
deprived of another crucial property: he is no longer immune to
treason. The escape of Callapine, Bajazeth's son and prisoner of
Tamburlaine, would have been unthinkable in the first part. Callapine
joins the Turkish army and, together with the other faithful contributory kings, meets Tamburlaine's army at Aleppo. The Turks
are defeated and most of their leaders taken prisoner, but again,
Tamburlaine's invincibility deteriorates, as Callapine manages to
escape. In a display of joyous cruelty, Tamburlaine has his chariot
drawn by the defeated kings, while their concubines are delivered to
the soldiers. It is the only occasion when Tamburlaine's savagery
regains some of its former cheerfulness. In an earlier episode, the hero
gloomily ordered that the city where his wife expired be destroyed

and never again rebuilt. Later, when his (diminishing) thirst for earthly power drives him to Babylon, his cruelty takes a more saturnian ring: he pointlessly shoots the captive kings, while the inhabitants of the city are drowned by the soldiers in an asphaltite lake. More involved in metaphysical endeavors, the power he is seeking toward the end of the second part is an inconceivable power over the gods: he defies the spirit of Mahomet and, at least rhetorically, expresses the desire to go "to war against the gods" (V, iii, v. 52).

Unmotivated by the plot (is this a semantic point to be made?), his death comes just when Callapine, the son of his former enemy, plans the largest war ever against Tamburlaine.[35] The outcome of the war will not be known: Tamburlaine dies prematurely, infringing an important Aristotelian rule, namely that all action started in a literary work must be satisfactorily ended within that work. But this is not an Aristotelian play,[36] and the action does not possess narrative unity. Where should one insert, for instance, the strange episode, unrelated to the main thread of the action, of Olympia and Theridamas? How do we account for Zenocrate's death? What is the role of Tamburlaine's slaying his eldest son, Calyphas? Is it an *attributive* element, the function of it being to show the audience *how* the character is? An implicit requirement of classical literature prescribes that the actions in which the characters reveal themselves should not be redundant, but relate in some well-motivated way to the main plot. The usual requirement that character show itself in action means that, inasfar as possible, no move should have the unique function of establishing an attributive truth. But the Caliphas episode has no other function than reinforcing an awareness that Tamburlaine is a near monster.[37]

The war against the Turks and the siege of Babylon can be taken as further solution to Tamburlaine's perpetual problem, the thirst for power. As for the last scene of the play, it can be represented, together with the episode of Zenocrate's death (and maybe with Calyphas' murder as well), as episodes in the unfair fight between Tamburlaine and Death. The poet explicitly indicates that this fight is the main theme of the second part of the tragedy:

> Where death cuts off the progress of his pomp
> And murderous Fates throws all his triumphs down.
> (Prologue, v. 4-5)

Indeed, as many critics have noticed, *Tamburlaine II* closely resembles medieval morality plays. To account for this, narrative tree (4.2) contains a nonanthropomorphic entity (Death), as index for the highest *Move.*

(4.2)

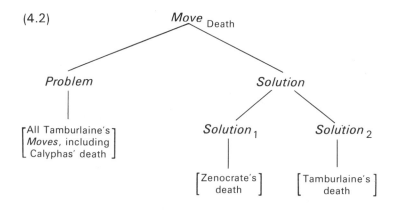

The main difficulty with tree (4.2) lies in the fact that its *Problem* does not stem from the definite action of a character, but is triggered by the general way in which a character solves his or her *Problem*. Death's "problem" is not caused by a specific violation by Tamburlaine, but by the hero's overall tendency to play Death's role. Tree (4.2) is an archaic narrative structure in that it uses supernatural or abstract actors. Renaissance tragedy dislikes the specific attribution, in the *Everyman* fashion, of tragic endings to symbolic cosmic forces only indirectly offended. This is why for the modern critic (and perhaps for Marlowe himself) the reading offered by tree (4.2) has an ironic tone. Illness comes suddenly upon Tamburlaine, in the middle of a speech: "But stay; I feel myself distempered suddenly" (V, i, v. 216), like a cruel irony.[38] Consequently, in order to show the link between Tamburlaine's actions and tree (4.2), one needs a more flexible way of interpreting the relation between *Problems* and *Solutions*.

In polemical configurations, where the *Solutions* of a given *Problem* constitutes in itself and in a very obvious way a violation in the domain to which the next *Move* belongs, the interpretation of the link between one *Move* and the succeeding one is rather simple. Each *Move* is a reaction to a previous violation, a kind of vengeance/ punishment calling for further vengeances/punishments. The *vendetta* structure of many narratives involves a conscious trespassing of someone else's rights or interests, and consequently a sort of acceptance of the risk of retaliation. This type of conflict is based on *explicit violations*.

Very early in the history of tragedy one finds another kind of relation between an action or a set of actions and the retaliation they call for: the involuntary infringement of some sacred or profane duty. In some cases, the violation is quite definite. Oedipus' crimes, although involuntary, can be designated unequivocally. Once exposed, their crystal-clarity literally blinds the hero. In other cases, perhaps even more primitive, the violation of the established order is not only unintentional, but also ill defined, sometimes indefinable. The malice of gods is such that they can decide to punish someone for the vague guilt of having been too happy. In such cases, divine retaliation punishes a *fuzzy violation*: the actions of the characters are liable to unexpected consequences from the most distant and unforeseen quarters. The fuzzy violation relates also to the perennial problem of power. A servant cannot be fuzzy-violated by his master, nor a man by his gods. Only the converse situation occurs: masters are indefinitely offended by their inferiors, as are gods by men. The fuzzy violation can be characterized as follows:

(4.3)   If actor X is hierarchically the superior of actor Y, then virtually any action or attribute of an action of Y can be interpreted as offensive by X. X's counter-action has the purpose of reasserting his supremacy over Y.

Proposition (4.3) accounts for the embedding of all Tamburlaine's moves under the *Problem* of Death's move. One can even assume that Tamburlaine's attempts to satisfy his thirst for power in the second part of the play are but a continuation of the first part of the tragedy. Death's privileges are violated by the whole career of Tamburlaine.

The assumption that the two parts of the tragedy are both embedded under the symbol *Problem* in tree (4.2) is acceptable from an intuitive point of view.[39] As for Callapine's plans of war against Tamburlaine, they can be attached as an *Auxiliary* under Death's *Move*. This reading is not compulsory, but it seems tolerably correct to assume that the purpose of the penultimate scene is to indicate how things become increasingly difficult for Tamburlaine and to what extent the future of his empire is an uncertain one. For the first time the hero is faced with a young enemy impossible to capture. The reading according to which the fall of the hero is the result of the irony and vengeance of death can accommodate the presence of Callapine as an *Auxiliary* to this irony.

The only episodes that are not included in the above analysis are those of Theridamas and Olympia, his unfortunate prisoner, who, rather than be unfaithful to the memory of her husband and marry his victor, prefers to die using an elaborate stratagem. Episodes that are not explicitly connected to the main thread of the action can have the semantic role of emphasizing a problem, a solution, the nature of a convention, etc. The most probable function of the

Theridamas and Olympia episodes is to insist on the spread of Death around Tamburlaine.[40] The lieutenants of the great hero pursue his work. But Theridamas' failure to conquer Olympia can be seen as signaling the absence of magic in the second part of the tragedy. The rising Tamburlaine diffused an irresistible charm around him. Now this is gone, and the aging hero, even if he can delegate to his vassals the power to win wars, does not imbue them with his dissipating charisma.

II

From a semantic point of view, the second part of *Tamburlaine* seems to contradict deliberately the maxims in force in the first part. First, it is no longer certain that all characters share the same ontology. It seems rather that toward the end of the play Tamburlaine's world changes its inventory of beings, or, at least, the inventory of essential properties. Consider a single, but crucial, passage, that of the book-burning (V, i). Tamburlaine repudiates his former faith in Mahomet, "Whom I have thought a God" (v. 174):

> In vain, I see, men worship Mahomet.
> My sword hath sent millions of Turks to hell.
> Slew all his priests, his kinsmen, and his friends,
> And yet I live untouched by Mahomet.
>
> (V, i, v. 177-80)

To test his new ontological hypothesis, Tamburlaine orders all the copies of the Alcoran found in Babylon to be burnt. Then he challenges Mahomet to come and defend his book. The prophet's failure to do so leads Tamburlaine to the conclusion that Mahomet is but another godhead, unworthy of being adored. Not later than the next scene, however, the king of Amasia proclaims, optimistically, his strong faith in Mahomet: "I see great Mahomet / . . . / Marching about the air with armed men / To join with you against this Tamburlaine" (V, ii, v. 31, 34-35), he declares to Callapine. In an epoch when saints and angels were believed to take part in battles and when ghosts were a familiar sight in the theater, these two opposite stands are certainly meant to be semantically pertinent.[41]

This ontologically partitioned play is epistemically divided into different groups as well. The main change with respect to the first tragedy is that Tamburlaine has lost his omniscience. Callapine is capable of coaxing his guard into freeing him without any interference from Tamburlaine. Remember, in contrast, the prompt appearance of the hero when, in the first part, Agydas tried to persuade Zenocrate into leaving with him. In the second part, information does not flow as easily as in the first; intentions can be hidden, while deliberate lies and cheating make an appearance. (Olympia's stratagem to get killed by Theridamas; the Christians' treason.) Moreover, while in the first part every character or group of characters was aware of everything that happened, here several events remain confined to the periphery of the play, without reaching all the groups involved. Thus, the details of the truce and subsequent war between the Turks and the Christians do not seem to reach Tamburlaine's headquarters. Nor is he briefed on the episode of Olympia. The hero no longer occupies the epistemic center of the play, knowing everything and planning the events according to copious information, as was the case in the first part. The second part does not even possess an epistemic center: no character knows everything the spectator knows.

This results in the lack of a "command" center in the second tragedy. In the first play it seemed that Tamburlaine had almost supernatural powers in perfectly planning his successes and bringing them about. Nothing after the first act happened without being caused to happen by the hero. He was fully in control and worked in a perfect identification with Providence. For this reason, in the first play one does not need a separate principle of action, apart from Tamburlaine's will. In the second part, on the contrary, the events impose themselves, so to speak, upon Tamburlaine, who does not control the main stream of the action. Consider tree (4.3), which represents most of the plot.

It is apparent that the hero takes but a single initiative: the siege of Babylon. All other events in the play either do not concern him at all (the conflict between Turks and Christians), or are initiated by forces outside him (Zenocrate's death, the war with the Turks, his own sickness and death). Some of these actions come from human opposition to his rule, the others look like providential intervention. Moreover, the *Solutions* figured out by Tamburlaine are far from efficient. His *Moves* lack the touch of assurance and perfect effectiveness they possessed in the first tragedy. He cannot prevent Zenocrate's death, is unable to change his eldest son's character and subsequently murders him, fails to keep Callapine prisoner, and despite the victory over the Turks, does not capture him again. Finally and most dramatically, he has no power over his own sickness.[42]

From the axiological point of view, earthly power has ceased to be the most desirable thing. In the second tragedy there is no such thing as a unanimously recognized supreme value. Tamburlaine still believes

(4.3)

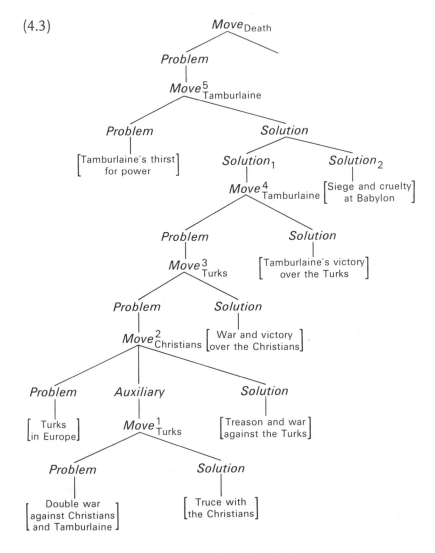

in secular dominion, since he preaches this single value to his sons on his deathbed. But during Zenocrate's illness he realizes that there is something that can "scourge the scourge of the immortal God" (II, iv, v. 80). In a weakly integrated *Move* that does not appear in tree (4.3), Tamburlaine's son Calyphas expresses his desire only to play and make love; he has to be killed in order for the ideals of his father to be justified. This sort of axiological conflict would have been unthinkable in the first tragedy, where people were not yet dying for opinions. In another significant episode, Olympia acts out of fidelity to her dead husband. Interestingly, Callapine, Bajazeth's son, wants not only his father's crown, but looks for vengeance as well: he does not accept that Tamburlaine's cruelty remains unpunished. Thus, the attitude toward cruelty, which in the first part of the tragedy was purely attributive, becomes now reason for action.

As for the distribution of success and failure, the play is less biased in favor of Tamburlaine. It must be noticed that the camps are not divided into power seekers and power keepers, but into conquerors and avengers. Tamburlaine still qualifies as a conqueror, and so do his lieutenants, as well as Sigismund, the king of Hungary. The avengers include Orcanes, his allies, and of course Callapine. By virtue of their common opposition to Tamburlaine, the avengers and Death are on the same side. The last act clearly suggests that what Callapine expects to accomplish by war, Death does in a less costly way. As for success, the only certain thing is that Death cannot be defeated. Further regularities prescribe that avengers can use deceit, that conquerors are always the victors, except when they commit treason, that Tamburlaine and those on his side invariably achieve military victory, but that they are unable to reach *all* their goals, and so on.

We are thus far removed from the monolithic structure of the first tragedy. *Tamburlaine II* is partitioned from the ontological and epistemic points of view, does not possess uniform rules for action, and has a pluralistic axiology. Add to this the fact that the plot has chaotic developments, that there is no epistemic and decision-making center in the play, and that a determining factor in the denouement is an abstract existential element: Death.

All this gives an indication of the amount of variation Marlowe was able to introduce into a new work in which almost every element was already present in the first part.[43] The second part of the play was dangerously predetermined: the characters, the problems, some aspects of the mood were already in place. The previous analysis helps to localize the devices used by Marlowe to produce a still novel and surprising play.

III

With *The Jew of Malta*, Marlowe again changes his mood. This time he chooses a tragico-sarcastic tone,[44] which will be much imitated by later Jacobean writers. *Tamburlaine I*'s effect derives from a subtle mixture of poetic rapture and very simple narrative rules. In *Tamburlaine II*, the poetic momentum is not yet lost, but the narrative mechanisms

are becoming more diversified. Both parts of *Tamburlaine* are mono-
tonal (and monotonous); Marlowe has not yet discovered the jumps
in mood and the fickle frivolity characteristic of *The Jew of Malta*
and *Doctor Faustus*.

The plot of *The Jew of Malta* is probably the most complex of the
playwright's whole career. It contains a great number of *Moves*, a
very peculiar set of rules for alliances, and a well-diversified set of
actors belonging to different social levels and obeying various norms
of behavior.

Barabas, a rich Jewish merchant in Malta, is summoned together
with his coreligionists to cede half of his property to the city, in
order to make possible the payment of a tribute to the Turks, ten
years past due. Because he refuses to pay the emergency contribution
and to become a Christian, the city hastily seizes all his wealth. In an
elaborate scheme to save some of it, Barabas persuades his daughter,
Abigail, to become a nun in the convent established by the city in his
own house. Abigail recovers a jewel-case hidden in the house, while
Barabas, with the help of a slave, manages to cause the death of the
Governor's son and to poison all the nuns.

A striking contrast opposes the martial brevity of Malta's dealing
with Barabas, at the abstract narrative level as well as in the text, to
the length and complexity of the vengeance. In order to achieve
vengeance, Barabas needs money. The episode of his daughter entering the nunnery and the recovery of the jewel-case are but an *Auxiliary Move* on the path of revenge. So is the hiring of Ithamore, the
Thracian slave who will help Barabas perform his plans. Then, Barabas
dedicates himself to the core of his search for vengeance. The first
step consists in sowing dissent among Lodowick and Mathias, Abigail's
suitors (one of whom is the Governor's son), and having them kill
each other. This deed convinces Abigail, who sincerely loved one of
them, that her father is unworthy of her devotion and that "there is
no love on earth." Consequently she decides to go to the nunnery.
Learning this, Barabas is upset to the point where, with Ithamore's
help, he sends a pot of poisoned rice porridge to the nuns. Before
dying, Abigail reveals everything concerning her father's deeds to two
monks. They have to be neutralized as well: one of them is killed and
the second is sent to prison following the accusation of having murdered his companion.

At this stage, Barabas starts having trouble with his slave, Ithamore.
Falling in love with a courtesan, the Thracian slave needs money,
which he raises from Barabas himself through blackmail. A series of
minor *Moves* and *Counter-Moves* provides for a release of the tension

of the play. In a comic interlude, Barabas appears disguised as a French musician. After a while, the blackmailers inform the authorities about Barabas' crimes. He feigns death, then hands the city of Malta to the Turks who, in the meantime, have laid siege to it.

After the conquest, submitting to an inexplicable urge to commit treason, Barabas tries to ambush the whole invading army, but instead is murdered himself. The authorities of the city have preferred to negotiate with the Turks rather than to deal again with the unpredictable merchant. The city of Malta uses Barabas as an agent of his own destruction, in the same way in which earlier he used his daughter's suitors.

The private tragicomedy of Barabas goes along with a serious civic conflict, that of Malta against the Turks. It is interesting to note that Malta's fight for independence has its own logical development, which intermingles with the destiny of the Jewish merchant. From the city's point of view, there is only one obsessive problem, that of the Turks' demand for money. At first, its solution seems to lie in raising the cash from the Jews and paying the debt. However, since later on a Spanish fleet approaches the island, the Governor changes his mind and refuses to pay. This brings about the siege of the island by the Turkish army, a siege that succeeds precisely due to Barabas' treason. Later, as he changes sides again, Malta takes advantage of Barabas' plot to get rid of the Turks while saving the lives of the enemy leaders. The end of the play thus solves in a satisfactory way the problem that brought it into being. Tree (4.4) is a simplified representation of the action.

The above analysis shows that, contrary to widespread opinion, the narrative structure of *The Jew of Malta* is not a simple, straightforward one.[45] Simplicity is, of course, a relative quality; Marlowe's tragedies are simpler than some by Shakespeare or Webster. But compared with the two *Tamburlaine* tragedies, with *Arden of Feversham*, or with some of Shakespeare's early historical plays, *The Jew of Malta* certainly displays considerable complexity. Under this analysis, which has not discussed all details of less essential episodes like the love story of Ithamore and Bellamira, nor some of the political problems of the city of Malta, the total number of *Moves* is sixteen, significantly more than could be found in each of the two parts of *Tamburlaine*.

Also, in contrast to *Tamburlaine II*, the play is perfectly coherent: the *Move*-structure can include all events of the play in a single tree. No event has to be explained by purely semantic reasoning. If one takes into account the fact that the play has two narrative centers of

(4.4)

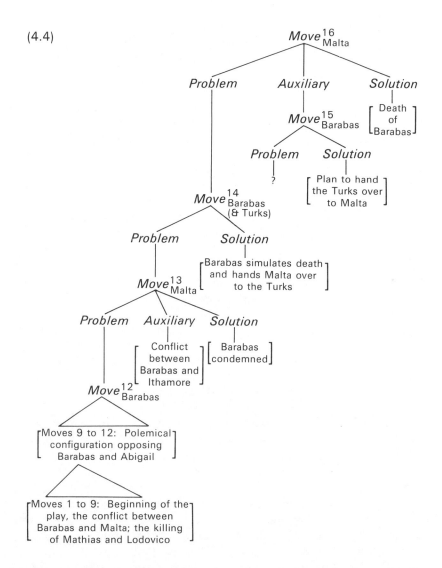

interest, namely the personal destiny of Barabas and the fate of Malta, the achievement of Marlowe seems even more remarkable. He constructs a plot that is neither monotonous, like that of *Tamburlaine I*, nor made up of entirely disconnected fragments, like the plot of *Tamburlaine II*.

Another aspect to be considered is the *narrative tempo* of the play. I take this notion to refer to the relationship between the number of *Moves*, the number of domains, and the length of the text. Thus, narrative tempo is different from the technique of cutting the plot into represented vs. narrated events and arranging the represented events in an entertaining way. This last capability relates to what should be called the *scenic tempo* of a play. To realize that narrative and scenic tempos are distinct, it is sufficient to think of a play like *Gordobuc*, in which a rich, dynamic plot takes the form of a slow, rhetorical scenic happening.

The number of *Moves* in *The Jew of Malta* is considerable. As the total length of a play is more or less circumscribed, the increase in the number of *Moves* results in a more lively plot. Elements contributing to this tendency are the number of major characters taking part, in other words, the number of narrative domains displayed in the plot, as well as the number of characters participating in each domain. In *The Jew of Malta* there are only four domains (or five, if one includes Ithamore's actions): those of Malta, the Turks, Barabas, and Abigail. A limited number of narrative domains in a plot containing many *Moves*, increases the chances that the characters are rather active and consequently the play well animated. If, moreover, the narrative domains contain more than a single character, the tempo of the play is likely to increase. Add to this the unstable nature of alliances in the play: Barabas changes his allegiance several times; his daughter, Abigail, belongs at first to his domain, but later founds her own domain, bringing about the best-defined polemical configuration of the play; Ithamore, who is also affiliated with Barabas, deserts him and establishes his own domain. The weak stability of alliances introduces a new set of unexpected changes to the strategic configuration and therefore significantly contributes to the dynamism of the play.[46]

In contrast with *Tamburlaine II*, there is no ontological disagreement in *The Jew of Malta*. With respect to its epistemic properties, however, the play is drastically partitioned. In no other play by Marlowe is information, its concealment, or its disclosure, given a comparably important place. Since every domain contains deception, except that of Abigail after she breaks with her father, concealing information is a frequent device. The most obvious occasions are Abigail's alleged desire to enter into a religious life (I, ii, when Abigail still belongs to the narrative domain of her father), Barabas' maneuvering of Lodowick and Mathias, and of course the final rapid succession of deceptions: Barabas' handling over Malta to the Turkish officers, and his being trapped by his own deceit. But information concealment goes beyond mere deception; it is crucial for Barabas' survival that his past activities remain unknown. Much effort is thus dedicated to preventing the truth from surfacing, and to neutralizing people who know about Barabas' crimes. Still, twice during the play, the way actors belonging to Barabas' domain leave it and establish their own domains is by disclosing facts about the vicious merchant: Abigail abandons her father and betrays him in III, vi, while Ithamore devises his blackmail and denunciation plans in act IV. Barabas' technique of deception is so powerful that even when, in V, i, the authorities of Malta learn about his past misdeeds, they do not know how to prevent him from further harming the city. Significantly enough, the fall of Barabas occurs only when his opponents resort to the same techniques of deception and use Barabas' projects against him.

A very effective device used by Marlowe to enhance the spectator's participation in the vicissitudes of the main character is based on the distinction between *narrative suspense* and *epistemic suspense*. Narrative suspense involves the mere ignorance of the outcome of a given *Move*. Even if the spectator knows everything about the intentions of all participants in a given action, he can still be ignorant of who will be successful and under what conditions. It is rather remarkable that *Tamburlaine I* and *II* almost completely lack narrative suspense. Most of the fascination these two tragedies exert on those who enjoy them is due to the amazing absence of surprise; every event acquires the compactness of necessity. *The Jew of Malta*, by contrast, is full of narrative suspense. One does not know with certainty what the outcome of Barabas' actions will be. After his failure to keep his estate, the series of successes against the city are far from taken for granted. The Jew is continuously on the verge of failing: first his daughter divulges his secrets, later Ithamore deserts him, still later he is caught by the city's system of justice. Each time he recovers, and his desperate successes against all odds pleasantly surprise the spectator.

Epistemic suspense occurs when the spectator is also denied crucial information on the organization of the *Move*. Take the case of deception. If the spectator knows that actor X intends to deceive actor Y, and waits to see if X will succeed in doing it, the work employs mere narrative suspense. If, however, the spectator does not know that X has treacherous intentions, the success of X's scheme against Y will constitute for the spectator a major surprise. In most cases, characters themselves are kept in ignorance of the plans and intentions of their adversaries. Epistemically open plots are a rarity. Consequently, one could (somewhat improperly) say that normal characters live under a strong epistemic suspense. Indeed, they are often ignorant of their opponents' secret objectives. It follows that in every situation in which a character X is in the dark about his adversaries' intrigues, the author has the choice of making known those intrigues to the spectator or keeping them covert. In the first case, the spectator will know more than the character. In the second, one can say that the character and the spectator "share" the epistemic suspense.[47]

In *The Jew of Malta*, the spectator is almost always informed in advance of Barabas' tricks. The only occasion when the audience is temporarily deceived by a feat of Barabas involves his false death in the last act. But even then, the spectator is the first to learn that Barabas is still alive and well and planning to ruin the city. (Nor should one minimize the whispered warnings Barabas offers to the spectator before his simulated death: v. 39 and 41 of scene V, i). In contrast, most of the actions planned *against* Barabas are kept from the audience. The spectator finds out that Bellamira and Pilia-Borza have at last made up their minds and gone to the Governor to denounce the Jew, only a few seconds before Barabas learns about it himself. As for the denouement, the spectator is, to the last instant, ignorant of the scheme devised by the Christians and the Turks to rid themselves of the dangerous merchant. The spectators are no less surprised than Barabas himself when he falls in the caldron prepared for Clymath, the son of the Turkish emperor.

To keep the spectator informed about *some* of the oncoming actions is certainly a powerful means of attaining certain effects. A spectator who knows everything tends to be ready to judge the characters. When one knows less, the usual tendency is to suspend judgment at least until all the relevant facts become known. But when the spectator shares all the knowledge and all the ignorance with a given character, it is only natural that a sort of complicity will establish itself between the audience and the character in question, a complicity that diminishes the repulsion the acts of the character would otherwise inspire. This "complicity through shared information" is often put to use by Elizabethan dramatists who want to make the villain of the play less repugnant. But never has a play been so constantly written *from the epistemic point of view of the villain.*

It is probably this peculiarity of Marlowe's play that has pushed commentators into somewhat anachronistically attributing to the author either sympathy for the main character, or at least a greater aversion for the hypocritical Christian behavior than for Barabas' open wickedness.[48] (Some think that the author feels an aversion for specifically Catholic behavior, although in this play at least, Marlowe never bothered to draw such distinctions.)

Another peculiar device employed in *The Jew of Malta* is the frequence of counter-normative maxims, that is of maxims going against the usual norms of situation-evaluation. Thus, although the way he applies it is both brutal and dishonest, the governor's principle according to which

> . . . better one want for a common good
> Than many perish for a private man.
>
> (I, ii; v. 99-100)

is not counter-normative. Nor are principles like those applied by Malta and the Turks in their conflict counter-normative. But Barabas' domain, and later Abigail's, gradually include more and more counter-normative rules. The first bizarre rule of the play is that of vengeance against the city. Not satisfied with recovering a substantial part of his possessions, Barabas proceeds with a complicated revenge. His behavior obeys the following maxims:

(4.5)   One is allowed to seek personal revenge against the agents of an arbitrary power;

(4.6)   In the process of revenge, one can use one's offspring as instruments;

(4.7)   The feelings or interests of the offspring may not be taken into account;

(4.8)   If, in the process of revenge, one's offspring change sides, they become enemies and may be treated accordingly;

(4.9)   Murdering innocent people is not prohibited when it is related, even indirectly, to revenge;

(4.10)   No alliance is to be respected.

From (4.5) to (4.10) there is a gradual aggravation of the counter-normative quality of Barabas' maxims. Maxim (4.5) is often acceptable. Principles (4.6) and (4.7) are forms of the general maxim of family allegiance, belonging to an archaic and cruel form of paternalism.[49] As applied by Barabas in III, iv, maxim (4.8) is repulsive, and so is (4.9). With (4.10) we reach the ultimate in Machiavellism.

This escalation corresponds to a steady deterioration in the character's moral standards. As the action goes on, Barabas commits crimes more and more heinous, and less and less motivated. The double murder of Lodowick and Mathias may look like revenge, although one does not see why Mathias, the son of a harmless widow, is included. Barabas claims causally that the young man's father was his chief enemy (II, iii, v. 247). The mass murder of the nuns exceeds the wickedness of previous actions, especially since Barabas' own daughter is among the victims. Still, it possesses the shadow of a reason: the resentment of a man deprived of his house and daughter by the representatives of an enemy religion. The murder of Fra Barnardine is slightly more justified (and more controlled: another monk is left alive and sent to prison). So is the handing over of Malta to the Turks. But the final change of allegiance, although superficially motivated through fear of the citizen's hate toward a Jewish Governor, looks rather like the climax of immorality. It is difficult to assess how real Marlowe's alleged enthusiasm for Machiavelli was;[50] it appears, however, that with his last treason Barabas steps outside of Machiavelli's teachings. Indeed, in its standard Elizabethan interpretation, Machiavellism argues that any action is justified provided it serves the interests of the agent; thus Machiavellism is merely a liberation from accepted moral standards. In this sense, almost all of Barabas' actions are examples of Machiavellism. The last change of sides, however, brings rejection of all reasonable considerations. Indeed, Barabas' last act is not justified by the interest of the agent: its only ground is the irresistible pleasure of manipulating destinies, of being an absolute master, beyond laws and conventions, in a way in which no official Governor of Malta can ever be. No wonder that in comparison with the exhilarating feeling of absolute amoral power, Barabas finds the governorship of Malta unattractive.[51] But in this play, only crime and spoliation may remain unpunished, whereas gratuitous acts cannot be allowed; thus Barabas must perish.[52]

Other action maxims in *The Jew of Malta* contribute as well to the overall effect. Consider, for instance, the breakdown of the relationship between master and slave: Ithamore blackmails Barabas, presumably because his master puts too much strain on a naturally fragile association. It is a major error of Barabas to ask too much of people with whom he has close affinity: Abigail, his daughter, leaves him and incriminates him for his deeds. Critics have noticed the parallelism between Abigail and Ithamore, each isolated from the influence of Barabas by an unhappy love for a Christian.[53]

Or think of a widespread gullibility, which asks every character dealing with Barabas to take his utterances at their face value, without suspecting anything. This regularity, although implausible, plays an important role in any story about deceivers.[54]

Stylistic and textual devices emphasize some of the syntactic and semantic properties of the plot. The following two examples are related to the tempo of the play and to its epistemic perspective. First, the rapidity of rhythm is confirmed by the textual arrangement. Moves come hastily, with minimal preparation. All of Barabas' schemes are put into practice at once. There is no long-term planning in the play, because there is no time for it. Toward the end of the drama time is so short that Barabas must abandon some of his machinations; for instance, he does not manage to murder Ithamore.

Second, although the scene is restricted to two main areas of action, namely Barabas' quarters (symbolically situated somewhere close to his former house) and the Governor's territory, occasionally a third place is brought to our attention: a less dignified district (the market?) where Barabas finds Ithamore and where Bellamira meets her customers and the Thracian slave. It is true that the variation of scenes appears rudimentary, especially when compared with Shakespeare's technique of space utilization. Nevertheless, the rhythm of the play is perfectly well emphasized within the limits of its system. Thus, a remarkable number of characters quickly traverse Barabas' dangerous space: some find their death there with notable rapidity.

The fact that the place of the action doesn't change too often is perhaps due to the previously noted epistemic perspective of the play. Centered around the epistemic outlook of Barabas, the play cannot stray for long from his dwellings. Notice also that in someone else's territory, Barabas becomes powerless: his failure to dispose of Ithamore could be related to the fact that instead of attempting it on his own premises, Barabas ventures into the neutral area of Bellamira and Pilia-Borza.

Finally, consider a detail related to the epistemic perspective of the play. We saw that the play is organized in such a way as to create a feeling of complicity between the spectator and the wicked hero. A textual device that strongly reinforces this feeling is the use of asides.[55] Such lines suggest, whenever used, the closeness of the character to the spectator. In *The Jew of Malta* the representatives of the authority never speak aside. This confirms the above remark about their being on the other side with respect to the spectator. The Jew addresses the spectator (or himself) as often as possible, to stress the ambiguity of his undertakings and to keep the spectator aware of his real intentions. Notably enough, Abigail's few aside lines are uttered while she is an ally of her father or when, later on, despite her change of sides, she has not yet resolved to expose his crimes. A most clear token of talking aside in connection with Barabas' interests which she still has at heart are the lines 73-75 at the end of act III, scene iii.

After having stated her intention of entering the nunnery, Abigail accuses her father of having forced her from the sisterhood. It is however only a slip of the tongue, for she immediately recants, adding aside:

> O Barabas,
> Though thou deservest hardly at my hands,
> Yet never shall these lips betray thy life.

The only other characters who speak aside are Ithamore, who does so a few times when confronted with Bellamira and Pilia-Borza, and the latter, always amongst themselves and only in front of Ithamore. It looks as if the neutral place (the market?) is the only one where all the characters can speak aside. Significantly, it is also the only spot where Barabas fails to bring about his dark intentions.

IV

In *Doctor Faustus* we are again confronted with a simple plot, simpler even than that of *Tamburlaine*, but liable to be read in two different ways. Harry Levin (1952) calls the play an "anticlimax of the parable"; R. M. Frye (1956) finds "no plot apart from the character." From the strictly narrative point of view, Goethe's famous remark on "how greatly it is all planned" is incomprehensible.

The explicit narrative *Problem* of the play is Faustus' merely *initial* dissatisfaction with everything except magic. (One major difference between Marlowe's and Goethe's heroes is the latter's *continuous* dissatisfaction with the objects of his fulfilled desires.) Thus, the structure of *Doctor Faustus* is definitely more rudimentary than that of *Tamburlaine I*. Tamburlaine's desire for power is an inextinguishable one. Each attempt to solve the initial *Problem* ends in military triumph and metaphysical disaster, for every victory shows more clearly to Tamburlaine that there is no limit to his earthly search. In that sense, one would say that, despite the theme, Goethe's tragedy is structurally more closely related to *Tamburlaine* than to *Doctor Faustus*.

Faustus' *Problem* is easily solved by the treaty with the devil and the subsequent episodes. The treaty itself constitutes a serious *Problem* from God's perspective. The final *Solution* will be Faustus damnation. Tree (4.11) sums up this unsophisticated narrative structure.

The episodes introduced under the *Solution* of *Move*[1] are the following:

(4.11)

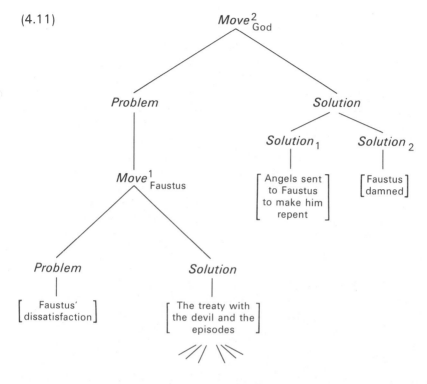

1. Faustus learns about the astronomical organization of the universe and watches the dance of the Seven Deadly Sins (II, ii);

2. Faustus takes an astronomical journey in the company of Mephistophilis (iii, i);

3. Faustus goes to Rome, where he plays tricks on the pope (III, ii);

4. Faustus arrives at the court of the German emperor, where he entertains the company with magic feats;

5. He provides fresh fruits in January to the pregnant Duchess of Anholt;

6. He deceives a group of peasants by selling them an imaginary horse and making them believe they broke his (Faustus') leg;

7. Back at home, he has Mephistophilis bring Helen of Troy to his study.

The lack of apparent logic in the progression of episodes may be attributed to the bad textual state of the play. Indeed, one can assume that the text of the play is so damaged that any attempt to judge on that basis Marlowe's intentions and achievement is refuted in advance. But if the text was damaged, plot-analysis may help us understand why it was subject to deterioration in the first place.[56]

A narrative or a dramatic text can be divided into *core* segments, which represent essential moments of the *Move*-structure, and collateral or "soft" segments, which represent secondary moments of that structure. The secondary segments are more easily eroded than the core ones, for obvious reasons: they are less indispensable for the comprehension of the plot. To give an example, in *Hamlet* the performance of the *Murder of Gonzaga* is an essential moment of the play, while the conversations of Hamlet with the First Player, with Rosencrantz and Guildenstern or with the two Clowns in the graveyard are less important for the advance of the plot. It is likely that a dramatic text, particularly when published long after its initial performance, will undergo an inevitable process of deformation. But in all probability, the deformation will affect first the secondary segments of the play, while the core fragments, those which are obligatory for the correct understanding of the plot, will prove more resistant.

If so, even a cursory glance at tree (4.11) shows why the episodes of Faustus' life after the signing of the treaty with the devil are more liable to editorial change than the beginning and the end of the play. The first act and the first scene of the second act are too crucial to the understanding of the plot to be significantly changed. They contain *Move*[1] almost in its entirety. Equally protected from deformation is the last act, which narrates the *Solution* of the problem raised by Faustus in God's domain. But the several episodes of Faustus' existence during his alliance with the devil do not have a momentous impact on the plot. Once the pact is signed, the only question in suspense is God's reaction to it. So, it is far from surprising that damage may have occurred in these "soft spots" of the play.

One can draw, moreover, a structural distinction between episodes that correspond to a newly introduced categorial symbol, such as *Problem, Auxiliary, Solution*, and episodes that result from the repetitive extension of an already introduced symbol (rules 1.12-14 of the *Move*-grammar). Let us call the last type *iterative* episodes. The narrative information brought by each iterative episode will be less than that corresponding to an independent episode. Accordingly, iterative episodes are more liable to lapses of memory and textual deformation. Faustus' adventures in the company of Mephistophilis are typical tokens of an *iterative* device. As such it is understandable they were felt as less unalterable than other segments of the play.[57]

In this particular case, the play, and especially the soft spots circumscribed above, sustain an almost unbearable metaphysical burden. The semantic load of the play is simply too heavy for its narrative structure. To localize the nature of the difficulty, notice that while the play contains only a few domains, its ontological structure is quite complicated. From the point of view of Faustus, who is the hero of the apparent story, the devil is just a dangerous instrument he uses to achieve certain goals. In Mephistophilis' view, however, the whole story of Faustus is only an episode in the perennial fight between Lucifer and God for the allegiance of men. This justifies perhaps the introduction of a polemical configuration involving God and Lucifer, something like tree (4.12).

(4.12)

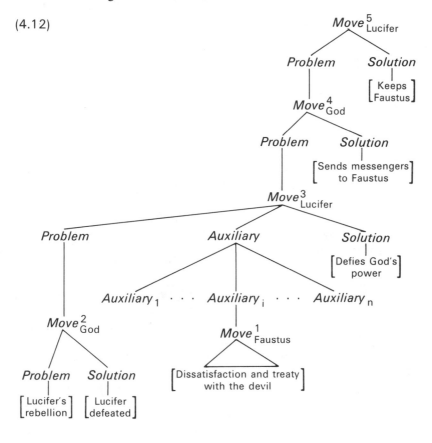

Tree (4.12), although much more complex than (4.11), is a faithful representation of the way Faustus' personal drama situates itself in the cosmic conflict of good and evil. With respect to Lucifer's purposes, as defined from time immemorial, Faustus' striving for knowledge and pleasure is but a local skirmish in a major war, the beginning and the end of which go beyond the limits of the play. It is also suggested that $Move^3$, which recounts Lucifer's attempts to somewhat overcome his previous defeat, contains under its *Auxiliary* symbol many stories similar to that of Faustus.

The narrative procedure represented in tree (4.12) consists in presenting a given element of a *Move*-structure as one among a series of coordinated similar elements. The reason for choosing this particular element, $Move^1_{Faustus}$ in our case, rather than any other element in the series $Move^i$, $Move^j$ . . . dominated by the *Auxiliary* of $Move^3$ but not narrated in the play, is not explicitly given. One tacitly accepts that the story which has been selected is among the most significant. Let us call it the *exemplum*. A structure like the *Auxiliary* or $Move^3$ in tree (4.12) will be called an *exemplary structure*. Exemplary structures are typical narrative mechanisms of late medieval morality plays, the semantic relevance of which comes precisely from the assumption that the story narrated is only one among countless other similar stories, and that its selection is the outcome of a process of focusing which constitutes the main contribution of the text. The larger cosmic setting belongs to the shared presuppositions of the society. Accordingly, it is alluded to only insofar as strictly required by the economy of the exemplum.

That *Doctor Faustus* may be described by both tree (4.11) and tree (4.12) indicates that the play has a double perspective. Tree (4.11) delineates the tragedy as seen from the human point of view, while tree (4.12) represents the cosmic conflict. The play has no strongly constituted vantage point in terms of which the different syntactic and semantic elements could be organized. Structural ambiguity reveals thus an important feature of the play, namely the hesitation between two perspectives, reinforcing the impression that this is a hybrid text, uncertain of its status, oscillating between morality plays and Renaissance tragedies. (For more remarks on perspective, see Appendix, section 5.)

This uncertainty reflects in the semantics of the plot as well. From the ontological point of view, *Doctor Faustus* takes place in a medieval world, marginally modified by the most recent geographic and astronomic discoveries. In this context, it is appropriate to distinguish between the *center* of an ontological outlook and its periphery. The center contains those propositions which are most present in the focus of attention and awareness of the community sharing the given outlook. The periphery contains propositions which are still within that ontology but which are less close to the main interests of the people who share it. Applied to literature, this distinction amounts to the separation of heavily used ontological propositions from propositions which are still held as true, but which fall out of grace with the writers and the public over a certain period. Problems concerning the relationship between the natural and the supernatural worlds were at the center of late medieval literary ontology. Writers and their public were intensely aware of the ontological propositions situating man in the middle of the chain of beings, and attributing to him a sizable set of properties following therefrom. Morality plays are largely based on these assumptions. Elizabethan theater, in contrast, without excluding the supernatural from its ontological outlook, pushes it to the periphery of its interests. God, the angels, the devils quit the theater, unable to interest the public. To remind people that there is a hereafter, Elizabethan playwrights sometimes introduce a ghost, the almost unique representative from beyond to be found in Elizabethan tragedy. The late medieval world is still there, in the peripheral shadows, but nobody thinks of exploring it. This shift of attention brings to the forefront the problems of human action and its relation to systems of values. For the treatment of these questions, the ontological propositions required by dramatists reduce to a bare minimum. It is in this context that the archaic character of *Doctor Faustus* appears more explicitly.[58] Indeed, taking for granted the evolution toward a new ontological center, what Marlowe tries to do in this play is to confront it with the ontological periphery. Hence, the amplitude of the ontological scope of the play, its lack of a precisely balanced axis, and ultimately its narrative incongruity.

As enough has been written on the semantic content of the play, I will not go into more detail. Let me only add that the play is epistemically open and that, after the signing of the treaty, there is no fundamental new risk taken in any of the actions of the hero. As for the axiology of the play, it lies precisely at the origin of the perplexity aroused by it: why should Faustus prefer a few scraps of uncertain astronomy supplemented by a ridiculous magician's tour of Europe to eternal salvation? That such a question could be asked says something about Marlowe's playful nihilism and about the scandalous message of the play.

V

With *Edward the Second* Marlowe again tries an entirely different enterprise. The structural dissimilarity between this tragedy and *Doctor Faustus* is so conspicuous that, for our purposes at least, it does not much matter which play was written first: they belong to different approaches to plot. While *Doctor Faustus'* tension comes in its entirety from the gravity of its thematic content and from the disastrous ending, in *Edward the Second*, in which the hero's desires are foolish and frivolous, the tragedy is calculated to stem from action and its unexpected consequences. And since the most powerful narrative device for action-based conflicts is polemical configuration, it is not surprising to see Marlowe use this type of narrative organization.

The new king of England, Edward the Second, has just called for his intimate friend, Gavestone, to return to London from exile. Since the relationship between the two young men is a strong infatuation with one another, the nobility is opposed to Gaveston's presence at the court. But Gaveston does not take into account the difficulties of his situation and instigates the king to imprison one of his moral censors, the bishop of Coventry. Thus, not only does Gaveston's return break a previous ordinance, but his and the king's first joint action is a serious violation of established order. The initial problem of this tragedy, Gaveston's exile, leads to the first *Move*: his return and the fight with the bishop of Coventry. The next *Move* consists in the reaction of the peers. It amounts to forcing the king into signing the exile of Gaveston (I, iv). After a harrowing scene of separation, the young king takes revenge on his persecutors by wilfully neglecting the queen. The *Move* brings the expected result: the queen persuades her friends to accept the return of Gaveston. The first act ends with the reconciliation between Edward and his earls. It is an act composed of numerous *Moves*, as can be seen from its representation in tree (4.13).

Tree (4.13) visibly constitutes a polemical configuration. The characters form two different groups, the *Moves* of each being dominated by the problem of the other group's *Moves*. An interesting feature of polemical configurations is that the stronger group indexes the last *Move* and that, when the outcome of the conflict is a compromise, the solution of this uppermost *Move* automatically becomes the solution of the opposite group, that is, of the penultimate *Move*. A transformation that may be called "*Solution*-generalization" copies the

(4.13)

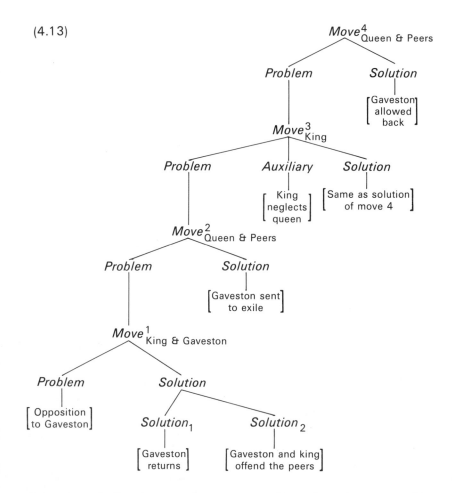

uppermost solution in every lower move where there is no narrative proposition under the symbol *Solution*.

The application of the *Solution*-generalization does not take place before the end of the plot. The *Solution* it generalizes belongs in most cases to the last move of the play. The application of the *Solution*-generalization at some point before the end of the plot may indicate a *fallacious denouement*, set only to emphasize further the vehemence of the renewed conflict.

Such is the case in *Edward the Second*. We saw that the *Solution*₁ of *Move*¹, Gaveston's return, is not strong enough to atone for the humiliation of the exile. The king and his friend need the more aggressive *Solution*₂ which, by offending the peers, is the immediate impetus for *Move*² initiated by the peers. A double *Solution* in which the second attempt prompts the outburts of a polemical configuration could be called a *Hubris-Solution*. Sometimes it constitutes the narrative consequence of the tragic flaw, especially in plays in which the nature of the tragic *Problem* is entirely presented through visible violent action. Back in the court of England for the second time, Gaveston cannot prevent himself from being inordinately arrogant with the peers who have just accepted him. A general rebellion follows, under the leadership of Mortimer Junior, one of the most intractable enemies of Gaveston. During a panicky retreat, the king and Gaveston separate, and the king's minion falls into the hands of the peers, who kill him (after some deliberation and an attempt by the king to see his beloved).

A most strange circumstance of the play is that the action does not stop with the death of the seemingly main villain. Edward mourns his friend, but not for long: in the meantime he has found a substitute for Gaveston in the person of Spencer Junior. It looks as if Gaveston had no role to play as an individual; he, as well as his successor, are temporary materializations of an abstract entity: the king's minion. The plot goes on as smoothly as before, with Spencer continuing to play Gaveston's part.⁵⁹ Later, the peers led by Mortimer and the queen achieve victory, take the king prisoner, and nominate Mortimer and the queen as regents. The deposition of the king does not satisfy Mortimer. When he arranges for Edward to be murdered, it becomes obvious that Mortimer wants the crown for himself. At the last moment, however, the young Edward the Third arrests him and orders his execution. The queen mother, who in the meantime had become intimately involved with Mortimer, will stand trial for alleged complicity in her husband's death.⁶⁰ See tree (4.14).

Tree (4.14), together with (4.13), exemplifies Marlowe's tendency to become obsessed with a single artistic mechanism that is overused in a given work and then totally abandoned. *Tamburlaine I* was constructed as an anticlimactic work, in which there were no surprises and no dramatic changes of situation. The predictability of Tamburlaine's victories and reactions becomes gradually obsessive, giving the play its hieratic tone. *The Jew of Malta* frenetically employs quick moves, deceptions, and violations of the most elementary rules of morality. In *Doctor Faustus* the succession of episodes that recount Faustus' life after signing of the demonic pact has no apparent logic. But this lack of logic is itself so obvious, so plain, that one cannot escape its monotonous spell. In *Edward the Second*, instead of disorder one finds a perfect concatenation of events, bound among themselves by

(4.14)

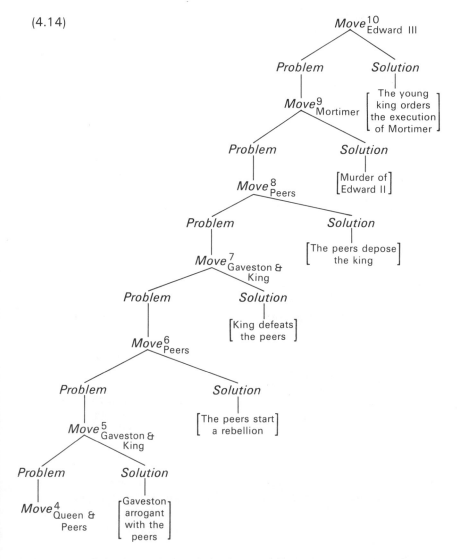

the most cohesive narrative tool: the polemical configuration.[61] Once again, however, there is too much of it.[62] As the plot advances, one feels kept prisoner of the repetitive device, of the unending sequence of *Moves* and *Counter-Moves*, not very different from the unavoidable triumphs of Tamburlaine, the breathtaking wiles of Barabas, or the irrelevant experiments of Faustus. These are haunting devices, impossible to employ more than once.

The insistence on a single narrative effect, thoroughly repeated throughout a whole play, cannot but influence its semantic aspects. Thus, it is not a matter of chance that in *Tamburlaine, Doctor Faustus*, and *The Jew of Malta*, most maxims are faithfully respected. The same situation prevails in *Edward the Second*. Here also, the play makes use of a stable set of maxims. The interest of Marlowe shifts again from epistemic and ontological problems to the maxims for situation evaluation and action. The play presents no particular ontological properties. From the epistemic point of view, it is fairly open. Every character is informed in due time about the planned or eventuated actions of others. Few secret plots are devised and implemented. The exceptions are the murder of Edward, secretly and cowardly planned by Mortimer (V, v), and that of Gaveston (III, ii). Their singularity in a world of open and defiant sin and rebellion makes them even more repulsive.[63]

The play's axiology is partitioned into at least three domains, obeying various sets of maxims: the domains of Edward the Second and Gaveston (or, later, Spencer Junior); that of the peers, Mortimer, and the queen; and that of Edward the Third. The king's evaluation of the situation regularly gives precedence to his personal feelings over the fragile equilibrium of the kingdom. He follows a maxim asserting that:

(4.15) The satisfaction of personal desires is inclusively preferable to the peace of the family or of the kingdom.

The presence of "inclusively" means that if both personal and public requirements can be simultaneously fulfilled, the king is ready to compromise. Gaveston follows a stronger form of the maxim:

(4.16) The satisfaction of personal desires is exclusively preferable to the peace of the kingdom.

Under (4.16) it is impossible to satisfy at the same time personal and public demands. Corollaries of these maxims bring about the neglect of marriage, lack of respect for private property, for established law, and so on.

The rival narrative domain finds these maxims abhorrent. The peers respect a converse of (4.15), containing an inclusive preference, and consequently the possibility of compromise:

(4.17) The respect of the laws and traditions of the kingdom is inclusively preferable to the respect of the king's person.

This rule is supplemented by a group of maxims requiring power shifts in cases of emergency.

(4.18) The subjects of a king who follows (4.16) may rebel against him.

(4.19) If rebellion occurs, the rebels may seek maximum power, even if this entails the deposition of the king.

A further rule lurks behind (4.19):

(4.20) Maximum power amounts to maximum personal power.

Since there are instances when the maximum of personal power cannot be achieved without breaking the laws and traditions of the kingdom, the successive application of maxims (4.17) and (4.20) may well lead to awkward choices. As in traditional feudal morality, the preference of personal interests receives a negative evaluation. Up to a certain moment, the peers have a monopoly on good behavior, while the king and Gaveston (later Spencer) live up to wicked principles. As Mortimer gains more power, he starts to use a set of maxims as evil as, if not worse than (4.16):

(4.21) A living king and his closest relations hinder one's progression toward maximum power;

(4.22) Achieving maximum personal power is exclusively preferable to any other law or consideration.

Hence the murder of the king and the execution of Kent. Maxim (4.22), a main rule in all Elizabethan historical and political tragedies, points toward a very likely execution of Edward the Third. The only action of the third domain of the play combines survival justice: when Edward the Third orders the execution of Mortimer and the removal of the Queen-Mother from the court, he apparently obeys a maxim like:

(4.23) A king must dispense justice.

A few more rules govern love, which plays a greater role in *Edward the Second* than in any other tragedy by Marlowe, except *Dido, Queen of Carthage*. In Edward's domain, love is exclusive in synchrony, but not in diachrony. At each moment of the story the king has a lover to whom he is faithful and whom he puts above everything else, but it is not necessary that at two successive moments, the king's lover be the same person. In the opposite domain, the queen and Mortimer follow the usual rules of courtly love. The queen is neglected by her husband, whose love she tries in vain to recover. Mortimer, who hates Edward, feels pity for Isabella and falls in love with her. After a long resistance, convinced that there is no hope in saving her marriage, Isabella gives in to Mortimer.[64] An unpleasant consequence is full complicity between lovers, which leads to the queen's being put to trial for Edward's violent death.

Among the ideas of structuralist poetics, one of the most successful opposes structure to individual freedom, and stresses the impersonal powers of grammar, linguistic or narrative, while playing down the role of the author. Contrary to such views, the preceding analyses suggest that a poetological perspective may well lead to interesting cosiderations about the artistic personality of individual writers. Marlowe's rebellious features have always impressed critics, favorably or not. His versatile, capricious stands, his taste for paradox and exaggeration, find an interesting confirmation in the structural analysis of his plots. Obsessed with continual exploration of entirely different plot techniques, Marlowe puts each to use in one drama until satiation, and then completely discards it. The frenzy with which he overuses his plot devices, turning to new ones with a savage desire to push them to their extreme consequences, strikingly resembles the violence of his poetic raptures.

Poetic grammars, like their linguistic counterparts, are oriented toward the general, impersonal features of a text; but just as linguistic grammars do not contradict the study of trends or individual styles, the description of plot-regularities should not make us neglect their idiosyncratic use by individual writers.

Chapter Five
Two Revenge Tragedies:
The Spanish Tragedy
and Arden of Feversham

I

The Spanish Tragedy by Thomas Kyd is contemporaneous with *Tamburlaine I*, but displays a much more complex narrative structure than any of Marlowe's tragedies, more complex even than *The Jew of Malta*. The modern reader is tempted to ask how the Elizabethan audience could remember all the details of such a ramified plot. A tentative answer is that it probably did *not*. The activity of plot-understanding presumably proceeds in two different stages: (1) the processing of local narrative information and the detailed understanding of parts of the narrative tree; and (2) an operation of schematization of clusters of past events rendered possible by the existence of domains and of their rivalries. Toward the end of a very complex tragedy, the spectators inevitably forget some of the material processed at the beginning by virtue of operation (1). The grasping of the global meaning is still possible due to operation (2), which sets apart the main conflicts from the many developments illustrating their intricacies (Lubbock 1921).

In *The Spanish Tragedy*, where the author purposely accumulates various features that complicate the plot, one may distinguish from the outset three different main narrative lines: the story of Andrea's death and its revenge, the story of the relations between Spain and Portugal, and the story of Horatio's death and its revenge.[65] Lateral miniplots, like Villuppo's attempt to destroy Alexander's reputation, or like Pedrigano's death, are but local devices for further perplexing the audience.

85

The prologue (or Induction) and several scenes related to it, narrate the story of Andrea, killed in the Spanish-Portuguese war by Don Balthazar, prince of Portugal. Andrea, former lover of Belimperia, niece of the Spanish king, comes back as a ghost, brought by Revenge, an allegorical character, to attend the "mystery" that tells the destinies of his murderer and of Belimperia. Although during the play Andrea often shows signs of impatience, at the end he seems satisfied with what has happened therein. Thus, the play itself is introduced as the solution to the unrevenged death. The adequacy of the solution can be seriously doubted: what satisfaction can Andrea derive from the fact that Belimperia falls in love with another man and ultimately dies in the midst of a generalized carnage? A maxim that explains the relevance of revenge and allows the abandonment of restraint could have the following form:

(5.1)   If X is guilty of Y's death, then X's death is a satisfactory revenge for Y or his allies, no matter what consequences accompany it.

Situations in which (5.1) works are noncompromise contexts, in which revenge takes precedence over everything else.

The political intrigue of the play appears as peripheral. At no time is there any genuine interaction between the personal tragedy of Horatio and Hieronimo and the political-military conflict opposing Spain and Portugal. The overplot has mainly the contingent capacity of bringing Don Balthazar to Spain and making him acquainted with Belimperia.

The main plot, much more complex than the other two, narrates the revenge taken by Hieronimo and Belimperia against Don Balthazar and his friend Lorenzo. After Andrea's death, Belimperia falls in love with Horatio, Hieronimo's son. Don Balthazar tries to make his way into Belimperia's heart. When he fails, his friend Lorenzo, Belimperia's own brother, discovers the identity of Belimperia's lover, and they kill Horatio. Belimperia's and Hieronimo's revenge amounts essentially to three operations. First, they must find out who is guilty of Horatio's murder. Second, they ineffectively try to obtain legal satisfaction. Third, they devise their own revenge.

The first operation is necessary because of the adverse epistemic conditions in the play. But after a series of unsuccessful inquiries, Hieronimo finds out the truth by mere chance. As has been suggested above, the intricacies of such an episode are easily forgotten. What is essential for the continuation of the play is the fact that Hieronimo discovers the murderer's identity.

Next comes Hieronimo's attempt to find justice at the royal court. But since he is now an old man affected by fits of lunacy, he misrepresents his case before the king and loses his credibility. Later he accepts a faked reconciliation with Lorenzo, which, incidentally, justifies the ghost's explicit impatience with the slowness of the revenge. In the meantime, moreover, Hieronimo's wife Isabella stabs herself from despair that the murderers of her son cannot be found.

At last, however, an occasion for revenge comes with the celebration of Belimperia's and Don Balthazar's marriage. Hieronimo accepts to organize the entertainment. He directs the performance of a play of his own, having as actors Lorenzo, Balthazar, Belimperia, and himself. The play-inside-the-play contains two murders and a suicide. The characters played by Hieronimo and Belimperia have to kill, respectively, those played by Lorenzo and Balthazar. The slayings actually take place. Belimperia then commits suicide, as her part demands, while Hieronimo explains the whole thing to the audience.

(5.2)

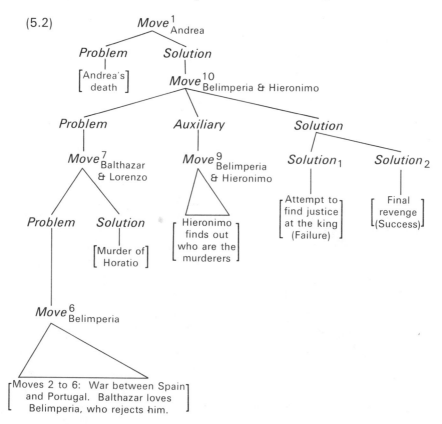

He then bites out his tongue, in order not to speak under torture, and surprisingly manages to stab Lorenzo's father and himself. Tree (5.2) is a simplified representation of the action.

Three episodes remain outside the representation in tree (5.2): Villuppo's defamation of Alexander at the Portuguese court, Isabella's suicide, and Hieronimo's public fits of lunacy. They are not reducible to any of the aforementioned moves. Indeed, Villuppo's episode lies completely outside the *Move*-structure,[66] while the two other episodes are lateral consequences of Horatio's death. As I noted previously, the presence of loosely connected episodes can be attributed to the need to stress various elements in the plot. Villuppo's actions are probably there in order to emphasize the play's epistemic partition, while Isabella's death and Hieronimo's despair function as reminders of the seriousness of Horatio's death. These episodes may be attached to the chronologically and polemically closest *Move* by a transformation that one may label the *Episode-Attachment Transformation.*

II

Ontologically, the play is divided into two partition cells: the domain of Andrea, which contains only supernatural beings, and the other domains, populated only by living humans. The two domains do not obey reciprocal restrictions. The ghost of Andrea belonged once to the human world. He still watches what happens there, hoping to derive some satisfaction from the events occurring after his death. In the human world, in contrast, nobody seems to remember him. His former betrothed, Belimperia, quickly falls in love with Horatio. Her indifference is still more striking when one realizes that she dedicates all her efforts to the revenge of her *second* love and even commits suicide after achieving it. On his side, Andrea does not appear jealous when he sees the idyll between Belimperia and Horatio. Indeed, the only comment he makes after the second act, in which Horatio and Belimperia unambiguously express their passionate love, is the regret for Horatio's death and certain worries about the fate of Belimperia, "on whom" he adds,

> I doted more than all the world,
> Because she loved me more than all the world.
>
> (II, vi, v. 4-5)

The only link between the two realms is revenge. Andrea does not perceive anything except what could lead to the death of his murderers.

He forgets however that for humans to die is not a happy event. Enumerating the slayings he has observed, including those of his friends: "Horatio murdered in his father's bower, / . . . / Fair Isabella by herself misdone, / . . . / My Belimperia fall'n as Dido fell / And good Hieronimo slain by himself," the ghost ends with the revealing words: "Ay, these were spectacles to please my soul" (IV, v, v. 3, 6, 10-12). Any death pleases him except his own.

In the human world, in contrast, death is consistently perceived as the major disaster. This amounts to a sort of ontological parochialism: since people know nothing about the other world, they consider that there is scarcely anything worse than to leave the present one. Their ignorance of the other world's existence and laws functions, incidentally, as a sort of barrier between the stage and the audience. Andrea's ghost stands proxy for the spectator: belonging to a different world than the actors, he still participates in their joys and sufferings; he can see and hear them, but the converse is impossible.

In both worlds a subtle distinction between *simple* and *generalized* revenge is in force. Andrea and Hieronimo first want simple revenge, which consists in the discovery and just punishment of the culprit. For various reasons, this cannot be done. Andrea's ghost is, if course, a mere spectator of events he cannot control. As for Hieronimo, after painfully discovering the identity of the murderers, he is clearly unable to make his case before the king. Simple revenge eludes him. Functionally, Hieronimo's madness is precisely the device that prevents him from looking further for a simple revenge. As if made aware of the impossibility for revenge to strike accurately the limited area inhabited by the culprits, Hieronimo changes his mind and proceeds to the staging of a generalized revenge. This second type of revenge looks more like a sacred frenzy, like a trance, during which the killing is indiscriminate. The violence of the trance is such that it suspends the laws of self-conservation: murder and suicide are but the manifestation of the same thirst for blood. It is thus unnecessary to construct complex rational explanations of the murder of the duke of Castille. Any spectator of violent movies understands perfectly well that the blood frenzy must not stop until every potential victim is reasonably or unreasonably slaughtered. This can as well explain Andrea's shocking remark "Ay, these were spectacles to please my soul" (IV, v, v. 12). Like Hieronimo, he had long awaited an unattainable limited revenge, and his exacerbated desire cannot be satisfied except by removal of restraints, and an overall indiscriminate spilling of blood. I do not claim here that the author approves or condemns this behavior: he merely correctly describes a primeval rage. The success of the play proves that he struck the proper note. Like Andrea, the public presumably felt liberated and "pleased" by the final carnage.[67]

If these considerations are accurate, then the lengthy delays through which Hieronimo goes before making up his mind to act receive a satisfactory explanation. These hesitations are inexcusable only when seen through the deforming glasses of psychology. Indeed, if Kyd was specially preoccupied with individual psychology, in the fashion of nineteenth-century dramatists, Hieronimo's procrastination would be difficult to explain. But this was not the case. Hieronimo's delay, after he knows with certainty the identity of his enemies, should not be attributed to psychological reasons. It may even be doubted whether the lapse of time between act III, scene vii, when Hieronimo reads Pedrigano's letter, and the penultimate scene is due to anything like genuine "hesitations."[68] Hieronimo's speeches in act III, scenes xii and xiii, are rather statements of the intention to act. A more acceptable explanation would start from purely structural considerations. As the author needed a final major splash of blood, he had to make it arrive after an exasperating period of waiting. Accordingly, Hieronimo's delay and his fits of madness are there in order to render the violence of the ending more satisfying. After the long wait, it is easier to understand why the frenzy of generalized revenge takes possession of both Hieronimo and Andrea.

The ontological division is accompanied by an epistemic one. Andrea's ghost sees everything that happens on the other side of the barrier, while the converse is not true. The epistemic barrier between the human world and the hereafter does not, however, play an important role in the play. More essential for the progress of the action is the epistemic partition that prevails in the human world: secrecy is the main rule here.[69] As long as their love is kept secret, Horatio and Belimperia have nothing to fear. Secrecy protects Horatio's murderers for a long time. Hieronimo's attempt to accuse them openly fails; he succeeds only by resorting to deception. Other plainly advertised developments lead to failure: the marriage of Balthazar and Belimperia is an example. As for Villuppo's episode, its dramatic function could be to ease the severity of the epistemic closeness, by providing an example of an evil action correctly planned in secret and still failing. If so, the episode is there to make the spectator feel homeopathically relieved that there can also be unsuccessful wicked plots. The situating of Villuppo's arrival just after Horatio's treacherous murder supports this reading.[70]

The play is epistemically closed, but not sealed off. In order to achieve success, the whereabouts of an action must be kept secret; it is never possible, however, to irreversibly hide information. News slowly but surely leaks out, if not through the efforts of the villains or heroes, then by fate's own intervention. Revenge herself tells Andrea's ghost who his murderer is (*pace* Empson!),[71] and sheer luck brings to Hieronimo Pedrigano's letter denouncing Lorenzo and Balthazar.

As for the audience, we already saw that it shares the perspective of Andrea's ghost. The spectator has early access to every piece of information, without regard to its origin. He knows that Lorenzo and Balthazar plan Horatio's death, that Pedrigano is doomed, that Villuppo lies, etc. As in *The Jew of Malta*, there remains, nonetheless, a last surprise. Although it is possible to guess in advance the substance of Hieronimo's plot, it is never explicitly revealed as such before its execution. I interpreted Barabas' uninterrupted complicity with the audience as a device meant to render him closer to the public and consequently more acceptable. Conversely, the fact that the spectators are not taken into Hieronimo's confidence, beside the obvious effect of strengthening the excitement of the denouement, results in isolating the audience from Hieronimo, precisely when his actions become highly reprehensible.

The evaluation and action rules of the play follow from the preeminence of revenge in both worlds. A general maxim of secrecy is in force in all domains:

(5.3)   Whatever you are doing, if you want it to succeed, do it secretly.

Not everybody listens to this maxim: Hieronimo, for one, tries vainly to obtain justice without recourse to it. In that, he differs from Balthazar and Lorenzo, who use the maxim for their wrongdoings, as well as from Horatio and Belimperia, who use a weaker form of it:

(5.4)   Delay making your actions public, until you are sure of the outcome.

These maxims derive from the grouping of characters into domains and the observation of the regularities inside each domain. For example, the statement

(5.5)   Hieronimo follows first the negation of (5.3) and later he follows (5.4).

is constructed by abstractly representing the character's behavior as compliance with a normative rule. At a higher level of abstraction literary critics often emit judgments like:

(5.6)   By making Hieronimo fail when he does not keep his plans secret and by having him accept finally the rule of secrecy, the author wants to show that personal revenge is unacceptable: even when justified, revenge compels the avenger to act as basely as his adversaries.

It is clear that for such a statement one has to take into account things other than the narrative domains and their content. Statement (5.6) makes an hypothesis about the author's intentions, about morality, etc. An even higher generalization

(5.7)   The condemnation by Kyd of personal revenge belongs to a widespread English Protestant attitude toward life and justice.

obviously derives from even more heterogeneous material. It involves hypotheses about the truth of fiction, or about fiction as a vehicle for moral opinions. My point here is that general statements like (5.7) make use, explicitly or implicitly, of statements like (5.3) and (5.4). Of course, the whole chain of deductions needs not be constantly explicated by critics and historians of literature and culture. Nevertheless, the need for examining its basis should not be lightly dismissed.

III

With *Arden of Feversham* we enter a wholly different realm, from the syntactic as well as from the semantic points of view. The *Move*-structure is so simple that if it is ever proved that its author was Thomas Kyd, certainly he must have had unparalleled ability to change his narrative patterns.[72] There are but two main *Moves*, the first of which occupies almost the whole play, while the second lasts only half an act. The solution of the first *Move* is divided into six subsolutions, each narrating an attempt to carry out the murder of the same person. Only the last attempt is successful. The second *Move*, much shorter, consists of the immediate discovery and arrest of the principal culprits. The narrative monotony makes one think of Marlowe, although in *Arden* each episode is individualized such that the textual outcome is more diversified than the *Move*-structure.[73]

Thomas Arden, a gentleman, worried by the love affair between his wife Alice and Mosbie, a rich commoner, decides to adopt a policy of patience and kindness toward the unfaithful wife and her friend. When Arden leaves the house, Alice and Mosbie plan to kill him. One of Alice's projects involves Michael, Arden's own servant. She promises the hand of Susan, Mosbie's beautiful sister, on the condition that he kill his master. Another project appeals to Clarke, a painter known for his ability with poisons. He too is promised Susan as a reward for his cooperation. Clarke gives the plotters a supposedly strong poison. Upon his return, Arden has a violent fight with Mosbie, but at the wicked man's protestations of innocence, he retracts and even agrees that Mosbie live in his house during Arden's impending journey to London. Despite this, Arden has not yet lost all of his suspicions, and as a consequence he takes some "mithridate" before supper, which saves his life. The first attempt to murder him fails. Following Arden's departure for London, Alice persuades Greene, a yeoman whom Arden has just ruined, into following her husband to London and murdering him there. Mosbie orders Clarke to paint a poisoned crucifix. Greene hires two murderers, Black Will and Shakebag to help. One of them is attacked just as they look for Arden, so the murder is postponed again. Next, Greene convinces Michael, the servant already corrupted by Alice, to leave the house unlocked at night. The servant acts accordingly, but Arden double-checks the locks, so this attempt fails too. A further ambush that Michael helps Greene and his accomplices to prepare does not bring about the expected result, because of the impromptu appearance of a friend of Arden's with his men. No greater success is achieved in the next attempt by Greene and his fellows, when a thick fog prevents them from eliminating Arden. As he returns home, Alice and Mosbie meet him, openly showing their intimacy. Driven mad, Arden attacks Mosbie, who has Greene and the two vagrants coming to help him. Arden and his friend Franklin drive them off, defeating another attempt at Arden's life. Alice manages to reconcile Arden and Mosbie, claiming that everything was an innocent joke. The final, successful try involves every plotter (except the painter, who makes a last short appearance in the fourth act). Arden is killed in his own house, while playing cards with Mosbie. The body is clumsily disposed of, which renders the task of the local mayor rather easy. The main wrongdoers are discovered and punished.

For Mosbie and Alice, the actors of the first main *Move*, the *Problem* consists in the fact that Arden is alive. Each attempt at Arden's life is a provisory *Solution*. See tree (5.8). This recalls *Doctor Faustus*, in which a similar repetitive structure relates the episodes of Faustus' happy life in the company of Mephistophilis. The only difference is

(5.8)

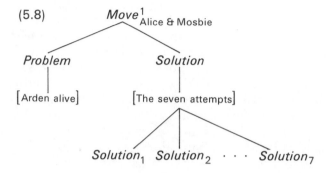

that here each solution takes place because of the failure of the previous one, while in *Doctor Faustus* there is no narrative link between the episodes.

An interesting characteristic of *Arden of Feversham*'s main plot is the absence of polemical configurations. Arden accepts all the far-fetched explanations his wife provides for her behavior. Indeed, Arden is no serious opponent for Alice and Mosbie. He escapes most of the attempts on his life merely by chance. Only twice are his own prudence or courage responsible for saving his life. This particular situation requires the use of rule (1.16) of the narrative grammar:

(1.16)   *Solution: (Pro-Solution + Counter-Solution)^n + Solution*

This rule specifies a *Solution*-symbol as a miniconflict, made up of propositions introducing the *Solution* and propositions countering it.

The semantic content of the plot substantially differs from that of Marlowe's and Kyd's tragedies. There is no special ontological proposition, as the play unfolds in the simplest of worlds. Epistemically, however, it manifests several interesting properties. But first, we should note that according to our definition of the domains, since Arden does not index any major *Move*, he is not entitled to possess his own domain, and this in a play that bears his name. To correct this unwanted consequence, the definition of narrative domains must be modified, so as to include *passive domains* as well. I will say that if a character does not index any major *Move*, but is both the origin of a major *Problem* and the target of a major *Solution* in the play, then he becomes the center of a passive domain. By "major" *Move* (*Problem, Solution*) I understand a *Move* (*Problem, Solution*) the deletion of which would prevent the overall action from reaching its present form. Since Arden does not index a major *Move*, but finds himself at the origin of the *Problem* of *Move*[1] and is the target of this

Move's solution, he qualifies as the center of a passive narrative domain. His friend Franklin is a member of the same domain, the passivity of which he greatly increases by his inept advice.

Now, a law of increase of susceptibility and of overestimation of adversaries' intentions is usually in force in many tragedies. Think for example of Tamburlaine's habit of interpreting the mere postponement of surrender as a major violation, punishable by collective death. Or remember Gaveston's unparalleled irritability, making him overreact to mere physical presence of his adversaries. Similar examples can be multiplied. In *Hamlet*, a vague suspicion is enough for the king to send the prince to his death. In *Le Cid*, one kills because of a slap in the face. This extraordinary irritability accounts for the need of epistemic closure in most tragedies. Since their adversaries are continuously on the alert, the characters must carry out their undertakings under the veil of secrecy. If, despite all risks, the play still remains epistemically open, one can foresee that serious clashes, murders, and overthrows will occur. Such is the case in *Edward the Second* and in many Greek tragedies (*Seven against Thebes, Antigone*).

One of the distinctive features of *Arden of Feversham* is that the hero utterly lacks the irritability so common among tragic characters. It is probably the only premodern tragedy where the tragic flaw is *dumbness*.[74] In this, *Arden of Feversham* is rather ahead of its time, and sometimes possesses a distinctive Brechtian overtone.[75] Arden's (passive) domain is indeed afflicted with an uncommon inability to read signs, to correctly and consistently match knowledge and perception, and to make likely predictions. Arden knows, for instance, that his wife and Mosbie have an affair. (How he reached this conclusion is a mystery, for the entire play shows him as unable to see the obvious.) This knowledge, which makes him moderately suspicious, and once or twice even considerate, does not prevent him from accepting in the first act the assurances Mosbie gives him. He even consents to Mosbie's living in the same house as Alice during his own absence, under the unlikely pretext of deterring malicious gossip. Later on, coincidences and chance protect him from being hurt in the numerous efforts Greene and Michael make to kill him; understandably, he does not grow more suspicious. That he accepts Alice's explanations for the clash in act IV, scene iv, indicates how reduced are his capacities for grasping situations. Moreover, he takes no precautions upon entering his home, where two more-than-potential enemies have every opportunity to plan his death.

Under these circumstances, no wonder that the efforts of his opponents toward secrecy are minimal. Alice openly sends killers to her husband, without the slightest fear that the news of it will reach his ears. This contrasts with the usual epistemic medium of tragedies. Indeed, more often than not, tragic events take place in a sort of transparent and overresounding medium. Recent undertakings are easily learned by distant people; between cities and camps news travels unusually quickly, the ground is full of messengers who rush, unseen and unheard, from one place to another, to keep the participants informed about their enemies' moves. Think for instance of *Agamemnon*, to which, incidentally, *Arden* has been ineptly compared. The first half of the Greek tragedy deals exclusively with the spreading of the news about Troy's fall and Agamemnon's return. The whole world strongly reverberates with the tidings. Nothing like that occurs in *Arden*, at least not until the death of the main character. The play's air is heavy, foggy, made out of thick felt. Sounds and images do not circulate through it. This could explain also the plotters' repeated failures: the dark, the epistemic fog prevent them from reaching Arden.

Notice that after Arden's murder, a sudden change in the quality of the medium takes place. It looks as if Arden's presence were the main factor responsible for the thickening of the atmosphere. As soon as the slaying is successfully carried out, unexpected guests knock at the door, as if drawn by the already visible crime. The corpse is first hidden in the countinghouse. But soon the major and the guard approach the house, looking for Black Will, one of Greene's accomplices. Mosbie and the company carry the body behind the abbey. The thick, foggy air dispels, making place for what one could call an epistemic snowfall: indeed, while the plotters carry the body, it snows, so that their footsteps can be followed. The snowing stops before they come back, so as not to cover the traces. Only nineteen lines later, Franklin, Arden's ill-advised friend, enters announcing that he has found the body. The accusatory signs do not fail to accumulate: a hand towel and a knife stained with blood in the room, and, decisively, the renewed bleeding of the corpse in the presence of Alice. In contrast with the trivial intentions and petty unsuccessful attempts nobody cared about, here stands the accomplished deed, in all its unavoidable compactness, visible from far away, attracting witnesses and punishment.[76]

As for the situation-evaluation and action maxims, we have just seen that in Arden's passive domain, the evaluation was most often incorrect, and action taken arbitrarily and imprudently. A maxim like:

(5.9)   Believe someone else's description and evaluation of the situation rather than your own[77]

governs Arden's judgment. Alice and Mosbie follow maxims like:

(5.10)   Once a course of action is decided, do not change your mind;

(5.11)   An unsuccessful attempt is nothing but a preparation for the next attempt.

Too concentrated on the execution of their project, Alice and Mosbie do not pay adequate attention to what they will have to do after the murder of Arden. Confident in the inexplicable impenetrability of their intentions, they seem to believe that their actions will stay equally unquestioned. Presumably they judge the whole universe in the likeness of Arden, credulous, easy to dissuade, blind. Arden's own incapacity is thus, paradoxically, what gains him an almost instantaneous revenge.

One last remark about the characters: the previous analyses did not insist on the particularization techniques employed by Marlowe or Kyd. This was mainly because in most cases no individual features, except those deductible from the participation in the *Move*-structure, were attached to the characters. Some attributive episodes may have added information concerning the characters, but in most cases they reinforced what the other *Moves* already expressed. Such was the episode of the slaying of Tamburlaine's own son in the second part of *Tamburlaine*. But in general, in Marlowe's and Kyd's plays, particularization devices independent of the plot are kept to a minimum. In this repspect, these plays resemble folktales, in which the actors have no properties except those implied or required by the actions they accomplish. In *Arden of Feversham*, on the other hand, one can notice rudimentary efforts to make the characters less dependent on their *Moves*. Arden, for example, who does not initiate any major *Move*, is several times made to look like a greedy man who causes the ruin of several yeomen, including a certain Reede, with whom Arden has a brief encounter (IV, iv). Significantly, his fall is not primarily due to this feature of his character, as would have been the case in the more economical Marlowian or Kydian outlook. Franklin, in the Epilogue, mentions again this trait:

Arden lay murdered in that plot of ground
which he by force and violence held from Reede

as if the author was careful to make the point that important aspects of actor's personalities are autonomous from the strictly causal logic of *Moves*, but nonetheless entertain a sort of global, or even symbolic, relationship to the tragedy's outcome.[78] Modern theater will appeal more and more often to this loose yet pregnant relationship.

Chapter Six
King Lear

I

Critics and commentators writing about *King Lear* have mentioned the unusual complexity of the plot.[79] It is the only major tragedy of Shakespeare to possess a secondary plot. Although it was possible for Charles Lamb to narrate *King Lear* with minimal reference to the second plot, most commentators emphasize the links and parallelisms between Gloucester's and Lear's stories.[80] In their narrative appearance, however, the two plots are largely different. Dramatic-effect derives, among other things, from the common problems of the two plots unfolding as *dissimilar* structures. Thus, while Lear's plot is basically a polemical configuration, Gloucester's plot starts with a deception, goes on as a complex revenge, and ends after an unusually rich embedding of *Auxiliary* structures. Lear's plot involves only the tragedy's main character and his opponents. It is a highly compact development, unfolding in the initially established structures, without much interference from outside forces. In contrast, Gloucester's plot is full of unexpected developments, interventions of previously uninvolved characters, new intentions and feelings. It is a frequent opinion of the critics that Gloucester's plot has less dramatic energy than the main plot. As the *Move*-analysis shows, in fact it possesses more diversity than its rival. But, precisely because of its diversity, it lacks the dynamism and the momentum of the main plot.

Lear's story starts as a fairy tale, with the king-father subjecting his daughters to a qualifying test. The usual moves involved in folktales containing this motif are: the qualifying test, a false answer given by the wicked son(s) or daughter(s), the misunderstanding of the sincere answer of the good sibling, the punishment by exile of the good son (daughter), the bad behavior of the wicked son(s) or daughter(s), the good behavior of the exiled son or daughter, the punishment of the wicked one(s), and the return of the good offspring. The main test consists of the behavior toward the father in some difficult situation.

The folktale structure is based on the king-father's continued power and authority. In *King Lear*, the shift of authority prevents Lear from revising his initial decision. Moreover, the arrangement reached with his older daughters contradicts the maxims of power generally in force in Elizabethan drama, in which:

(6.1)   Supreme power does not tolerate limitations on the territory where it applies.

This maxim justifies Goneril and Regan's decision to limit the number of knights in their father's retinue. In the first plot of the tragedy, the two daughters are constant allies. See tree (6.2).

The first two acts are thus particularly dynamic from the point of view of the main plot: they contain eight *Moves*, six of which belong to a polemical configuration. The third act, in contrast, provides for a tragic respite. During this act, Lear wanders around in the storm, finds shelter in a hovel, is then moved to a farmhouse adjoining Gloucester's castle, is told again to leave. Let us call the narrative episodes in which the hero's situation changes randomly without improving, the *Tribulations* of the hero.

During the unfolding of the action, the spectator is too caught by the sequence of *Moves* to scrutinize carefully every resulting configuration and to listen to gnomic comments. After the final catastrophe, the spectators cannot bear more than a small sampling of moral considerations. But *Tribulations*, both long before the end, and somewhat outside the swiftest plot developments, provide the best opportunity for the elaboration of tragic statements. (Notice that recent theatrical creation has again made us responsive to static suffering on the stage.)

Lear's tribulations consist of three stages: Lear's wanderings in the storm, the scene in the hovel, and the short stay at Gloucester's farmhouse. When the king's company leaves the area, it does so in order to avoid the murder plans of Goneril and Regan, and to head toward Dover, where, it is by now clear, lies the only hope. *Move*[9] contains as its *Problem* the preceding *Move* of Goneril and Regan; it includes

(6.2)

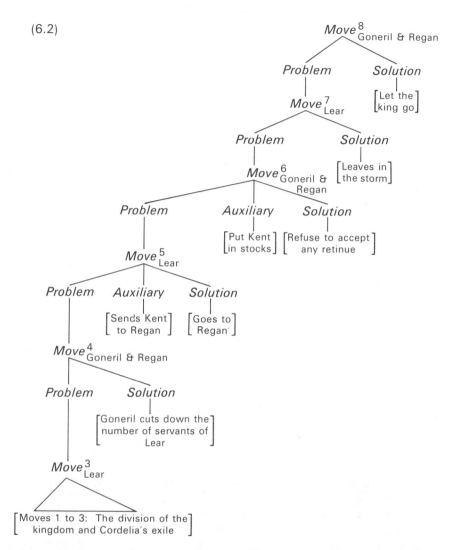

the *Tribulations* and, as an *Auxiliary*, Gloucester's warning about Goneril's and Regan's dark intentions. See tree (6.3).

The strategic situation at the end of *Move*[3] offends Cordelia less by depriving her of her heritage than by alienating Lear from her. It is equally reasonable to attribute the early presence of the French army at Dover not only to the French king's awareness of the latent conflict between Albany and Cornwall, but also to Cordelia's

(6.3)

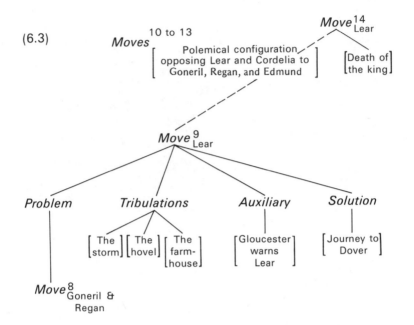

foreboding of the breakdown of Lear's arrangements with his older daughters. ("I would prefer him to a better place," I, i, v. 276, she says before leaving for France. Kent has the same fears, as he stays with the king, disguised, after having been driven away.) Her sister's behavior, together with her father's tribulations, constitute *Problems* of Cordelia's domain. The attempted *Solutions* include finding Lear, putting him to rest and, as soon as he recovers from his madness, making peace with him; then regarding her sisters and the conflict between them and Lear, waging war against the British. The first group of *Solutions* succeeds, but the outcome of the war favors the opposite party. Notably, Cordelia's death is ordered by Edmund, a character who, despite his prominence in the second plot, has no independent impact on the main plot. But something as important as a final *Move* in a long and complex polemical configuration is usually expected to have deep roots in the past of the configuration itself. The logic of the main plot, left to itself, already points to a solution: Albany, now in charge of the British army, announces his intention of exercising leniency toward his father- and sister-in-law. In view of this, Edmund's intervention may appear as insufficiently prepared inside the first plot. This could explain why for more than a century the play was performed in a milder version, which ended with Lear's restoration and Cordelia's marriage to Edgar.

The main plot, which dominates the beginning of the play, gradually gives way to the second plot, the Edmund vs. Edgar story, to the point that toward the end of the play, the king is forgotten about in his prison (V, iii, v. 238). The secondary plot starts as a family intrigue, without clearly foreseeable consequences. In contrast with the main plot, which is an epistemically open polemical configuration, Edmund's plot, being based on cunning, initiative, and improvisation, triggers much less immediate polemical response. Revenge and punishment come here quite late and in unexpected ways.

The beginning of Edmund's undertakings lies in a rapid move, by which he usurps his brother's place in the heart and bequest of Gloucester. Second, Edmund opens another move that brings about the ruin of his father. Gloucester, who hosts in his castle Cornwall and Regan (and later Goneril as well), witnesses with disapproval the expulsion of the king and follows him in order to offer help. Knowing all about the matter, Edmund denounces his father to the duke, who blinds the old man, throws him out of the castle, and gives Edmund the earldom of Gloucester. The role of Edmund in this episode is that of a mere auxiliary, as can be seen from tree (6.4).

Without yet openly affecting him, Edmund's machinations start to have remote results. Separated from his father, Edgar goes through a period of tribulations, out of which he is able to extricate himself only after an auxiliary element helps him unexpectedly: the presence of his blind, banished father.

(6.4)

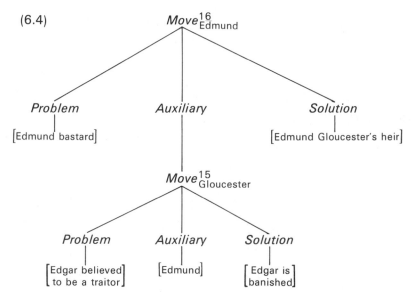

Edmund's last operation consists in his simultaneously trying to marry Goneril and Regan. But Regan's projects are unbearable for Goneril. Before her own treason is discovered by Albany, at a moment when she still hopes to marry Edmund, she poisons her sister. The evil people devour each other. Consequently, Goneril's action indirectly helps the global effort of justice initiated by Albany and Edgar. Tree (6.5) show this clearly, since $Move^{25}_{Goneril}$ is embedded as an *Auxiliary* to $Move^{27}$. The latter has found his father, but must still revenge the humiliations and the wrongs Edmund has inflicted on him and Gloucester. He knows that Edmund is the most wicked man in the world, but needs an instrument to prove this to the mighty protectors of his brother. The occasion for the attempt to overthrow Edmund presents itself when Oswald, Goneril's servant, tries to murder Gloucester. Edgar kills the man and finds on him a compromising letter from Goneril to Edmund. His next step consists in informing Albany about the letter and asking the duke to let him fight against Edmund. The narrative contribution of the final *Move* amounts to more than the local punishment of a few misdeeds. Albany and Edgar's *Problem* is the presence of evil in the world they inhabit. Consequently every event that helps the setting up of a new order must come under this *Move*, as an auxiliary to the final solution. See tree (6.5).

II

I have already remarked that the secondary plot influences the main one toward the end of the play, when Edmund orders the secret execution of Cordelia. Conversely, the Lear plot has only a limited influence on the secondary plot. The only event unambiguously related to the secondary plot is Gloucester's attempt to help the king. But, in contrast with Cordelia's death, which has an important role in the termination of Lear's plot, Gloucester's involvement with the king is only indirectly associated with the solution of the secondary plot. Between it and the final solution there is a tortuous chain of *Move* embeddings: Cornwall banishes Gloucester, which indirectly helps Edgar find his father. By means of an attempt to Gloucester's life, which can ultimately be traced to Cornwall's hate for the earl, Edgar finds the means to dispose of Edmund. Notice also that while Gloucester's action genuinely helps Lear, Edmund's interference with the development of the first plot does not have a direct impact on the second.

Still, the two plots share common characters. Not only are many

(6.5)

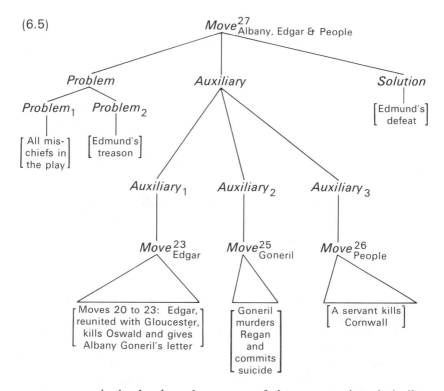

actors present in both plots, but some of them are assigned similar functions. Edmund, for instance, is always the villain. The characters may thus be divided into two categories: one-plot actors and two-plot actors. The *dramatis personae* restricted to a single plot are Lear and Cordelia in the first plot and Edgar in the second. (Incidentally, Nahum Tate's having Edgar marry Cordelia improved the links between the two lines of action.) All the other characters appear in both plots. One doubtful case is that of Albany. As Goneril's husband, he takes part in the *Solution* of *Move*[4] (the harassment of Lear in act I, scene iv), but later on he changes sides and finds himself as the main opponent of the two sisters. The fact that Albany hesitates and changes sides is felt as unique in the play, where other characters' evolution is either purely interior, without incidence on the alliance affiliation of the actor (Edgar), or, if they do affect the alliance system, the modification looks rather like a recognition of a *de facto* association foolishly ignored (Lear, Gloucester). This suggests that the main device for linking the two plots is the alliance system.

The villains, at least, are quick to find each other. Edmund acts alone only in the first deception against his brother. From then on, he is constantly coupled with the Goneril and Regan group. The enlarged group (Goneril, Regan, Cornwall, Edmund, Oswald) functions as a powerful evil squad in both plots. In contrast, a major strategic disadvantage of the good characters lies in the fact that their alliances are loose and slow to emerge. The good people are scattered throughout the play, without knowing each other, and have great difficulty in reaching one another. Indeed, many of Lear's tribulations take place because of the physical distance at which Cordelia dwells and because of the king's ignorance of her being in Britain. Albany does not recognize the knight who defeats Edmund. Gloucester ignores the fact that his guide is his own son. His late meeting with Lear (IV, vi) is that of a blind man and of a madman. Throughout the plot there is an apparent spell against good people knowing each other. Here lies the possible explanation for Edgar's choice of hiding his identity from his father. This could equally explain why Kent stays disguised long after this stratagem is needed.

Strategically, the play looks therefore like an uneven battle between a shock force (the evil squad), well armed and with good intelligence, and two isolated groups (Lear's and Gloucester's), poorly organized, unaware of each other, both having serious logistic and intelligence problems. It is only natural that the successes of the shock force be spectacular and constant. A disastrous rift develops, however, between two factions of the shock force, the moderates and the extremists. As the extremists (Edmund and the women) plan to do away with the moderate chief (Albany), a member of the adversary group (Edgar) discovers by chance the inner division of the shock force and in a suicidal action tries to defeat the extremists by exposing their intentions to the moderate chief. This leads to the destruction of the extremist group and to the disbanding of the shock force. Despite the enormous losses suffered by the less organized groups, the moderates and the survivors from the opposite camp form a new alliance.[81]

One of the striking features of the secondary plot is the large number of *Auxiliaries*. See trees (6.4 and 6.5). They may be either slightly modified forms of the classic action of help; or an independent action involuntarily leading to the same general result as the undertakings of the character who indexes the move, for example, the killing of Oswald unexpectedly helping Edgar's revenge; or, finally, elements which do not help the *Solution*, but rather lead to it. For instance, it cannot be said that the conflict between Goneril and Regan constitutes the *Problem* that makes Gloucester act. It is rather an *Auxiliary* that functions as a catalyst for the action, different from the *Problem* of the *Move*.

The *Solution* of the last *Move* can be labeled Syntactic Denoument. In a play as complex as *King Lear*, the Syntactic Denoument is only part of the larger General Denoument. The conclusion of the play cannot be limited to the victory over Edmund. What spectators understand by denoument is something that cannot be duly localized at a single point of the *Move*-structure. A question like "How did it all end?" is satisfactorily answered only by a list of events: "A servant killed Cornwall; Goneril poisoned Regan and then killed herself; Edmund was defeated and killed by his brother Edgar; Cordelia was put to death in prison; Lear died short afterwards, etc." Apart from sentences referring to the characters' individual destinies, a satisfactory outline of the denoument can include sentences that evaluate different moves and projects: "Regan's and Goneril's projects to marry Edmund broke down; Edmund failed to murder Albany and to become the most powerful man in Britain; Lear and Coredlia failed to survive in prison; Edgar managed to recover his name and fortune, etc." If we exclude from the definition of the denoument moral conclusions and other kinds of semantic elaborations, the General Denoument should refer to the success or failure of the main actions and projects of the characters and to the state in which the actors are found at the end of the play. A tentative definition is proposed here:

(6.6)   The General Denoument of a plot is a set of sentences describing (1) the last Bremond-stage of the last two *Moves* of any polemical configuration as well as of any other *Move* not included in a polemical configuration, and (2) the state in which the characters are found at the end of the plot.

A remarkable device of the text is the alternation between movement and stagnation. The *Move*-structure is not matched by a congruent text progression; rather, the dramatic text capriciously changes its rhythm independently of the *Move*-structure. Thus, more than half of Lear's plot fills the first two acts and develops at a remarkable speed. (The haste is brought into relief by such details as Lear's arrival at Gloucester's castle before the receipt of an answer through his messenger.) Then, suddenly the movements come to a standstill: the third act presents in full detail the king's tribulations. Significantly, while a kind of brake is put on Lear's plot development, the secondary plot just starts to advance. The first two acts contain only two *Moves* of the secondary plot. The other eleven *Moves* fill the last three acts. Meanwhile, Lear's plot does not recover its lost momentum. Act IV deals mostly with the second plot. The last act concentrates again on Lear's plot: its last four *Moves* are all present here. In contrast, the secondary plot exhibits only two *Moves* in the last act: Goneril's poisoning of Regan and the final *Move* of the play. But due to the importance it gained during the third and the fourth acts, the great number of characters involved in it, and the complex lines along which it advances, in the last act the secondary plot still appears as more substantial than the main one. This feeling cannot but increase when its last *Move* embeds Lear's plot.

III

The ontology of the play is more economical than that of other major Shakespearian tragedies. In *King Lear* not only is God absent, but also ghosts, witches, even foreboding signs. The inventory of the tragedy is strictly natural.[82]

But what is saved in inventory is spent on the special characters with which natural phenomena are invested. First, and most obviously, the natural disasters have a special malignity, striking with precision defenseless people and only when they are at their lowest ebb. The significance of the storm has been so often discussed that there is no need to insist on it here. The special nature of the space of the tragedy, however, has attracted less attention from the critics. One can notice two main contrasts on which space effects in the play are based: shelter vs. open space, and magnetic vs. nonmagnetic space. Subtler nuances can also be detected. Shelters are either fortified castles or military camps. Since the contrast between the castles and the landscape surrounding them is greater than that between an army camp and its vicinity, more protected shelters make for more savage environments. The surroundings of Gloucester's castle is unbearably severe, while next to the French army camp one finds pleasant, flowery meadows. Here we have a sign that not only the opening of the play was borrowed from folktales: the spatial opposition between the domain of the king and that of the villain is not unfrequently reinforced in folktales by strong contrastive elements, usually linked to the landscape.

A typical Learian property of space is its magnetism. Several times in the play characters are attracted to places where they have no obligation to go. Actors gather in areas seemingly chosen in advance without their knowledge. There are at least four such locales: the opening space (Lear's palace) the conflict space (Gloucester's castle), the tribulation space (the heath outside Gloucester's castle), and the solution space (the area near Dover). That everybody is present at the royal palace for the beginning of the play is understandable. Less clear is why Cornwall and Regan live at Gloucester's castle. Many commentators have noticed that no reason is given for their presence there. The above-mentioned magnetism of space is the only likely explanation: actors head there allured by the vortex of oncoming conflict. Equally improbable is Edgar's presence so close to his father's domain. He must stay there, however, since this is the place marked in advance for tribulations. Soon, Lear and his party will join him. Again, critics have asked why should Gloucester decide that the only appropriate place to commit suicide is precisely at Dover. But this does not involve a conscious decision on his part. The place designated for the solution attracted him, as it attracted all other characters toward the end of the play. Needless to say, this peculiarity of space adds to the ritual atmosphere so often noticed in the tragedy.[83]

From the epistemic point of view, the play is perfectly transparent to the spectator. No privileged character knows more than the public. Even the surprising death of Cordelia is arranged on stage and it looks unexpected only because the intervening events make the audience lose Cordelia from sight. This transparency is a more general feature of Shakespeare's tragedies, which adds to the feeling that Shakespeare is a friendly, dependable author for his public. This is so especially since the plays themselves are always epistemically partitioned and the spectator very often finds himself privileged in comparison with the characters.

The actors form at least two epistemic classes. In the main plot the circulation of information between opposite camps is amazingly free. Sometimes we see the channels used: the play is continually crossed by Oswald, who carries news from one place to another. But quite often things are simply known to everybody, through some unexplained spreading of the news, characteristic only to the first plot. Thus, early in the play, Kent is able to speak about the French landing at Dover, while Gloucester knows where to find the king in the storm. In addition, the characters in the first plot feel that their actions are spectacular, in the open, visible to anyone. The possible origin of this lies in the royal position of Lear: accustomed to be the center of his country's attention, Lear speaks so arrogantly to his daughters because he still wants his voice to be heard. And it is heard, for, directly or by means of messengers, every item of information needed in the first plot reaches its destination in time. Accordingly, there is no conflict or malfunctioning due to undisclosed or ignored information.

The only spot where the epistemic limpidity of the first plot seems to become troubled is in proximity to Cordelia. Indeed, in the first scene, she is unable to make herself understood by her father. Then, despite the epistemic security in this plot, in which everybody faces one another courageously, only once does a character hesitate to meet another: Lear, according to Kent, "by no means / Will yield to see his daughter" (IV, iii, v. 41-42). Notice also that the only secret action in the first plot is Cordelia's execution at Edmund's orders. True, the epistemic nature of the act can be attributed to Edmund's way of concealing his infamous dealings, but the coincidence is still puzzling.

Cordelia's failure to win her father's approval in the first scene may relate to the previously noted inability of good people to recognize one another. A generalized variety of Stoll's (1933) Calumniator Credited convention prevails here: not only are evil people believed and cohesive, but the good people have the fundamental incapacity of making themselves credible. It is in this context that Kent's (and for that matter Edgar's) disguises should be understood. These are devices meant to overcome the character's handicap of being good.[84]

The epistemic openness of the first plot does not preclude madness; there we find three mad characters: the Fool, Edgar as Tom, and Lear himself. Notice, however, that madness never interferes with the *Move*-structure. No decision having the slightest impact on the progress of the plot is made under the influence of madness. Consider as well that, with the exception of the Fool, who is continuously a bit out of his mind (and, characteristically, has no actual role in the *Move*-structure), the two other characters who either become mad (Lear), or simulate folly (Edgar) have this trait only during their tribulations, namely at a moment when the advance of the action stops. These remarks should help us clarify the function of the tribulations in the play, their relation to madness, and the two-level epistemic structure of the first plot.

In folk and medieval stories, the tribulations of the hero represent, as has been pointed out many times, the trials he has to undergo on his way to knowledge. Comparable to a set of initiation rites (to which they have been traced), the tribulations confer on the hero the wisdom he initially lacks.[85] One has no need to insist on how often in medieval and Renaissance literature the external expression of wisdom takes the form of folly. In *King Lear* the first plot unfolds at two different epistemic levels, and both levels are carefully signaled with the help of unambiguous narrative devices. One of the levels could bear the label "factual knowledge." It consists of statements about the actions of the opponents or allies, as well as of the conventional wisdom that the characters (minimally) employ when they are reasonably happy. Beyond a certain limit of adversity, though, the characters enter a special state that prevents them from acting; it even somewhat prevents them from reasoning. It is called madness by people who still dwell in the world of action, the world exterior to the scene of tribulation. But to the characters who go through the tribulations, it represents a time of intense, painful contemplation, leading to what may be called the level of "transfactual knowledge." This state can descend on someone only to leave him later, or it can be called forth through the simulation of its symptoms. Lear becomes mad; Edgar pretends to be mad in order to capture the violent visions the second level of knowlege imparts. There is no other explanation for the frenzy with which he plays the role of Poor Tom: much more than a disguise, it becomes a shamanic trance.

We thus arrive at the question of the laws of expression. In the special state induced by the second level of knowledge, the characters speak another language than that of the rest of the play. They use wild metaphors, obscene expressions; they jump illogically from one field to another; they do not entirely participate in the conversation, but use the other actor's line as a mere stimulus for their own divagations. In this special state, the laws of common speech are suspended.

We can divide the king's plot accordingly into three linguistic periods. The first one, which lasts until Cordelia's departure, allows for misunderstandings and linguistic excesses. It represents the usual, spontaneous, poorly constrained linguistic practices. Suggestively, the tragic error of Lear has something to do with careless listening. The next period, starting with the conflict between Lear and his elder daughters, obeys the laws of transparency. It is as if the tension of the confrontation dispels the previous misunderstandings and lays the language brutally bare. In the third period, expression is clouded again, but this time not because of carelessness and lack of consideration for the interlocutor. The new obscurity of language sets its roots in the very inexpressibility of the tragic visions that the characters contemplate during their tribulations. The third period also has a transplot magnetism, comparable to the similar quality of space. Since the tribulation space, in the vicinity of Gloucester's castle, attracts all outcasts regardless of the plot from which they come, the special contemplative state and the language of trance is shared by all those who find themselves there. Edgar, for one, originates in a plot in which the laws of language are drastically different. Once in the tribulation region, he, like Lear, looks for the special knowledge imparted there, and, perhaps even more conspicuously than other characters, adopts the local idiom.

In the second plot, by contrast, false language is well entrenched. This follows from the main epistemic property of the second plot, which is information unavailability. A characteristic contrast between the free flow of the news in the first plot and the severe penury of intelligence in the secondary plot arises in connection with the French landing at Dover. Although banished and excluded from the social structure, Kent knows about the event. As a potential helper of Lear, Gloucester receives a letter from a "neutral heart," reporting the French presence. But the main representatives of power in the second plot, despite the numerous messengers that surround them, are ignorant of this important fact for a long time. Similarly, while the French king quickly learns about the developing rift between Albany and Cornwall, the two dukes discover only quite late his warlike intentions. Events taking place inside the same castle are no better known. For a long time Gloucester and Edgar have no idea that they are being deceived by Edmund. Gloucester finds out the truth about his younger son only after Cornwall and Regan have blinded him. Regan is unable to discover the truth about Edmund's affair with Goneril. This medium is fully favorable to Edmund's techniques of manipulating information. It is striking that in the second plot he remains for a long period the only character to know everything and to dole out true or false intelligence, according to his interest of the moment.

Edmund's epistemic supremacy does not last until the end, however. Edgar, who at the beginning of the secondary plot was so easily deceived, acquires, after his tribulations, a kind of spontaneous access to information. The "unsubstantial air" of the tribulation area makes him sense better than anyone else the structure and the quality of the surrounding world. That Oswald happens to cross his path, enabling him to discover the decisive letter from Goneril to Edmund, may be only the outcome of his new awareness. Shortly before, Regan, who still obeyed the law of unavailability of information, was unable to obtain the same letter. In the final fight against Edmund, Edgar keeps his identity secret, which decides the results of the combat. Never before was Edmund confronted with an opponent epistemically superior. Since all the achievements of the natural son of Gloucester were based on exclusive mastery of intelligence, the lack of it cannot but herald his end.

Compared to the simplicity of *Tamburlaine I*, in which all characters obsessively followed the same maxims, respected the same values, and used the same strategies, *King Lear* displays much more diversity. But the basic rules have not yet changed significantly.

In contrast with the average Renaissance tragedy, power here is *not* the most desirable thing for every participant. Power is still essential for an important group of people belonging to the two plots (Goneril, Regan, Cornwall, Edmund). But it is less clearly so for the one-plot actors: Lear, Cordelia, or Edgar. Lear explicitly wants only a limited amount of power: a retinue of a hundred knights. His calamities spring from the fact that there is no such thing as limited power. More subtly, with additional variations and individual preferences, we are still close to *Tamburlaine*. The change lies more in the development of personal attitudes than in the structure of power. As we have already seen, supreme power does not tolerate limitations on the territory where it applies, but also, as in *Tamburlaine*, power does not tolerate power in its vicinity. Cordelia, among others, acts several times in accordance with this last maxim.

The maxims that separate the camps refer to the means of gaining and keeping power. Goneril, Regan, and Cornwall practice a policy of total disregard toward previous understandings and existing customs. For them, agreements regarding limitations of supreme power are not binding. Lear's retinue is cut in half not long after the division of the country. Gloucester's independent activities are cruelly punished in spite of the laws of hospitality.

Edgar and Cordelia act less ruthlessly. Their maxims prescribe that where there is no agreement in force, or where previous contracts have been unilaterally canceled, fair confrontation is permissible. By "fair confrontation" I understand a conflict in which both opponents have the same chances of winning. The war between the French and the British, and the individual combat of Edgar and Edmund belong to this category.

Edmund's actions imply the Machiavellian principle that the purpose of gaining power allows one to undertake any action whatsoever. But the nature of power being indivisible and the fighters for it having to be ruthless, the fight for power will be a desperate one. It is so strong that no system of alliances can survive.

Indeed, one of the most striking features of the play is the fragility of the family alliances. No family link overcomes the challenge of the fight for power. But even more generally, with two exceptions (the Lear-Kent link and the fidelity of Oswald to Goneril), no alliance lasts for the whole length of the play. And of Lear's link to Kent, it must be said that it is disowned by Lear and survives only due to Kent's disguise. The fragility of the alliance system is one of the reasons why the overall plot is so difficult to remember. What is gained is a greater mobility of the actors and a feeling that they function as individuals rather than as members of a polemic group.

Chapter Seven
Move-Grammars
and Styles of Plot

A formal plot-grammar can be viewed as a *model* in terms of which certain properties of literary texts can be better brought to attention and understood. A major way of gauging the value of such a grammar is to check the structural descriptions it supplies against the literary intuitions the text elicits in the reader.

The proposed *Move*-grammar and its semantics are subject to this kind of intuitive evaluation. Their categorial load, abstract as it is, still has an intuitive correspondence: one "naturally" knows when a certain action is an important *Move*, or an inconsequential one. In addition to the intuitive knowledge about the narrative significance of actions in context, the reader has available an elaborate mechanism for the understanding of the *links* between various important actions in the narrative. By producing narrative trees that are supposed to account correctly for the link-intuitions, the grammar provides a model of certain aspects of the knowledge the reader has about the organization of the plot. The very unfolding of the analyses of this essay brings to light this kind of knowledge. (About independent ways of checking the validity of the categories, see note 97.)

It should not be forgotten, however, that during a formal analysis, new properties may appear, not all of which are reducible to existing knowledge.

A specific case of narrative regularity better enhanced in *Move*-grammar than in traditional criticism, and perhaps even than in some competing narrative theories, is the hierarchical dependency into which narrative units (events, propositions) enter. The naive view of a plot as a linear sequence of events proves inadequate when dependencies at a distance must be accounted for. Although the present work does not insist on purely formal considerations, it may be useful to briefly discuss the difference between the *Move*-grammar hereby proposed (and its immediate predecessor presented in Pavel 1976a), and linear sequence narrative grammars.

A linear sequence narrative grammar produces strings of events whose unique theoretically significant property is that they fill a certain position in the string. Propp's (1928) grammar, for instance, describes a set of Russian folktales as materializations of a sequence of abstract categories (called "functions" by Propp) that combine among themselves in only one possible way. Consequently, every Proppian function can be defined by and only by its position in the sequence. Various critics have pointed out that for the current description of a story it is crucial that events be defined not only according to their position in the sequence, but also to the dependencies at a distance that arise between pairs of functions. Propp himself realized that some of his functions go by pairs. The link he set up between them was, however, an isolated device. Other students of narrative structure consider that coupling, far from being an isolated phenomenon, pervades any plot. Think indeed, of the ever-present relations between interdiction and violation, lack and lack liquidation, etc. What the *Move*-structure grammar adds to this is the idea that dependencies at a distance between narrative elements are themselves hierarchically organized, in a way not too different from the articulation of natural-language sentences into syntactic hierarchies.

The results of *Move*-grammars can also be relevant to the study of cultural and stylistic phenomena, in particular to the problem of period-style.

Beside the task of explicating texts, poetics and literary theory have long since dedicated a considerable amount of energy to the definition of their own categories. But many of these categories, primarily those designating period-styles, relate to vague notions, having a minimal factual coverage. Yet, such categories often possess the remarkable power of triggering strong cultural intuitions. Such notions do not unequivocally distinguish their objects; on the contrary, more often than not they are all-embracing and fuzzy. Nevertheless, they display a kind of hypnotic quality: they stimulate the perception of stylistic phenomena and enhance their understanding.

Take the distinction between the classic and the baroque styles, characterized by Heinrich Wölfflin in terms of five dimensions: the linear vs. the painterly, the plane vs. the recession, the closed vs. the open form, the multiplicity vs. the unity, and the absolute vs. the relative clarity of the subject.[86] Wölfflin's criteria are not governed by a set of necessary and sufficient conditions. None of these five criteria is *operational* in the usual sense of the term; one cannot securely reach a definite conclusion about the stylistic membership of an artistic piece only by virtue of Wölfflin's criteria.[87] With enough critical brio, one can claim about almost any painting that it is both linear and painterly, closed and open, multiple and coherent, clear and ambiguous, etc.

True, Wölfflin did not devise his criteria for a blind, mechanical application. Belonging to the world of culture, they presupppose a certain familiarity with the field, an initial agreement about their correctness. They function as illuminating notions for the believer, rather than as descriptive concepts. The fact that taxonomy uses vague distinctions is of lesser import than its purpose of shaping of the artistic percpetion of the works: these categories are not there to be verified, but to be internalized. Once their meaning is captured, the structural properties that instantiate this or that feature will be identified without much trouble.

This relative freedom may play a role in the proliferation of the more extreme notions of period-style. The recent history of the term *baroque* is particularly instructive in this respect. As delineated by René Wellek, it is the history of a quick proliferation: the extension of the concept grew to that of an *eon*, while its intension became more and more imprecise. One man's baroque features are the opposite to another's. The antithetic feeling of life, the opposition between worldliness and asceticism, the tensions between realism and idealism, between classical form and Christian sentimentality, between Circe (the principle of metamorphosis) and the Peacock (the principle of ostentation), were in turn proposed as definitions of baroque.[88]

Some of these suggestions met with strong resistance. J. Mueller argued in 1954 that a historical period must be delimited according to "a single or a small number of significant traits which differentiate the period from its neighbours," or to "a configuration of traits which constitutes a meaningful whole."[89] Bernard Heyl suggests that the use of the term *baroque* should be flexible; he introduces the idea of degree of baroque, as well as the notion of multiple baroques.[90] Similarly, A. Bucker, while showing that for every thesis concerning the baroque, there is an antithesis, reaches the prudent conclusion that the *Zeitgeist* notion is "neither entirely reliable, nor entirely mythical." To accept it uncritically may lead to a loss of important distinctions, but a flat rejection of the notion can result in lack in vision.[91]

The development of a balanced approach would certainly be helped by a clarification of the variables on which the characterization of broad stylistic categories, such as baroque, rests. We should broaden and render more precise the study of various structural properties that manifest the category in question. Progress in the understanding of period-stylistic notions requires a richer, more detailed set of structural parameters.[92]

Move-grammars can provide interesting criteria for period-stylistic considerations. The relevance of plot-style is not something previously neglected. As early as 1916, Oskar Walzel studied the style of Shakespeare's dramatic form, showing that classic authors prefer *tectonic* constructions, as opposed to baroque *nontectonicity*.[93] Walzel's distinction can be related to the *narrative complexity* of a *Move*-structure.

A simple variable, already examined by critics from William Empson to Richard Levin, is the number of plots in the play.[94] Traditionally a device for epics and comedies, multiple plots came to be heavily used in tragedies only in English Renaissance dramatic literature.

Defined in terms of our grammar, a *plot* is a structure of moves characterized by a stable number of actors and the exhaustion of a problem load by means of successful or unsuccessful solutions. Under this definition, a plot is a set of actions intended to overcome a certain number of problems, some of which can derive from actions initiated inside the plot itself. As long as the problems are not even tentatively solved, the plot is unfinished. The definition allows for more than one plot in a literary text.

Plots should be distinguished from other narrative developments. Thus, I would call a *pseudo-plot* a coherent line of action which is characterized by a constant set of actors, but which either (1) contains no more than one or two moves, or (2) plays a secondary narrative function in a major plot. In accordance with the first case, the secondary comic line of action in many Renaissance dramas are pseudo-plots: they have a single, parodic problem and only one or two mock attempts to solve it. Their function is often purely ornamental. The second case is designed for episodes involving a detailed preparation of an effect in the major plot. The procedure is often used in comic movies: a car race, for instance, is set against lateral happenings with which it interferes.

An interesting question about the construction of a dramatic work is how well integrated are the secondary plots and the pseudo-plots. The integration of the secondary plot into the main one can be of different degrees. The secondary plot of *King Lear* is strongly integrated into the main plot: a whole group of characters is of prime importance in both plots, then the end of the main plot derives from a character belonging to the second. The two plots can be represented as a single narrative tree without offending the elementary intuitions on which the *Move*-grammar is based. In contrast, Villuppo's episode in Kyd's *The Spanish Tragedy* is weakly integrated. It takes place far away from the scene of the main plot; it involves only characters of secondary importance in the main plot; and it does not have any kind of impact on the main action, to the point that it cannot be represented as part of the play's main *Move*-structure.

An interesting case of smooth integration of a secondary plot into the main one is the *continuation* of Edward's plot by that of Mortimer in Marlowe's *Edward the Second*. The transition remains almost imperceptible: once the king loses his crown, he is divested also of the quality of main character. The tragedy continues as the story of Mortimer's rise and fall.

Pseudo-plots can play a merely ornamental role, as is most often the case with clown subplots, or they may be *exempla*, inserted in the play as a typical case of relationship between the main plot and the rest of the world, or else they can be lateral developments with definite syntactic or semantic functions. The comic pseudo-plot of *Doctor Faustus* is only loosely related to the main development. No narrative link connects the clown-plot of *Doctor Faustus* to the main plot. (But this is not always the case. In *The Jew of Malta*, the comic subplot has a decisive influence on the destiny of the main actor.) The pope vs. the antipope episode is better integrated. It has a distinct place in the sequence of experiments undertaken by Faustus. Still, one feels that it could be deleted or substituted with something entirely different, without the plot losing anything essential to its unfolding. Exemplary pseudo-plots have, of course, this peculiarity; their very function calls for their replaceability by something else. As for lateral developments, they are generally well integrated by virtue of their role in the main plot.

Table (7.1) shows all this in detail. A cursory glance at this table suggests that those plays with few slots filled are more "tectonic" (to use Walzel's term) than those with several kinds of secondary plots and pseudo-plots. The simplest structure, with the least lateral ramifications, is the first part of *Tamburlaine*. This coincides well

(7.1)

Plays	Secondary Plots			Pseudo-plots				
	Weakly Integrated	Strongly Integrated			Lateral Developments		Clown Subplots	Exempla
		Semantically	Syntactically	Tribulations	Syntactic	Semantic		
Tamburlaine I					Bajazeth's agony; Agydas' plot Christians			
Tamburlaine II	Theridamas & Olympia					Calyphas' killing		
The Jew of Malta			Ithamore & Bellamira; Malta					
Faustus					Benvolio's plot		Dick & Robin; The Horse Courser	Pope vs. Anti-Pope
Edward II			Mortimer					
The Spanish Tragedy	Villupo; Spain & Portugal			Hieronimus' madness		Andrea's plot		
Arden					Michael, Painter & Susan	Reede's plot		
King Lear		Edmund's plot		Lear; Edgar	Cornwall's killing	Kent's story	The Fool	

with the austere narrative impression the play leaves on the public. Close to *Tamburlaine I* stands *Edward the Second*. In my reading, according to which Mortimer's adventures after Edward's overthrow constitute a secondary plot skillfully attached to the main one, the play has a high degree of tectonicity. Notice, however, that while *Tamburlaine I*'s massivity is troubled only by entirely lateral developments, in *Edward the Second* the additional material comes in the center of table (7.1), where the more important categories are set. Still, *Edward the Second* is a bit more unified than *The Jew of Malta*, where *two* secondary plots relate to the main action. The classification of table (7.1) could be supplemented with indications concerning the nature and size of the secondary developments involved. Thus, the two secondary plots of *The Jew of Malta* have probably a more disruptive effect than Mortimer's plot in *Edward the Second*. They develop at different social levels than the main plot, and one of them has a different, comic tone as well. Next on the scale comes *Doctor Faustus*, with at least three types of pseudo-plots: clown developments, *exempla*, and lateral developments. The least coherent play by Marlowe is, according to table (7.1), *Tamburlaine II*, which has a secondary plot marked to the left of the table as weakly integrated, in addition to syntactic and semantic lateral developments to the right.

Among plays by authors other than Marlowe, *Arden of Feversham* has the simplest design, almost as simple as the first *Tamburlaine*. Its only lateral developments are Reede's episode, which is there as an exemplum characterizing Arden's behavior outside the main plot, and the rudimentary plot involving Michael the painter and Mosbie's sister. To differentiate *Arden of Feversham* from *Tamburlaine I*, one has to appeal to features belonging to the semantic level. Clearly, table (7.1) may not be used in isolation from other criteria.

The collateral lines of action of *The Spanish Tragedy* are comparable to those of *Tamburlaine II*, only that the textual arrangement and better syntactic links of some of them to the main course of action help make *The Spanish Tragedy* look more unified. The play contains two weakly integrated secondary plots: Villuppo's episode and the postwar matrimonial arrangements between Spain and Portugal, a lateral pseudo-plot semantically related to the main plot (Andrea's prologue and epilogue), and a short series of tribulations.

The most complex play of the group is *King Lear*. It has five distinct types of developments outside the main *Move*-structure: a strong secondary plot, well integrated from the syntactic as well as from the semantic point of view, two parallel series of tribulations, a small comic line of action (the story and comments of the Fool), and two lateral pseudo-plots, one with a syntactic function (Cornwall's murder) and the other having probably a mere semantic role (Kent's story). Notice, nevertheless, that the play has no weakly integrated plots nor *exempla*. As for the developments mentioned here, all are well connected with the main stream of the play. Certainly, if by "nontectonic" we understand a type of construction opposed to that of *Tamburlaine I*, then *King Lear* is a nontectonic play. However, table (7.1) shows that *King Lear* is still a well-integrated play and that it employs an unusually wide scale of lateral devices, each being rather limited in scope.

Is this due to the baroque *Zeitgeist* or to the skill of the dramatist? Between the first part of *Tamburlaine* and *King Lear* no more than fifteen to eighteen years elapsed. If one wishes to subsume all these structures under the same period-sytlistic category, this category certainly has to display quite a remarkable flexibility.

The criterion of the plot-complexity allowed us to sketch a detailed stylistic taxonomy of the plays under consideration. Further remarks can be derived from focusing on the inner organization of the *Move*-structures. Indeed, far from being uniformly constructed, plots show clear preferences toward one or another of their major syntactic categories. Thus, one can distinguish between plots in which emphasis falls on the *Solution*, those which insist on *Problem* creation, and those in which the most-developed part is the *Auxiliary*.

In *Solution*-oriented plots, the solutions looked for are particularly difficult. The task either surpasses the hero's capability, or is made up of many subparts that need individual treatment. A solution-oriented plot can consist, like *Tamburlaine I* or *Arden of Feversham*, of a sequence of solution-attempts, each but the last one ending in failure. In *Tamburlaine I*, every episode is an attempt to satisfy Tamburlaine's inexhaustible thirst for power. In *Arden of Feversham*, the episodes narrate unsuccessful attempts on the hero's life. A further distinction can set aside the *cumulative solutions* from the *repetitive* ones. Tamburlaine's taste for power is never fully satisfied, despite the fact that each military undertaking of the hero is, in a sense, a success. The sequence of his partial accomplishments forms an accumulation of deeds, a series that by virtue of the type of problem Tamburlaine faces cannot but end in compromise (first part of the tragedy) or failure (second part). This structure is schematically represented by tree (7.2).

(7.2)

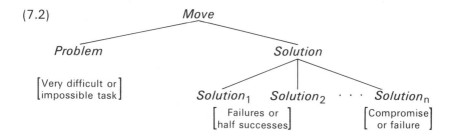

In contrast, a *repetitive* solution is one in which several attempts are made, each unsuccessful, such that every time the task remains unfulfilled. As shown in tree (7.3), *Arden of Feversham* displays a beautiful example of "failure and new attempt" repetition.

(7.3)

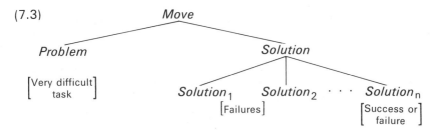

Another type of solution-oriented plot is the *algorithmic* plot, in which, as in complex computation, every step presupposes the correct

(7.4)

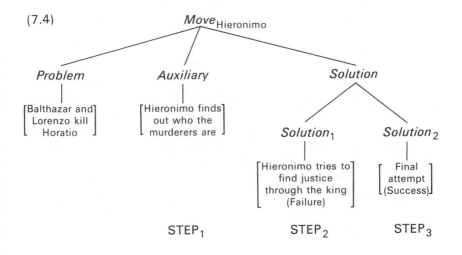

'solution to the preceding step. The closest approximation is found in *The Spanish Tragedy* and in the secondary plot of *King Lear*. Consider tree (7.4), representing Hieronimo's efforts to revenge Horatio's death. The solution Hieronimo is attempting to implement divides into three steps: the finding of Horatio's murderers, an attempt to find royal justice, and the complicated revenge at the end. In *King Lear*, Edgar's revenge, represented by tree (1.7) in chapter 1, proceeds in at least two steps: the killing of Oswald and the victory over Edmund. Now, that to kill Oswald and find Goneril's letter is a necessary step of his revenge is, of course, something Edgar doesn't know at the outset. But what a character happens to know or to ignore in advance is of secondary interest here. An algorithmic solution can be initially devised as such by a careful and considerate actor, or it can derive from an unexpected inadequacy of a first move, which, instead of accomplishing the whole solution, achieves only a first step, or else it can relate to a later discovery that the task was more complex than believed in the first place, etc. Structurally, these possibilities are closely interrelated.

Most often, revenge tragedies are *Solution* oriented. However, from *The Spanish Tragedy*, in which revenge is relatively straightforward, with some variation coming from the unsuccessful appeal to the crown, to such intricate plays as *The White Devil* and *The Revenger's Tragedy*, there is a tremendous syntactic evolution. In Webster's *The White Devil*, the revenge of the duke of Florence and of Monticelso has at least four stages, not necessarily related to one another by an algorithmic progression, although some kind of chronological order must be respected: Brachiano must first be induced into marrying a strumpet and excommunicated, and only then murdered. As for the concrete steps of the murder itself, they are so elaborate that they may be interpreted as merely ornamental.

In contrast with plots stressing the solution, there are texts mostly based on *Auxiliary* effects. Such is the case of Tourneur's *The Revenger's Tragedy*. Without going into the details of its extremely elaborate *Move*-structure, one can say that the play emphasizes less the various conflicts or the structure of their solutions, than the random interactions of the groups involved. Tourneur focuses attention on the various ways in which the parties are, voluntarily or involuntarily, linked to one another in rather unconnected activities. Each group pursues its own interests, usually without any awareness of the other's purposes, except when the latter may be employed as an *Auxiliary*. One could say that the play has no conflict in the sense of "open confrontation." Everything happens rather by chance, and each move is related to some unwise move of another character. A universe where the links between the actions of the different groups are mainly circumstantial may be called a *narratively chaotic universe*. Narratively chaotic universes lack the cohesion of open confrontations or of fully controlled purposeful actions. The characters' trajectories look like Brownian motions, with fortuitous interactions and entirely unexpected consequences. Modern sensibility is fascinated by this type of narrative organization, which probably explains why T. S. Eliot praised so highly *The Revenger's Tragedy*.[95] The extensive use of auxiliary developments, combined with a quite large number of mutually independent groups of characters, conveys a sense of instability and unpredictability. The prominence of *Auxiliaries* in *The Revenger's Tragedy* not only reveals a special type of narrative organization, but also indicates the lines along which it can be artistically exploited.

Besides *Solution*-oriented plots and plots rich in auxiliary developments, a third category of plots emphasizes *polemical configurations*. In such a configuration, two opposite groups of characters successively inflict blows upon one another: one group's solution is the other's problem and vice versa. Being an essentially epic organization of events, the polemical configuration is at its best in drama only when combined with other types of structures. Among the tragedies considered here, only one exclusively employs the polemical configuration scheme for its plot: *Edward the Second*. But this is a consequence of Marlowe's habit of overusing a given narrative procedure, only to later on turn to entirely different devices.

A most interesting circumvention of the monotony of polemical configurations occurs in *King Lear*. Here, the primary plot narrates a conflict whose syntactic structure is not unlike that of *Edward the Second*. The two camps, that of Lear and that of his elder daughters, rhythmically exchange blows, until a spurious denouement brings Lear close to Cordelia. Then, following a short pause, the fight resumes, only to end in catastrophe a few scenes later. The backbone of the tragedy is thus a polemical configuration. To minimize its tedium, the author counts on at least three narrative diversions. The first and most visible is the alternation of scenes belonging to the first plot with scenes of Edmund's story. The secondary plot, by its complexity and omnipresence, renders the flatness of the main story less conspicuous. A second way of enlivening the polemical configuration consists in interrupting it with Lear's tribulations in the wilderness.

These episodes, by arresting the ineluctable advance of the configuration, provide some narrative relief for the audience. Third, the polemical configuration is not allowed to capture the attention of the public from the beginning of the play to its end with the same intensity. As the play advances, the first plot fades away, so to speak, while Edmund's plot becomes more and more emphasized. By gradually withdrawing Lear's plot from the forestage, Shakespeare somewhat arouses interest in the polemical configuration. The more scarce the information about it, the more welcome. Lear and his retinue slowly fade away, until the shock of Cordelia's death brings the polemical configurations to a violent and again fully emphasized end.

This typology can be of interest for the definition of the plot-styles of an author, of a genre, or of a period. Marlowe's plots are, each, constructed around a single prominent device: *Doctor Faustus* and *Tamburlaine I* use successions of repetitive solutions, *Edward the Second* is a long polemical configuration, *The Jew of Malta* employs the same strategies over and over. However, as if he wanted to compensate for monotony inside each play, Marlowe radically changes his plot-patterning from one tragedy to the next. Shakespeare, on the contrary, combines all available devices into ample, ramified plots, rich in *Problems* as well as in *Auxiliaries* and *Solutions*. Notably, the overall proportion of these categories does not considerably vary from one play to another.

In relation to genre, we saw that revenge tragedies prefer *Solution*-oriented plots. The *Auxiliary*-oriented plots are usually employed in comedy, where the means of obtaining some strongly desired object receives much attention. The presence of this type in *The Revenger's Tragedy* is puzzling; it may be interpreted as a stylistic hint of what we called a narratively chaotic universe.

But can we use the proposed typology to close in on the notion of baroque style? On this point I have some doubts. It may be that the inner organization of the grammar is too deeply built into the poetics of plot to be liable to much historical variation. Syntactic forms like those unveiled here must exist in every period, independently of any particular period-style. Plots in which emphasis lies on any of the three aspects previously mentioned are probably indispensable constitutes of a healthy and complete narrative culture.

Plot-semantics too can serve for systematization of existing knowledge, and, perhaps, as a stimulus for new intuitions as well. A detailed exploration of its potential would go beyond the purpose of the present essay; here are nonetheless a few proposals.

The ontology of domains can lead to a better definition of the type of representation involved by the work. Realist texts tend to restrict the ontological inventory, while mythological, fantastic, and marvelous texts use rich ontologies, spread over natural and supernatural worlds. Finer observations may result from analysis: in many Renaissance dramas, the supernatural is present only in one domain, usually that belonging to the most important character or group of characters. Thus, in *Hamlet*, the Ghost visits and influences only Hamlet's domain; in *The Spanish Tragedy*, Andrea has links to Belimperia and Horatio; in *Macbeth*, only the hero can see the Ghost of Banquo. This could be related to the strength of supernatural effects: their impact is such that they not only are best located in the dramatic center of the text, but also must be tempered by restricting ghosts and supernatural elements from interfering too much with other, less conspicuous, domains. Hence the particular feeling one experiences when apparitions from beyond play only an episodic role, like the mysterious god visiting Anthony's camp before the battle (*Anthony and Cleopatra*): such delicate intervention pleasantly contrasts with the heavy ontological duality of *Doctor Faustus* or *Macbeth*.

The flow of information, one of the major epistemic regularities, may also be related to significant distinctions. Hamon (1973) and Brooke-Rose (1980) noticed that an important characteristic of realist writing is plethora of information. This observation could be refined by introducing a distinction between information about the real world and information about the plot. Plot-information can be generally distributed, as in *Tamburlaine I*, or scarce, as in Tourneur's plays. Scarcity of information may affect some domains, as in *King Lear*, or all domains, as in *The Spanish Tragedy*. It may be shared or not by the reader/spectator, according to the strategy embraced by the author. Shakespeare keeps the audience in his confidence; later writers are more diffident and dispense knowledge with more circumspection. Still, until quite late in the nineteenth century, the author remains perfectly in control of the information and dispatches it according to his own priorities. It is only later that we meet with plots that lack an epistemic authority: in Kafka's novels, for instance, one cannot be certain that the author masters all the relevant information about the plot. Such authors are not just unreliable—they are simply as ignorant as is the audience.

Most of traditional critical interpretations of literary texts have been preoccupied with the axiological systems within a plot and with the rules for action. Dividing plots into domains and analyzing axiological partition may help us answer such questions as what sets a *Move* in motion? or, more specifically, what counts as transgression? as lack? Conversely, one may ask what is an acceptable *Solution* to a narrative *Problem*? The answers would contribute to genre theory, for each genre not only has its own battery of transgressions and desires, but also the comic solutions to a similar problem are different from the tragic ones. According to generic conventions, desire to marry may lead to stratagems, to elopement, or to suicide. Historical development can also be followed along the same lines: the range of problems/solutions evolves in close parallelism to changes in mentality and social systems.

Appendix

Appendix:
A Few Considerations
on the Formalism
of *Move*-Grammars

A formal definition of the *Move*-grammar can be adapted from Chomsky's (1963) and Chomsky and Miller's (1963) definition of context-free grammars, by replacing the axiom and the vocabulary with the appropriate symbols. Since the details of such a definition are too technical for the purpose of the present book, I will limit myself to a few comments on the formalism of the *Move*-grammars.

1. *Recursivity*. It has been pointed out in the early 1960s that in order to represent embedding correctly, the base component of a generative transformational grammar must allow for the axioms to appear to the right of the arrow ("column" in my notation) in some rules (Fillmore 1963). Chomsky (1965) calls the trees that embed the axiom *generalized trees*. It is clear that by allowing the embedding of the axiom under another nonterminal node, the generative power of the base component has been greatly increased. Recursivity in the *Move*-grammar may be justified in properly narrative terms. Since the grammar has as its axiom the symbol *Move*, the objects it generates do not belong to a highly restricted class, as is the case with sentences generated by sentence-grammars: plots are made up of series of *Moves*; a powerful base is thus indispensable for their representation. More important from an empirical point of view is the fact that constraints on possible stories seem to be much less powerful than constraints on possible sentences. Studies of special cases have shown that embedding

of stories within stories can be achieved practically without limit. One paper on *The Arabian Nights*, which used a stronger syntactic pattern than *Move*-grammar, indicated how whole stories can be variously embedded within other stories (S. Pavel 1975); the conclusion of that study amounted to an introduction of multiple recursiveness in the narrative base. Since the study made use of a grammar which had as its axiom the symbol *Story*, its conclusions are true *a fortiori* for a grammar which has the axiom *Move*. A *Move*-grammar needs to be more powerful than a *Story*-grammar, if only because any story is made up of several moves.

From the above remarks it becomes clear that *Move*-grammars are not directly related to grammars of discourse. The latter strive to account for *linguistic* trans-sentential phenomena, while *Move*-grammars generate *narrative* structures, which are independent of their linguistic manifestation. A narrative structure can be manifested as a series of paintings, or sculptures, or as a silent movie. The textualization of a narrative structure is a complex operation, obeying structural, cultural, and linguistic constraints. Its study, however, goes beyond the purpose of this book.

2. *Formal relations.* A constituent tree is a formal object on which one can define several formal relations. Some of these are general, uniform relations, such as dominance or precedence. Others can be described, as the need arises, as more restricted relations. Since different grammatical theories use labeled trees as *models* for various kinds of grammatical statements, the formal relations on the tree receive in each case a different theoretical interpretation. Thus, for instance, the formal relation of dominance in a constituent tree is theoretically interpreted by Chomsky (1963 and 1965) as a model of the grammatical relation "is a."[96]

The interpretation given here to the dominance relation is somewhat more refined than the "is a" relation. Although it is entirely possible to say that a problem plus a solution "are" a move, or "constitute" a move, it appears more advantageous when taking into consideration chains of moves to interpret the leftmost branch as "leading to" the move, and the other branches as "constituting" the move. From a formal point of view, this amounts to introducing a distinction between left-dominance and non-left-dominance and giving this formal distinction a theoretical interpretation. Further differentiation may be made between *Solution*-dominance, which can be properly interpreted as the relation of "constituting" and *Auxiliary*-dominance, which means "helping to."

An important property of constituent trees as theoretical models involves the labels assigned to nonterminal nodes. In linguistic trees, these labels bear theoretical categories, for instance, *Noun Phrase, Noun, Verb* (in Chomsky's 1965 model), or *Proposition, Modal, Verb, Case, Actor, Object, Dative*, etc. (in Fillmore's 1968 model). In these two examples, the theoretical notions used as labels are distributional classes (syntactic categories, in Chomsky's terminology) and syntactic functions, respectively. Clearly, distributional classes can be formally defined, at least up to a certain degree of approximation. Functional labels are less well defined; in order to take notions such as *Subject, Object, Indirect Object* as primitives, one must rely more on semantic intuitions. This is the situation of our narrative labels: *Problem, Solution*, etc., are "functional" notions that cannot be defined in a purely distributional way. That narratology has always worked with these types of notions may be attributed to the fact that a story is an abstract object which can be understood and repeated, but which does not depend on a particular textual manifestation. The intuitive evidence that some action in a story constitutes a problem for some character is taken to be of the same type as the notion that a verb determines a constellation of cases, some of which may not be manifested in a particular sentence. Semi-formal definitions are nevertheless traditional in narratology. Thus, the *Move* corresponds to Dorfman's *narreme*, and to Barthes' *nucleic* functions. The pair *Problem* and *Solution* originate in Greimas' distinction between inverted and posited content and in Todorov's notions of disequilibrium vs. equilibrium. Maranda's terminology also influenced my choices. The analysis of the *Problem* relates to Propp's and Dundes' notions of *lack* and *violation*, while the *Solution* benefits from Bremond's analyses. Such examples can be multiplied.[97]

3. *Indexing*. Once the primary labels and relations have been defined, the constituent tree can be further manipulated for theoretical reasons. Thus, almost every proposal in transformational generative grammar since 1965 has included some form of Noun Phrase co-reference indexing. More generally, an indexing may be defined as a relation between a finite set of indexes and a (sub) set of labeled nodes. *Move*-grammars contain two types of indexing. One is the purely numerical indexing of moves. In addition to this, the grammar employs indices designating characters or groups of characters assigned to specific occurrences of the label *Move*. The character-indexing function is a function from the set of nodes labeled *Move* into the set of subsets of the set of characters. (The set of subsets is needed since we

assign groups of characters to some of the *Moves*.) In several cases, special constraints limit the range of values of the function. Polemic configurations and conventions regarding the alliance systems may rule out some possible values of the character-indexing function.

4. *Subconfigurations.* Another important way of exploiting the constituent tree for theoretical purposes is to define on it formal subconfigurations that have interesting theoretical properties. The most common such narrative subconfiguration is the polemical configuration, which consists of a series of *Moves*, each embedded under the *Problem* of the next *Move*, such that every even *Move* is assigned to a (group of) character(s) and every odd *Move* to another (group of) character(s).

5. *The hierarchy of nodes.* Notice that situating the root of a narrative tree at the top and arranging the other nodes under it is a conventional representation that does not necessarily imply that the top node is hierarchically more important or more comprehensive than the nodes it dominates. One can easily turn narrative trees on their side. Consider the variant of tree (1.8) shown in tree (1.8′). One can

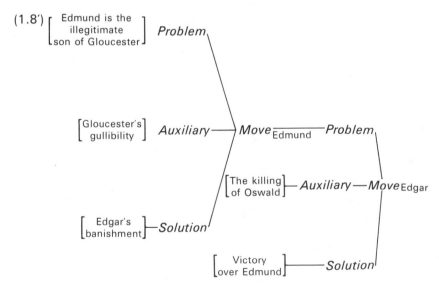

read tree (1.8′) from left to right and from top to bottom, noticing, for instance, that the leftmost *Moves* chronologically precede the *Moves* situated on their right. In fact, as the previous analyses showed, chronological sequence is reducible to a left-to-right *Move*-sequence only in the case of *Moves* embedded under one branch of the leftmost *Move*. Under the above interpretation of the dominance relation, higher *Moves* (or in the above tree, *Moves* situated to the right) are "caused" by lower *Moves* embedded under their *Problem*, "helped" by *Moves* embedded under the *Auxiliary*, and "constituted" of *Moves* embedded under *Solution*.

By going from a lower *Move* to a higher one, one does not necessarily reach a "more important" *Move*, but simply a later one. The highest *Move* is not the most important, but the one that concludes the series. It might be the case that the highest *Move* is related to a hierarchically important character, but this is not obligatory. This remark suggests a way of understanding the perspective of the plot. Since each *Move* is indexed, the character to which the *Move* belongs is affected by the *Problem* of the *Move* and undertakes the *Solution*. The perspective of each *Move* is thus the point of view of the character indexed to the *Move*. The "highest" *Move* is the one the *Solution* of which concludes the series. In some cases the last *Move* indicates the general or dominant perspective under which the plot is constructed, as in *Tamburlaine I*, for instance. But in other occurrences, this does not apply. What the *Move*-grammar can represent is the *local* perspective of every *Move*. The general or dominant perspective may well be a semantic notion, depending on various ways of emphasizing narrative or non-narrative elements.

Notes

Notes

Foreword

1. *Le Miroir persan* (Paris: Denoël, 1978).
2. *Inflexions de voix* (Montréal: Les Presses le l'Université de Montréal, 1976).
3. Most notably, *La Syntaxe narrative des tragédies de Corneille* (Paris: Klincksieck, 1976).
4. This account excludes such nonhistorical endeavors as the *Grammaire* of Port-Royal.
5. For a remarkable recent study, see Marc Fumaroli, *L'Age de l'éloquence: Rhétorique et "res literaria" de la renaissance au seuil de l'époque classique* (Geneva: Droz, 1980).
6. Such a tendency becomes particularly marked in the histories of literature of nations on the periphery of cultural power. For a parodistic treatment of these tendencies, see Witold Gombrowicz, *Dziennik* (Paris: Institut Littéraire, 1956).
7. I am not trying to suggest a cause-and-effect relation between these demographic phenomena and the developments in literary theory, but to draw attention to the background of these phenomena. The history of literary theory will have to take into account the changes in patterns and scopes of literacy.
8. Most notably V. N. Voloshinov, *Marxism and the Philosophy of Language* (New York: Seminar Press, 1973).
9. Cf. my "Semiotics of Semiotics," forthcoming in *Australian Journal of Cultural Studies*.
10. Roland Barthes, *Elements de Sémiologie* in *Le Degré zéro de l'écriture* suivi de *Eléments de sémiologie* (Paris: Gonthier, 1965).
11. This discussion excludes those concerned with speech-act theory and with text-linguistics. It also leaves aside the important work of the scholars of the Porter Institute of Poetics.
12. Among the exceptions stand the work of Nicolas Ruwet and that of Gerald Prince.
13. The exception here is the unjustly neglected work of Guillaume on the psycho-mechanics of language. See Gustave Guillaume, *Langage et science du langage* (Québec: Presses de l'Université Laval, 1964).

14. G. E. M. Anscombe, *Metaphysics and the Philosophy of Mind* (Minneapolis: University of Minnesota Press, 1981), p. 57.

15. Noam Chomsky, *Language and Mind* (New York: Harcourt, Brace and World, 1968).

16. J. Margolis, *Philosophy of Psychology* (Englewood Cliffs, N.J.: Prentice-Hall, 1984), pp. 84-85.

17. Ibid. p. 88.

18. Ibid. p. 90.

19. Fredric Jameson, "Reification and Utopia in Mass Culture," *Social Text* 1 (1979): 130-48.

20. See Mieke Bal, *Narratologie* (Paris: Klincksieck, 1977); Seymour Chatman, *Story and Discourse* (Ithaca, N.Y.: Cornell University Press, 1978); Shlomith Rimmon-Kenan, *Narrative Fiction* (London: Methuen, 1983).

21. Aleksandr N. Veselovskij, *Poetika sjužetov* in *Sobranie sočinenij*, series 1, vol. 2, first part (Saint Petersburg: Akademija Nauk, 1913).

22. *Morfologija skazki* (Leningrad: Akademija, 1928). For a thorough discussion of Propp's contribution to this area and to the misunderstandings that have attended this work, see Antoly Liberman, "Introduction" to Vladimir Propp, *Theory and History of Folklore* (Minneapolis: University of Minnesota Press, 1984), pp. ix-lxxxi.

23. Claude Brémond and Jean Verrier, "Afanassiev et Propp," *Littérature* 45 (1981): 61-78.

24. Hayden White, *Metahistory: The Historical Imagination in Nineteenth-Century Europe* (Baltimore: The Johns Hopkins University Press, 1973), p. 6, note 5.

25. Peter Brooks, "Fictions of the Wolfman," *Diacritics* 9:1 (Spring 1979): 72-86. See also his "Freud's Masterplot: Questions of Narrative," *Yale French Studies* 55/56 (1977): 280-300.

26. Gérard Genette, *Nouveau Discours du récit* (Paris: Seuil, 1983).

27. Peter Brooks, *Reading for the Plot* (New York: Knopf, 1984).

28. Claude Brémond, *Logique du récit* (Paris: Seuil, 1973).

29. Martin Heidegger, *Nietzsche*, trans. D. F. Krell (San Francisco: Harper and Row, 1979), p. 64. The German original is to be found in *Nietzsche*, vol. 1 (Pfullingen: Neske, 1961), pp. 76-77.

Chapter 1. Introduction

1. An extensive discussion of the notion of literary competence is to be found in Culler (1975), pp. 113-30. "To read a text as literature," Culler argues, "is not to make one's mind a *tabula rasa* and approach it without preconceptions; one must bring to it an implicit understanding of the operations of literary discourse which tells one what to look for. Anyone lacking this knowledge . . . would for example be baffled if presented with a poem. He would be unable to read it *as* literature . . . because he lacks the complex 'literary competence' which enables others to proceed. He has not internalized the 'grammar' of literature which would permit him to convert linguistic sequences into literary structures and meanings" (pp. 113-14). See also Ihwe (1970 and 1972).

2. A reassessment of this distinction, made from the point of view of philosophical logic, is to be found in Von Wright (1971). Itkonen (1975) discusses the status of linguistics as a formal, yet hermeneutic science. See the discussion in Chomsky (1980).

3. Jakobson (1970) discusses this question and reaches the following conclusion: "Phonology and grammar of oral poetry offer a system of complex and elaborate correspondences which come into being, take effect, and are handed down through generations without anyone's cognizance of the rules governing this intricate network. . . . Such structures, particularly powerful on the sublimal level, can function without any assistance of

logical reflection and patent apprehension both in the poet's creative work and in its perception by the sensitive reader" (p. 308).

4. Culler (1975) writes: "The ideal reader is, of course, a theoretical construct, perhaps best thought of as a representation of the central notion of acceptability. . . . The meaning of a poem within the institution of literature is not, one might say, the immediate and spontaneous reaction of individual readers but the meanings which they are willing to accept as both plausible and justifiable when they are explained" (p. 124). An important paper on the role of the reader is Prince (1973b). For a presentation of the various trends in reader-oriented criticism, see Suleiman's "Introduction" to Suleiman and Crossman, eds. (1981).

5. Thus, Fish (1973) argues that "the way to repair the ruins of stylistics" is to be found "not by linking the descriptive and interpretive acts, but by making them one" (p. 150).

6. According to Halliday (1954), in the last plays of Shakespeare "the bleakness of the diction is emphasized by the free use of light and weak endings — that, and — completely breaking down the architectural form of the verse by sweeping one line into another without any definition of pause" (p. 181).

7. Culler (1975) argues along the same lines: "This would not need to be said if interpretive criticism had not tried to persuade us that the study of literature means the elucidation of individual works. But in this cultural context it is important to reflect on what has been lost or obscured in the practice of an interpretive criticism which treats each work as an autonomous artefact, an organic whole whose parts all contribute to a complex thematic statement. . . . Nor has discourse on literature always been so imperiously committed to interpretation. It used to be possible in the days before poem became preeminently the act of an individual . . . , to study its interaction with norms of rhetoric and genre, the relation of its formal features to those of the tradition, without feeling immediately compelled to produce an interpretation which would demonstrate their thematic relevance."

8. Thus, Chomsky (1972) appears to agree on the need for more than one grammar to account for natural language structure. Fillmore (1972) claims that incomplete grammars are unavoidable.

9. This does not mean that textual properties are not a highly interesting subject of investigation. Text-grammar, as developed by J. Ihwe, T. Van Dijk, H. Rieser, J. Petöfi, S. Schmidt, and others, takes precisely as its object general text-properties. See, among other contributions, Van Dijk (1972) and Petöfi and Rieser (1973).

10. Narratology as one of the most dynamic fields in structuralist poetics is linked to its bias in favor of highly regular phenomena. To mention only a few contributions, Propp (1928), Dundes (1964), Barthes (1966), Todorov (1966, 1969, and 1971), Greimas (1966, 1970, 1976, and 1977), Greimas and Courtés (1982), Bremond (1964, 1966, 1968 and 1973), Maranda and Köngäs (1971), have developed a cluster of notions, categories, and methods of narratological description related to the theoretical advances in structural linguistics. Transformational-generative grammar has in turn influenced progress in narratology. Lakoff (1972), Prince (1973a), and Van Dijk (1975) are among those proposing narrative models based on transformational generative research. Other theoretical trends lead to Fotino's and Marcus' (1975) formal narrative models; to the psycho- and sociolinguistic research on narratives proposed by Labov and Valetzky (1967), Sacks (1972), Rumelhart (1975 and 1977), Shank (1975), Van Dijk et al. (1975), and Kintsch (1977); and to text-grammar formal methodology proposed in Van Dijk (1973) and (1975). Narrative syntax has been supplemented by various contributions to narrative semantics such as Greimas (1966 and 1970), Todorov (1966), Doležel (1976a, b, and c), Pavel (1976b). Scholes (1974) and Chatman (1978) offer critical presentations of the French school of narratology. An extensive study — which would include material on the Dutch and German schools, on recent Russian semiotics, and on transformational-generative research — is still needed.

11. See Jackendoff (1977a and b) and Chomsky (1977 and 1980).

12. See Rapoport (1966), pp. 13-21.

13. For the discussion of narratively significant vs. insignificant actions, see Barthes' (1966) distinction between *functions* and *indexes*. Dorfman (1969) proposes a similar criterion for the definition of the *narreme*.

14. It is not difficult to see that the proposed grammar takes into account both "principles of stories" described by Todorov (1978). According to Todorov, narrative units are related by *succession* and *transformation* (p. 66). In our grammar, the relationship between the *Problem* and the *Solution* of the same move refers to Todorov's *transformation* (but see note 16 below), while *succession* is represented by the embedding of *Moves* one under another.

15. Van Dijk (1972), Lakoff (1972), Prince (1973a), and Pavel (1973 and 1976a) have shown that narrative structures present transformational aspects, and that an adequte narrative grammar must include a transformational component.

16. Incidentally, writers like Lévi-Strauss or Greimas use the term *transformation* to refer to an entirely different notion. One can find in Pavel (1976a), pp. 131-47, a critical review of the use of the term in narrative studies.

Chapter 2. Plot-Grammar: Marlowe's *Tamburlaine I*

17. Rumelhart (1975) labels the direct impact *cause* and the contingent impact *allow*.

18. Throughout this book, the term *act* will be used only in order to simplify reference to the most common editions of Marlowe's and other Elizabethan dramatists' plays. Accordingly, the term does not have a structural significance. For different stands on the reality of the division into acts, see Jewkes (1958) and Baldwin (1965).

19. This principle, as here formulated, allows for cases like tree (2.2), in which $Move^2$ and $Move^3$ do not obey any strict chronological order. Indeed, Cosroe's successful attempt to become king ($Move^3$) ends long after $Move^2$, Theridamas' conversion, has taken place. But the two *Moves* do not belong to the relation of dominance, so the principle of Solution Postponement does not apply to them. The solution of $Move^4$ in the same tree does obey the principle. It comes only after the completion of everything in the *Moves* dominated by $Move^4$. Similarly, $Move^2$ concludes only after $Move^1$ has ended.

20. Greimas (1970), Van Dijk (1973), Prince (1973a) all show how a prechronological order can be related to a temporal sequence of events.

21. This threefold distinction originates in Propp (1928). See also Greimas' introduction to Cortés (1976), p. 9.

22. There are other devices for the elevation of the hero above the realm of humanity: Menaphon's description of him has been so analyzed by Meehan (1974). Battenhouse (1941) shows how the initial raptures gradually become "false flames spiritual but infernal," subject to condemnation in the eyes of Elizabethan moralists.

23. "The drama is built up on rivalries like a tournament, where each new contender is more formidable than the last" (H. Levin 1952, p. 34); ". . . in defiance of dramatic expectation, Tamburlaine defeats each of them and acquires with each victory the power over his opponent. These opponents are carefully ordered, each representing a different kind of monarch, and Tamburlaine's progressive victories represent . . . a triumph measured primarily in terms of political sovereignty" (Summers [1974], pp. 41-42).

24. The exchange probably has the attributive function of rendering Bajazeth as hateful as possible. Tamburlaine's self-image as "the Scourge and Wrath of God" (v. 1142) is thus vindicated. Knoll (1969) shows how carefully constructed is the dramatic case in favor of Tamburlaine. Among other features, one may cite the accusations Tamburlaine makes against Bajazeth's cruel treatment of the Christians.

25. It can be argued that an episodic nature is a common feature of *De Casibus* tragedies. Indeed, Cole (1962) has shown the historical relationship between *Tamburlaine* and the *De Casibus* genre, which "dealt chiefly with the fall of princes and kings, notably wicked ones" (p. 42). One has to keep in mind, however, that if the second part of the play respects the rules of the genre, the first part, as Farnham (1936) has pointed out, "is a rebellious violation of all that *De Casibus* tragedy has set out to convey" (p. 369). On this type of tragedy, see Doran (1954), pp. 116-28.

26. For a more detailed analysis of acts III to V, see Pavel (1978), pp. 44-51.

Chapter 3. Semantic Considerations: Narrative Domains

27. In two innovative and stimulating works, Hendricks (1976 and 1977) proposes a narrative system in which characters in a story are grouped into two (or more?) sets, prior to the analysis of its plot-structure. In the analysis of "A Rose for Emily" by Faulkner, Hendricks discovers two main sets of characters: the protagonist and the antagonist set. The assignment of a given character to one of these sets presupposes, however, some knowledge of the character's place in the plot. In addition a character can change his or her place from one set to another. The system of alliances is often very fragile, especially in complex narrative structures, where it is not easy to define the protagonist and antagonist sets, except by relativizing them with respect to different episodes. But this would amount to analyzing the plot *before* describing the sets of characters.

28. For a discussion of tragic plots in relation to chances of success in a conflict, see Pavel (1981).

29. It has been pointed out (Summers 1974) that verbally Bajazeth is more cruel than Tamburlaine. Still, in this rhetorical play, Bajazeth's speeches are mere words, while Tamburlaine's cruelty is the only one to achieve palpable results.

30. Battenhouse (1941) believes that these "ornamental" aspects are more important than the plot itself: "the *Tamburlaine* drama may be likened to a fabric set with jewels. The fabric, the history of a mighty conqueror, would be bald spectacle if it were not decorated with resplendent scenes of moral instruction, sewn in with care to create the tapestry. Their presence in the drama gives it its 'purple patches,' makes it seem episodic and a thing of parts." He goes on to claim, like many others, that "Indeed, it is plain that the *Tamburlaine* has no plot in the modern sense of entanglement and resolution. The play is a pageant" (p. 150).

31. Many critics have noticed the "special" character of the plot. Among those who do not attribute it to the rules of the *De Casibus* genre, Meehan (1974) makes a typical judgment: "It seems clear that the soul of this play is not the plot; Marlowe's principal concern is not the construction of victory upon victory" (p. 40). A century ago, Legouis was already disturbed by what he called the monotony of the play. On the other hand, it is worth noting that about such a highly stylized and conventional play, it was possible to write that "*Tamburlaine*, so far from interpreting life by indicating its form, appears as formless and incoherent as life itself" (Ellis-Fermor 1927, p. 44).

Chapter 4. Marlowe—An Exercise in Inconstancy

32. Critics have seldom been aware of the deep dissimilarities between the two plays. Several sections of the following analysis can be taken as an argument against those who see in *Tamburlaine* a single grandiose ten-act tragedy (Battenhouse 1941; Steane 1964).

33. The parallelism was noticed by Harry Levin (1952): ". . . as in the preceding play, the structure is tripartite, and the central act pits Tamburlaine against a Turkish foe: this

time it is Callapine, the son of Bajazeth, crowned and accompanied by an avenging host. Again, the last two acts march toward the culminating siege; and where the locale was Damascus in the First Part, it is now Babylon" (p. 35). See also Waith (1962) in Leech, ed. (1964), pp. 81-82.

34. Boas (1940) notices that in the second part "there is less concentration of interest upon the central figure" (p. 100).

35. It has been argued that after "fulfilling the pattern of a Scourge of God, Tamburlaine boasts himself proudly against God and burns the Scriptures. Then within minutes, he finds himself strangely distempered . . . God is now casting his Scourge into the fire" (Battenhouse 1941, p. 257). This reading appears to be a typically uneconomical one: there is no indication in the play that the qualification of "Scourge of God" is taken otherwise than in a purely rhetorical way. Moreover, Tamburlaine's obsession with godlike power pervades the play. Finally, there is no concrete indication that his death comes from God, and even less from an annoyed God. Steane (1964) is another partisan of "God as the great unseen actor of the play" (p. 114). Again, at least at the level of the plot, there is no support for this view. Kocher (1946) gives a stimulating account of the diversity of religious attitudes in *Tamburlaine*.

36. Bevington (1962) analyzes the structural properties of popular moral and chronicle plays before Marlowe. Among their most common features is the linear and episodic structure of the plot, its progressive (as opposed to repetitive) character, its pervasive symmetry, and the systematic use of the soliloquy. He convincingly argues that *Tamburlaine* displays these features. The primitive structure of *Tamburlaine* is seen as imperfectly adapted to the radically new vision of the world that Marlowe conveys.

37. H. Levin (1952) describes the episode as "ineffectual" (p. 36). Battenhouse (1941) does not even mention it in the interpretation of *Tamburlaine* that closes his book. Boas (1940) considers that it is "somewhat irrelevantly intermingled" with the rest of the play (p. 95). Notice that the informal analysis of plots often leads critics to recognize poorly integrated episodes containing secondary characters. However, none of the above-mentioned writers, or for that matter none of the critics writing on *Tamburlaine*, have adequately described the poorly integrated episodes containing *central* characters, such as the slaying of Calyphas. Battenhouse (1941), who is the most sensitive to morality-like episodes, does not insist on the exemplary nature of the Calyphas episode.

38. Again, this is a commonplace in Marlowian criticism. Battenhouse (1941), p. 258, and Waith (1962) underline the pathos of the ending.

39. This stresses the ambiguity of the relationship between the first and the second part of the tragedy. Earlier, we saw plot-based arguments *against* the interpretation of Tamburlaine as a simple ten-act play. Here we have evidence to partially support this view.

40. For Battenhouse (1941), Olympia "seems plainly to be introduced by Marlowe as a foil to the character of Zenocrate" (p. 167). In an ingenious alternative to this commonly accepted view, Steane (1964) argues that "Olympia's virtues are to some extent a reflection of Tamburlaine's own; the strong-minded killing of her son compares with Tamburlaine's killing of Calyphas" (pp. 68-69).

41. Kocher (1946) should have insisted more on this highly suggestive contrast, which is probably even more revealing of Marlowe's religious attitude than the often quoted anti-Christian episode of Orcan vs. Sigismund.

42. This suggests that the "Scourge of God" theory (Battenhouse 1941; Kocher 1946), covers only the first part of the tragedy, and so does the "herculean hero" theory (Waith 1962).

43. Of all critics dealing with Marlowe, Harry Levin is the most sensitive to Marlowe's preoccupation with artistic change. In his book of 1952, the chapter dedicated to *The Jew*

of Malta starts with the words: "What next? That has always been the crucial question for the creative mind. How can it continue to surprise the audience captured by its early boldness?" (p. 56). The question appears to have preoccupied Marlowe even before he started to work on *The Jew of Malta*. How can we otherwise explain the drastic changes in the semantics of *Tamburlaine II*?

44. T. S. Eliot (1932) called the play a "savage farce." Cf. ". . . the diction is plainer and much saltier . . . [Barabas] dissembles his shrewdness, plays the Eiron, . . . Often he utters no more than a line at a time and engages in stichotymy — in capping line for line — with his interlocutors. . . . The climax of ironic dissimulation comes with the scene where the two Friars 'exclame against' Barabas" (H. Levin 1952, pp. 72-73).

45. "The narrative of *The Jew of Malta* moves along straightforwardly, bare of the artful richness achieved by Shakespeare through development of imagery and juxtaposition of scenes" (Rothstein 1966, p. 271).

46. At the textual level, it has been noticed that, while in *Tamburlaine* the average length of a cue is 6.3 lines, in *The Jew of Malta* it reduces to 2.8 lines (H. Levin 1952, p. 72).

47. The notions of *narrative* and *epistemic suspense* approximately correspond to two types of games, called *gambling* and *strategy* games. Gambling requires only the calculation of odds, while strategy games involve consideration of possible but often unknown actions of an opponent (Rapoport 1974). *Tamburlaine I*, from the point of view of the main character, is merely gambling. *The Jew of Malta*, in contrast, looks like an elaborate strategy game.

48. That the villain's sincerity toward the audience is but a convention could not escape the notion of H. Levin (1952), who believes it to be "less and less convincing." He argues that "Life would be considerably less tragic, . . . if villainy announced itself in such resounding tones" (p. 58). However, the dramatic explanation of the villain's sincerity convention does not lie in its psychological exactness, but in its function of rendering the villain closer to the spectator, as Levin himself points out several pages later.

49. Boas (1940) compares Barabas' attitude toward his daughter with Agamemnon's readiness to sacrifice Iphigenia.

50. According to Ellis-Fermor (1927): "The dauntless courage and ruthlessness of Machiavelli's doctrines seem at first to have made a strong appeal to Marlowe: and in *The Jew of Malta*, which may have been written in the first burst of this enthusiasm, he invests them with a certain poetic splendour" (p. 89). See the chapter on *The Jew of Malta* in Summers (1974).

51. It may be argued with much more plausibility that Barabas' opponents are true Machiavellian characters. Summers (1974) shows that Ferneze is an "accomplished Machiavellian" of a "more serious kind" than Barabas (p. 105). Summers slightly misinterprets, however, the function of Barabas' self-confessed (to the public) evil. He attributes to a variety of "open" evil, what is in fact a purely conventional stage device.

52. Notice that in the perspective of the plot, *cupiditas*, which according to some critics (Steane 1964 among them) is the main vice in the play, does not have a major role. Money provides only a motive for revenge and a means to its accomplishment. Bevington (1962) convincingly argues that the play is not a mere "vice" tragedy.

53. See Rothstein (1966), for a most lively and stimulating essay on this play.

54. One recognizes here the *Calumniator Credited* convention as formulated by Stoll (1933).

55. "*The Jew of Malta* requires some means of private comment, as well as public speech, to express the cross-purposes between policy and profession, deed and words. It leans much more upon the soliloquy, which the extroverted Tamburlaine hardly needed, and its characteristic mode is the aside. . . . We, who overhear his asides and soliloquies, are his only trustworthy confidants. We are therefore in collusion with Barabas. We revel in his malice,

we share his guilt. We are the 'worldlings' to whom he addresses himself" (H. Levin 1952, p. 73).

56. See the discussion in H. Levin (1952), p. 21ff.

57. Brooks' (1966) powerful insights into the construction of the play support this reading: "In his *Poetics*, Aristotle observed that a tragedy should have a beginning, a middle and an end. The statement makes a point that seems obvious. . . . Yet the play without a middle does occur . . . Marlowe's *Doctor Faustus* may seem to show . . . [this] defect, for very early in the play the learned doctor makes the decision to sell his soul to the devil, and after that there seems little to do except to fill in the time before the mortgage falls due and the devil comes to collect the forfeited soul. If the consequences of Faustus' bargain is inevitable, and if nothing can be done to alter it, then it doesn't much matter what one puts in as filler. Hence one can stuff in comedy and farce more or less *ad libitum*, the taste of the audience and its patience in sitting through the play being the only limiting factors" (pp. 208-9).

58. For a discussion of the morality play aspect of the piece, see Brockbank (1962).

59. Psychologically oriented criticism was shocked by the smoothness of the substitution. Reluctant to attribute it to Marlowe, Boas (1940) symptomatically writes: "It was unfortunate for Marlowe that the death of Gaveston was immediately followed in the Chronicle by prominent mention of the king's new favorites, the Spencers, father and son" (p. 183), as if the Chronicle has forced the dramatist's hand.

60. Steane (1964) proposes a similar analysis: "At a performance one has the impression that there are really two plays: in the first half the subject is the homosexual king and his favourite; in the second it is the rise of Mortimer and the fall of Edward. The impression is not quite accurate, however, partly because the interval has cut across the middle. Actually the construction includes an important middle section marked out from the rest by the fact that in it the king is for a short time strong, determined and victorious" (pp. 2-3). It is precisely the need to clarify the basis for such intuitions that justifies the construction of plot-grammars.

61. According to Bevington (1962), *Edward the Second* is "generally acclaimed as Marlowe's most carefully constructed play" (p. 234).

62. "*Edward II*, despite its acclaimed superiority of structure over Marlowe's earlier plays, is still linear in movement" (Bevington 1962, p. 238). The skill in its construction attracted the retaliation of M. C. Bradbrook, who, rather abruptly, claims that "by Elizabethan standards [?] it is an inferior play" (Bradbrook 1935, p. 160). The most explicit criticism of the weaknesses in *Edward the Second*'s plot is to be found in Clemen (1961): "For all his skill in complicating the plot, the composition, especially in the first two-thirds of the play is hurried and breathless, and nothing is carried through to its proper conclusion." Boas (1940) found the third and the fourth acts "overcrowded" (p. 186).

63. Wilson (1953) pertinently notices that "It adds to the horror that on the last two acts Edward is never brought face to face with his two tormentors." Should one assume the existence of a violent Death-rule asking for doomed people to be far removed from their friends, as well as from their persecutors?

64. Perhaps this is a too naive view of Isabella's character. Bevington (1962) suggests that, during the play, Isabella is gradually unmasked as fundamentally evil. It could be so, however in the case of Mortimer one can indeed speak of a "transition from rationally motivated behaviour to pure viciousness" (p. 241), while Isabella's initial viciousness is nowhere suggested in the play. For H. Levin (1952), she is a "split personality . . . who starts by being ungallantly abused [and] ends by justifying [the king's] antipathy" (p. 98). Critics are quite harsh on women's misdemeanors.

Chapter 5. Two Revenge Tragedies: *The Spanish Tragedy* and *Arden of Feversham*

65. Bowers (1940), p. 73, enumerates twelve basic Kydian formulas for the tragedy of revenge, one of them being the use of a ghost only loosely related to the rest of the play. He does not mention the use of the historico-political overplot. (H. Levin 1952, p. 67, calls *overplot* "the stuff of history as it impinges upon the more personal concerns of the characters.") One writer who challenges the reduction of *The Spanish Tragedy* to a mere revenge tragedy is Hunter (1965, p. 241).

66. Biesterfeld (1936) sees little connection between the subplot and the main line of action. In a similar vein, Edwards (1959) thinks that the subplot "could have been introduced more economically and the relevance of theme is very slight" (p. 49). Freeman (1967) argues, however, that the Portuguese scenes warn against a too-hasty judgment and justify Hieronimo's temporizations to the audience. They also "serve the dramatic function of establishing some sympathy with Balthazar" (p. 85). See also Wiatt (1958).

67. This is independent of psychological and moral considerations: "what an Elizabethan might think of Hieronimo's actions in real life may be irrelevant of *The Spanish Tragedy*. Hieronimo may still be a sympathetic hero, in spite of Elizabethan indignation against private revenge" (Edwards 1959, p. 53).

68. See the insightful study of Edwards (1959): "that Belimperia and Isabella should speak of delay (III, 9 and IV, 2, 3) is a measure only of their understandable impatience and does not mean that Hieronimo *could* have acted more quickly. It is the sense of delay which is real, and not delay itself." However, the next assertion: "Hieronimo does everything possible as quickly as possible" (p. 51) is an exaggeration since Hieronimo too blames himself for the delay.

69. Murray (1969) submits that "the Central image of man in *The Spanish Tragedy* is . . . a figure standing alone in semidarkness, able to see and apparently able to control those below him in the hierarchy of power, although without understanding them, but often unable even to *see* those above him" (p. 31).

70. This interpretation is different from that of Freeman (1967). Indeed, why would Kyd wish to warn his audience against too hasty conclusions as Freeman suggests? Was he conveying moral and psychological information? Is it not more natural (and closer to the craft of writing plays) to think that if the main plot ends in catastrophy, a subplot with a limited happy ending provides some respite, and some *inconsequential* hope about the possibility of justice?

71. Empson (1956) argues that "the Duke (of Castille) had arranged the death of Andrea" (p. 63).

72. See the discussion of the authorship in Wine (1973), p. lxxxif.

73. "So much, in fact, does the structure of the play resemble the episodic and unstructured quality of life itself that not a few critics have been beguiled into thinking the play 'singularly devoid of constructive art,' 'in danger of becoming as dull as life,' . . ." (Wine 1973, p. lxxv).

74. Holinshed's narrative of the event shows that the real Arden was entirely aware of the situation, but that he accepted it out of avarice: he did not want to antagonize the family of his wealthy wife.

75. Gillet (1940) provides an existentialist-flavored reading of the play, centered on the character of Alice.

76. This contrast, as well as Reede's episode, suggests that the author, besides having a remarkable sensitivity to social reality, has a discrete moral message to convey.

77. This precept is related to Stoll's (1933) maxim: believe "at the critical moment the

detrimental thing that is cunningly told" (p. 6). Arden, the reverse of Othello, believes that his wife is innocent.

78. In fact, as the comparison with Holinshed shows, the author tried to *play down* Arden's greed, to the point that it is no longer, as in the real incident, a motive for action in connection with Alice and Mosbie. Ironically, the character of Arden looks more realistic on stage because there he displays qualities not immediately related to the plot. This, however, is the result of a change the author operated in the real-life material.

Chapter 6. *King Lear*

79. Shakespeare criticism is so developed that I have to neglect a discussion of details and a confrontation with other points of view. The decision is not due only to the material difficulty of dealing with such a multitude of insights on Shakespeare, but also to the theoretical problem that almost anything has been said on this author and his works. My chapter owes a great deal to Bradley (1904); see also Mack (1970). Nonetheless, the results of the present work should not be labeled neo-Bradleyan, since plot is not considered here to be as intimately connected with character as Bradley thought. Situated in the Proppian tradition of narrative analysis, my inquiry is primarily interested in the basic structure of plot, to which individualization procedures are mere late additions, beautiful ornaments that a certain kind of literary practice can afford, but certainly not essentially present in any plot. Consequently, it is close to the initial project of Stoll (1933) of finding the conventional, nonpsychological elements in Shakespearian drama. Unfortunately, as remarkable as Stoll's intentions are, his concrete analyses yield disappointingly few results. In fact, beyond the statement of intention, Stoll establishes merely two Shakespearian conventions: the postulate of improbability, and the convention of the Calumniator Credited. For a semiotic interpretation of these, see Steinmann (1977). My arguments are also close to Fergusson (1949), to Crane's (1953) ideas on hypothesis and refutation in criticism, as well as to the School of Chicago's preoccupation with plot. In a different vein, one may take a sort of naive delight in the studies of Moulton (1893) and Lounsbury (1901). These authors are certainly much less sophisticated than more recent critics; still they help one understand the basics of the plot and the elementary features of the characters in a reassuringly solid way.

80. See the authoritative work of Richard Levin (1971) on multiple plot.

81. One finds the following note in Ribner (1960, p. 135): "See the excellent discussion in Enid Welsford, *The Fool: His Social and Literary History* (New York, 1935), pp. 253-69. Miss Welsford has pointed out to me that whereas at the beginning of the play the good characters are disorganized and separate from one another and the evil characters closely joined in a compact group, at the end of the play, the evil characters are dispersed and the good characters have come together."

82. Elton (1966) analyzes the attitudes toward religion and the gods in the play. He finds a complex syncretism in which the unrevealed god plays an important role. On the relationship between Shakespeare and Christianity, see R. M. Frye (1963). The strict naturalism of the play does not refer to what the characters say or believe in, but only to the inventory of elements manifested in the plot.

83. The above theory of space in *King Lear* explains away most of the questions subtly raised by Bradley (1904) in connection with the incongruities of scenery in the play. He himself points out that the "very vagueness in the sense of locality . . . [has] a positive value for the imagination. [It gives] the feeling of vastness, the feeling not of a scene or particular place, but of a world" (pp. 213-14). For the ritual atmosphere of the play, see Frost (1952).

84. See Cavell's essay "The Avoidance of Love: A Reading of *King Lear*," in Cavell (1976), pp. 267-53.

85. See Eliade (1955 and 1958). Eliade (1963) discusses "renewal" myths in connection with the cyclical view of life. He describes apocalyptical experiences as the destruction of an old cycle in order to better implant the new cycle. Should one speak of *King Lear* as an "apocalyptical" play? The tribulations period certainly suggests it; however, the old order is not destroyed during or via the tribulations. We have already noticed that the tribulations do not have a direct narrative impact: their significance is purely spiritual. Northrop Frye (1967) calls *King Lear* a tragedy of isolation, focusing thus on the tribulations as the semantic center of the play. A description of these as part of a larger "gethsemane" of the king is found in Harbage (1958), p. 118.

Chapter 7. *Move*-Grammars and Styles of Plot

86. H. Wölfflin (1915).

87. For an attempt to give Wölfflin's criteria an objective foundation, see Cupchik (1974).

88. See Wellek (1963). The features mentioned were proposed respectively by A. Hübscher, E. Ermatinger, H. Cyzarz, L. Pfandl, and J. Rousset. See also Hatzfeld (1955), Bucker (1964) and Warnke (1972). An interesting attempt to circumscribe a literary period objectively is Remak's (1971) study of romanticism.

89. Mueller (1954), p. 428.

90. Heyl (1961), p. 283.

91. Bucker (1964), pp. 311-14.

92. This stand comes close to the position expressed by Brady (1972).

93. See Walzel (1916). Heyl (1961) remarks that art historians don't always agree on the applicability of these notions. While Wölfflin considers that baroque art lacks tectonicity, Sypher (1955) assigns the attribute "tectonic" to the baroque style, in connection with the "mighty decorum" and the "august equilibrium" of baroque art. Heyl argues that the two writers dwell on the different aspects of the style, by focusing on different works, or on different components of the same work.

94. Empson (1935); R. Levin (1971).

95. T. S. Eliot, "Cyril Tourneur" in Eliot (1932).

Appendix: A Few Considerations on the Formalism of *Move*-Grammars

96. Notice that, within linguistics, this theoretical interpretation of the dominance relation is not always applicable. Thus, in dependency trees of "stemmas," dominance has to be interpreted as a subtype of dependency, which is not a part-whole relation. The reason for not adopting here a dependency type of grammar for narrative structure, involves the fact that the classical dependency grammar of Tesnière (1959) does not use nonterminal symbols and thus cannot represent theoretical categories such as *Noun Phrase, Verb*, etc. (or, in our case, *Move, Problem, Solution*, etc.). This is a particularly damaging lack, since the narrative meaning of a given narrative proposition cannot be grasped without taking into account the nonterminal node that dominates it. More recently, several dependency grammars have been proposed that borrow some of the characteristics of constituent grammars, including the use of nonterminal symbols (Hays 1964; Robinson 1970). It is not clear however, whether these grammars are more than notational variants of constituent grammars. Robinson (1970) has argued that the two types are formally equivalent.

97. Colby (1970) discusses this problem and suggests ways of formally constraining the identification of narrative abstract categories, which he calls "eidons": "How does one go about identifying eidons? Propp never tells us how he began his own analysis of Russian fairy tales. Obviously it is necessary to begin with a good intuition. . . . It may be precisely through structural regularities in the more easily recognizable themes that we may find

the best clues to eidons. In these statistical studies [Colby 1966a and b], themes were indicated by the appearance of words used to express each theme. . . . Correlated themes, when revealed through statistical operations, can indicate eidochronic narrative points for identifying the remaining eidons in a folktale, by showing statistical summaries and graphs of themes which are used in establishing these anchor eidons. The initial selection of tentative eidons prior to the final distributional tests can be clearly documented" (p. 183).

References

References

Bal, Mieke. 1977. *Narratologie*. Paris: Klincksieck.

Baldwin, T. W. 1965. *On Act and Scene Division in the Shakspere first folio*. Carbondale, Ill.: Southern Illinois University Press.

Barthes, Roland. 1963. *Sur Racine*. Paris: Seuil.

_____. 1966. "Introduction à l'analyse structurale des récits." *Communications* 8: 1-27. (English translation in *New Literary History* 6[1975]: 237-72.)

Battenhouse, R. W. 1941. *Marlowe's Tamburlaine: A Study of Renaissance Moral Theology*. Nashville: Vanderbilt University Press.

Bevington, David M. 1962. *From Mankind to Marlowe: Growth of Structure in the Popular Drama of Tudor England*. Cambridge, Mass.: Harvard University Press.

Biesterfeld, Peter W. 1936. *Die dramatische Technik Thomas Kyd: Studien zur inneren Struktur und szenische Form des elisabetanischen Drama*. Halle: Niemeyer.

Boas, F. S. 1940. *Christopher Marlowe: A Biographical and Critical Study*. Oxford: Clarendon Press.

Bowers, Fredson. 1940. *Elizabethan Revenge Tragedy*. Princeton: Princeton University Press.

Bradbrook, M. C. 1935. *Themes and Conventions of Elizabethan Tragedy*. Cambridge: Cambridge University Press.

Bradley, A. C. 1904. *Shakespearian Tragedy*. London: MacMillan, 1974.

Brady, P. 1972. "From Traditional Fallacies to Structural Hypotheses: Old and New Conceptions in Period-Style Research." *Neophilologus* 56: 1-11.

Bremond, Claude. 1964. "Le message narratif." *Communications* 4: 4-32.

_____. 1966. "La logique des possibles narratifs." *Communications* 8: 60-76.

_____. 1968. "Posterité américaine de Propp." *Communications* 11: 148-64.

_____. 1973. *Logique du récit*. Paris: Editions du Seuil.

Brockbank, J. P. 1962. *Marlowe: Doctor Faustus*. London: Arnold.

Brooke-Rose, Christine. 1980. "The Evil Ring: Realism and the Marvellous." *Poetics Today* 1, no. 4: 67-90.

154 □ REFERENCES

Brooks, Cleanth. 1947. "The Naked Babe and the Cloak of Manliness." In *The Well Wrought Urn*, pp. 22-49. New York: Harcourt, Harvest Book.
————. 1966. "The Unity of Marlowe's Doctor Faustus." In *Marlowe, Doctor Faustus: A Casebook*, edited by John Jump, pp. 208-221. London: MacMillan, 1969.
Brooks, Peter. 1977. "Freud's Masterplot," *Yale French Studies* 55-56: 280-300.
————. Forthcoming. "Narrative Desire." *Style*.
Bucker, A. 1964. "The Baroque S-T-O-R-M: A Study in the Limits of the Culture-Epoch Theory." *The Journal of Aesthetics and Art Criticism* 22: 103-313.
Burckhardt, Sigurd. 1968. *Shakespearian Meanings*. Princeton: Princeton University Press.
Burke, Kenneth. 1945. *A Grammar of Motives*. Englewood Cliffs, N. J.: Prentice-Hall.
Cavell, Stanley. 1976. *Must We Mean What We Say?* Cambridge: Cambridge University Press.
Chatman, Seymour. 1978. *Story and Discourse*. Ithaca, N.Y.: Cornell University Press.
Chomsky, Noam. 1956. "Three Models of the Description of Language." In *I. R. E. Transactions on Information Theory*, vol. IT-2, pp. 113-24.
————. 1957. *Syntactic Structures*. The Hague: Mouton.
————. 1963. "Formal Properties of Grammar." In *Handbook of Mathematical Psychology*, edited by D. R. Luce, vol. 12, pp. 187-94. New York: Wiley.
————. 1965. *Aspects of the Theory of Syntax*. Cambridge, Mass.: M.I.T. Press.
————. 1972. "Some Empirical Issues in the Theory of Transformational Grammar." In *Studies on Semantics in Generative Grammar*, pp. 120-202. The Hague: Mouton.
————. 1977. *Essays on Form and Interpretation*. New York: North-Holland.
————. 1980. *Rules and Representations*. New York: Columbia University Press.
Chomsky, Noam, and G. A. Miller. 1963. "Introduction to the Formal Analysis of Natural Languages." In *Handbook of Mathematical Psychology*, edited by D. R. Luce, R. Bush, and E. Galanter, vol. 2, pp. 269-321. New York: Wiley.
Clemen, Wolfgang. 1961. *English Tragedy before Shakespeare*. London: Methuen.
Colby, Benjamin N. 1966a. "Cultural Patterns in Narrative." *Science* 151: 793-98.
————. 1966b. "The Analysis of Culture Content and the Patterning of Narrative Concern in Texts." *American Anthropologist* 68: 374-88.
————. 1970. "The Description of Narrative Structures." In *Cognition: A Multiple View*, edited by Paul L. Garvin, pp. 172-92. New York: Spartan Books.
Cole, Douglas. 1962. *Suffering and Evil in the Plays of Christopher Marlowe*. Princeton: Princeton University Press.
Courtés, J. 1976. *Introduction à la sémiotique narrative et discursive*. Paris: Hachette.
Crane, R. S. 1953. *The Language of Criticism and the Structure of Poetry*. Toronto: The University of Toronto Press.
Culler, Jonathan. 1975. *Structuralist Poetics: Structuralism, Linguistics and the Study of Literature*. Ithaca, N.Y.: Cornell University Press.
Cupchik, G. C. 1974. "An Experimental Investigation of Perceptual and Stylistic Dimensions of Paintings Suggested by Art History." In *Studies in the New Experimental Aesthetics*, edited by D. E. Berlyne, pp. 235-57. New York: Wiley.
Dipple, Elizabeth. 1970. *Plot*. London: Methuen.
Doležel, Lubomír. 1976a. "Narrative Modalities." *Journal of Literary Semantics* 5, no. 1: 5-14.
————. 1976b. "Narrative Semantics." *PTL* 1: 129-51.
————. 1976c. "Narrative Worlds." In *Sound, Sign and Meaning*, edited by L. Matejka, pp. 542-53. Ann Arbor: Michigan Slavic Publications.
Doran, Madeleine. 1954. *Endeavors of Art: A Study of Form in Elizabethan Drama*. Madison: The University of Wisconsin Press.
Dorfman, Eugene. 1969. *Narreme in the Medieval Romance Epic: An Introduction to Narrative Structures*. Toronto: The University of Toronto Press.

Dundes, Alan. 1964. *The Morphology of North American Indian Folktales*. Helsinki: Academia Scientiarum Fenica.

Edwards, Philip. 1959. "The Theme and Structure of *The Spanish Tragedy*." In *Shakespeare's Contemporaries*, edited by M. Bluestone and N. Rabkin, pp. 44-55. Englewood Cliffs, N.J.: Prentice-Hall, 1961.

Eliade, Mircea. 1955. "Littérature orale." In *Histoire des littératures*, vol. 1: *Littératures anciennes et orales*. Encyclopédie de la Pléiade, edited by R. Queneau, pp. 3-26. Paris: Gallimard.

_____. 1958. *Rites and Symbols of Initiation: The Mysteries of Birth and Rebirth*. New York: Harper.

_____. 1963. *Aspects du mythe*. Paris: Gallimard.

Eliot, T. S. 1932. *Essays on Elizabethan Drama*. New York: Harcourt.

Ellis-Fermor, Ulla. 1927. *Christopher Marlowe*. London: Methuen.

Elton, W. R. 1966. *King Lear and the Gods*. San Marino, Ca.: Huntington Library.

Empson, William. 1935. "Double Plots: Heroic and Pastoral in the Main Plot and Sub-plot." In *Some Versions of the Pastoral*. London: Chatto & Windus.

_____ 1956. "The Spanish Tragedy." In *Elizabethan Drama: Modern Essays in Criticism*, edited by R. J. Kaufmann, pp. 60-80. New York: Oxford University Press, 1961.

Farnham, Willard. 1936. *The Medieval Heritage of Elizabethan Tragedy*. Berkeley: University of California Press; reprint, Oxford: Blackwell, 1963.

Fergusson, Francis. 1949. *The Idea of a Theater*. Princeton: Princeton University Press.

Fillmore, Charles. 1963. "The Position of Embedding Transformations in a Grammar." *Word* 19: 208-31.

_____. 1968. "The Case for Case." In *Universals in Linguistic Theory*, edited by E. Bach and R. T. Harms, pp. 1-90. New York: Holt, Rinehart and Winston.

_____. 1972. "On Generativity." In *Goals of Linguistic Theory*, edited by S. Peters, pp. 1-19. Englewood Cliffs, N.J.: Prentice-Hall.

Fish, Stanley. 1973. "What Is Stylistics and Why Are They Saying Such Terrible Things about It?" In *Approaches to Poetics*, edited by S. Chatman, pp. 109-52. New York: Columbia University Press.

Fotino, Stanca, and Solomon Marcus. 1978. "Les mecanismes génératifs du conte populaire: La Grammaire du conte." In *La sémiotique formelle du folklore: Approche linguistico-mathématique*, edited by Solomon Marcus, pp. 105-41. Paris: Klincksieck & Bucharest, Editura Academiei.

Freeman, Arthur. 1967. *Thomas Kyd: Facts and Problems*. Oxford: Clarendon Press.

Frost, William. 1952. "Shakespeare's Rituals and the Opening of *King Lear*." In *Shakespeare: The Tragedies. A Collection of Critical Essays*, edited by C. Leech, pp. 190-200. Toronto: The University of Toronto Press.

Frye, Northrop. 1967. *Fools of Time: Studies in Shakespearian Tragedy*. Toronto: University of Toronto Press.

Frye, R. M. 1956. "Marlowe's *Doctor Faustus*: The Repudiation of Humanity." In *Twentieth Century Interpretations of Doctor Faustus*, edited by W. Farnham, Englewood Cliffs, N.J.: Prentice-Hall, 1969.

_____. 1963. *Shakespeare and Christian Doctrine*. Princeton: Princeton University Press.

Genette, Gérard. 1972. *Figures III*. Paris: Seuil.

_____. 1983. *Nouveau discours du récit*. Paris: Seuil.

Gillet, Louis. 1940. "Arden of Feversham. In *Le Théâtre Elizabéthain*, edited by Georgette Camille and Pierre d'Exideuil, pp. 197-207. Paris: Corti.

Greimas, A. J. 1966. *Sémantique structurale*. Paris: Larousse.

156 □ REFERENCES

————. 1970. *Du sens*. Paris: Seuil.

————. 1977. "Elements of a Narrative Grammar." *Diacritics*, Spring 1977, pp. 23-40.

Greimas, A. J., and J. Courtés. 1976. "The Cognitive Dimension of Narrative Discourses." *New Literary History* 7: 433-38.

————. 1982. *Semiotics and Language: An Analytical Dictionary*. Bloomington: Indiana University Press.

Halliday, F. E. 1954. *The Poetry of Shakespeare's Plays*. London: Duckworth.

Hamon, Philippe. 1973. "Un discours contraint." In R. Barthes et al. *Littérature et réalité*, pp. 119-81. Paris: Seuil, 1982.

Harbage, Alfred. 1958. "*King Lear*: An Introduction." In *Shakespeare: The Tragedies. A Collection of Critical Essays*, edited by A. Harbage, pp. 113-22. Englewood Cliifs, N.J.: Prentice-Hall, 1964.

Hatzfeld, H. 1927. *Don Quijote als Kunstwerk*. Leipzig: Teubner.

————. 1955. "The Baroque from the Point of View of the Literary Historian." *The Journal of Aesthetics and Art Criticism* 14: 156-64.

Hays, David. 1964. "Dependency Theory: A Formalism and Some Observations." *Language* 40:211-25.

Hendricks, William O. 1976. *Grammars of Style and Styles of Grammar*. Amsterdam: North Holland.

————. 1977. "*A Rose for Emily*: A Syntagmatic Analysis." *PTL* 2: 257-95.

Heyl, Bernard. 1961. "Meanings of Baroque." *The Journal of Aesthetics and Art Criticism* 19: 275-87.

Hunter, G. K. 1965. "Ironies of Justice in *The Spanish Tragedy*." *Renaissance Drama* 8: 89-104.

Ihwe, Jens. 1970. "Kompetenz und Performanz in der Literaturtheorie." In *Texte, Bedeutung, Aesthetik*, edited by S. Schmidt, pp. 136-52. München: Bayerischer Schulbuch Verlag.

————. 1972. "On the Foundation of a General Theory of Narrative Structure." *Poetics* 3: 5-14.

Itkonen, Esa. 1975. "Concerning the Relationship between Linguistics and Logic." Indiana University Linguistic Club, mimeo.

Jackendoff, Ray. 1977a. $\bar{X}$ *Syntax: A Study of Phrase-Structure*. Cambridge, Mass.: M.I.T. Press.

————. 1977b. "Constraints on Phrase Structure Rules." In *Formal Syntax*, edited by P. Cullicover, T. Wasow, and A. Akmajian, pp. 249-83. New York: Academic Press.

Jakobson, Roman. 1960. "Linguistics and poetics." In *Style in Language*, edited by T. A. Sebeok, pp. 350-77. Cambridge, Mass.: M.I.T. Press.

————. 1970. "Subliminal Verbal Patterning in Poetry." In *Studies in General and Oriental Linguistics Presented to Shirô Hattori*, pp. 302-8. Tokyo: TEC.

Jakobson, Roman, and Lawrence G. Jones. 1970. *Shakespeare's Verbal Art in Th'expence of spirit*. The Hague: Mouton.

Jakobson, Roman, and Claude Lévi-Strauss. 1962. "*Les Chats* de Baudelaire." *L'homme* 2: 5-21.

Jewkes, W. T. 1958. *Act Division in Elizabethan and Jacobean Plays*. Hamden, Conn.: Shoe String Press.

Kintsch, W. 1977. "On Comprehending Stories." In *Cognitive Processes in Comprehension*, edited by M. Just and P. Carpenter, pp. 33-62. Hillsdale, N.J.: Erlbaum.

Knoll, Robert E. 1969. *Christopher Marlowe*. New York: Twayne.

Kocher, Paul H. 1946. *Chistopher Marlowe: A Study of His Thought, Learning and Character*. Chapel Hill: The University of North Carolina Press.

Labov, William, and J. Valetzky. 1967. "Narrative Analysis: Oral Versions of Personal Experience. In *Essays on the Verbal and Visual Arts*, edited by J. Helm, pp. 12-44. Seattle: American Ethnological Society.

Lakoff, George. 1972. "Structural Complexity in Fairy Tales." *The Study of Man* 1: 128-50.

Leech, Clifford, ed. 1964. *Marlowe: A Collection of Critical Essays*. Englewood Cliffs, N.J.: Prentice-Hall.

Levin, Harry. 1952. *The Overreacher: A Study of Christopher Marlowe*. Cambridge, Mass.: Harvard University Press.

Levin, Richard. 1971. *The Multiple Plot in English Renaissance Drama*. Chicago: The University of Chicago Press.

Lévi-Strauss, Claude. 1963. *Structural Anthropology*, translated from the French by C. Jacobson and B. Grundfest Schoepf. New York: Basic Books.

_____. 1964-1971. *Mythologiques*, vol. 1-4. Paris: Plon.

Lounsbury, Thomas R. 1901. *Shakespeare as a Dramatic Artist*. New Haven, Conn.: Yale University Press.

Lubbock, Percy. 1921. *The Craft of Fiction*. London: J. Cape.

Mack, Maynard. 1970. "*The Jacobean Shakespeare: Some Observations on the Construction of the Tragedies*." In *Modern Shakespearian Criticism*, edited by A. B. Kernan, pp. 323-50. New York: Harcourt.

Maranda, Pierre, and Elli Köngäs. 1971. *Structural Models in Folklore and Transformational Essays*. The Hague: Mouton.

Meehan, V. M. 1974. *Christopher Marlowe Poet and Playwright: Studies in Poetical Method*. The Hague: Mouton.

Moulton, Richard. 1893. *Shakespeare as Dramatic Artist*. Oxford: Clarendon Press.

Mueller, J. 1954. "Baroque—Is It a Datum, Hypothesis or Tautology?" *The Journal of Aesthetics and Art Criticism* 12: 421-37.

Murray, Peter B. 1969. *Thomas Kyd*. New York: Twayne.

Pavel, Silvia. 1975. "La prolifération narrative dans les *Mille et une nuits*." *The Canadian Journal of Research in Semiotics* 4: 21-40.

Pavel, Thomas G. 1973. "Remarks on Narrative Grammars." *Poetics* 8: 5-30.

_____. 1976a. *La syntaxe narrative des tragédies de Corneille*. Paris: Klincksieck and Ottawa: Editions de l'Université d'Ottawa.

_____1976b. "Possible Worlds in Literary Semantics." *The Journal of Aesthetics and Art Criticism* 34: 165-76.

_____. 1978. "Move-Grammar: Explorations in Literary Semiotics." In *Monographs, Working Papers and Prepublications of the Toronto Semiotic Circle*, vol. 4. Victoria University, Toronto.

_____. 1981. "Tragedy and the Sacred: Notes Towards a Semantic Characterization of a Fictional Genre." *Poetics* 10: 231-42.

_____. 1983. "Incomplete Worlds, Ritual Emotions." *Philosophy and Literature*, Spring 1983, pp. 48-58.

_____ Forthcoming. "Origin and Articulation." *Style*.

Petöfi, J., and H. Rieser, eds. 1973. *Studies in Text Grammar*. Dordrecht: Reidel.

Polanyi, Michael. 1966. *The Tacit Dimension*. Garden City, N.Y.: Doubleday.

Prince, Gerald. 1973. *A Grammar of Stories*. The Hague: Mouton.

_____. 1973b. "Introduction to the Study of the Narratee." In *Reader-Response Criticism*, edited by J. Tompkins, pp. 7-25. Baltimore: Johns Hopkins University Press, 1980.

_____. 1982. *Narratology*. The Hague: Mouton.

Propp, Vladimir. 1928. *Morphology of the Folktale*. Bloomington: Indiana Research Center in Anthropology, 1958.

Rapoport, Anatol. 1966. *Two-Persons Game Theory: The Essential Ideas*. Ann Arbor: The University of Michigan Press.
_____. 1974. *Fights, Games and Debates*. Ann Arbor: The University of Michigan Press.
Remak, H. H. H. 1971. "West European Romanticism: Definition and Scope." In *Comparative Literature: Method and Perspective*, edited by N. P. Stallknecht and H. Frenz, pp. 275-311. Edwardsville: Southern Illinois University Press.
Ribner, Irving. 1960. *Patterns in Shakespearian Tragedy*. London: Methuen.
Riffaterre, Michael. 1960. "Criteria for Style Analysis." *Word* 15: 154-74.
_____. 1971. *Essais de stylistique structurale*. Paris: Flammarion.
Robinson, Jane J. 1970. "Dependency Structures and Transformational Rules." *Language* 46: 259-85.
Rothstein, Eric. 1966. "Structure as Meaning in *The Jew of Malta*." *Journal of English and Germanic Philology* 65: 260-73.
Rumelhart, D. E. 1975. "Notes on a Schema for Stories." In *Representation and Understanding*, edited by D. Bobrow and A. Collins, pp. 211-36. New York: Academic Press.
_____. 1977. "Understanding and Summarizing Brief Stories." in *Basic Processes in Reading*, edited by D. LaBerge and S. J. Samuels, pp. 265-363. Hillsdale, N.J.: Erlbaum.
Ryan, Marie-Laurie. Forthcoming. "The Modal Structure of Narrative Universes." *Poetics Today*.
Sacks, Harvey. 1972. "On the Analyzability of Stories by Children." In *Directions in Sociolinguistics*, edited by John J. Gumperz and Dell Hymes, pp. 325-45. New York: Holt, Rinehart and Winston.
Schank, R. C. 1975. "The Structure of Episodes in Memory." In *Representation and Understanding*, edited by D. Bobrow and A. Collins, pp. 237-72. New York: Academic Press.
Scholes, Robert. 1974. *Structuralism in Literature*. New Haven: Yale University Press.
Spence, Leslie. 1927. "Taburlaine and Marlowe." *PMLA* 42: 604-22.
Spitzer, Leo. 1948. "Perspectivism in *Don Quijote*." In *Linguistics and Literary History*. Princeton University Press.
Steane, J. B. 1964. *Marlowe: A Critical Study*. Cambridge: Cambridge University Press.
Steinmann, Martin, Jr. 1977. "The Semiotics of Elizabethan Drama." Paper read at the Second Annual Conference of the Semiotic Society of America, Denver, October 1977, mimeo.
Stoll, E. E. 1933. *Art and Artifice in Shakespeare*. Cambridge: Cambridge University Press.
Suleiman, Susan. 1980. "Introduction." In *The Reader in the Text*, edited by S. Suleiman and I. Crossman, pp. 3-45. Princeton: Princeton University Press.
Summers, Claude J. 1974. *Christopher Marlowe and the Politics of Power*. Salzburg: Institut für Englische Sprache und Literatur, Universität Salzburg.
Sypher, W. 1955. *Four Stages of Renaissance Style*. New York: Doubleday.
Tesnière, L. 1959. *Eléments de syntaxe structurale*. Paris: Klincksieck.
Todorov, Tzvetan. 1966. "Les catégories du récit littéraire." *Communications* 8: 125-51.
_____. "Poétique." In *Qu'est que le structuralisme*, edited by O. Ducrot et al., pp. 99-166. Paris: Seuil. A modified version has been translated into English as *Introduction to Poetics*, trans. Richard Howard (Minneapolis: University of Minnesota Press, 1981).
_____. 1969. *La Grammaire du Décaméron*. The Hague: Mouton.
_____. 1971. *The Poetics of Prose*. English translation by Richard Howard. Ithaca, N.Y.: Cornell University Press, 1977.
_____. 1978. *Les genres du discours*. Paris: Seuil.
Van Dijk, T. A. 1972. *Some Aspects of Text Grammars*. The Hague: Mouton.
_____. 1973. "Grammaires textuelles et structures narratives. In *Sémiotique narrative et textuelle*, edited by C. Chabrol, pp. 177-207. Paris: Larousse, 1973.

_____. 1975. "Narrative Macro-Structure: Logical and Cognitive Foundations." University of Amsterdam, mimeo.

Van Dijk, T. A., et al. 1975. "Recalling and Summarizing Complex Discourse." University of Amsterdam, mimeo.

Venesoen, Constant. 1976. "*Athalie* ou le demi-échec de la théologie tragique." In *Racine: Mythe et Réalités*, edited by C. Venesoen, pp. 25-48. Société d'étude du XVIIIe siècle et Université de Western Ontario.

Von Wright, Georg H. 1963. *Norm and Action*. London: Routledge.

_____. 1971. *Explanation and Understanding*. London: Routledge.

Waith, Eugene M. 1962. *The Herculean Hero in Marlowe, Chapman, Shakespeare and Dryden*. London: Chatto & Windus.

Walzel, Oskar. 1916. "Shakespeares Dramatische Baukunst." In *Wege der Shakespeare-Forschung*, edited by K. Klein, pp. 103-37. Darmstadt: Wissenschaftliche Buchgesellschaft, 1971.

Warnke, Frank. 1972. *Versions of Baroque: European Literature in the 17th Century*. New Haven, Conn.: Yale University Press.

Wellek, René. 1963. "The Concept of Baroque in Literary Scholarship." In *Concepts of Criticism*. New Haven, Conn.: Yale University Press.

Welsford, Enid. 1935. *The Fool: His Social and Literary History*. London: Faber.

Wiatt, William H. 1958. "The Dramatic Function of the Alexandro-Villuppo Episode in *The Spanish Tragedy*." *Notes and Queries* 5: 327-29.

Wilson, F. P. 1953. *Marlowe and the Early Shakespeare*. Oxford: Clarendon Press.

Wine, M. L. 1973. "Introduction" to the *Tragedy of Master Arden of Feversham*, pp. xix-xcii. London: Methuen.

Wölfflin, Heinrich. 1915. *Principles of Art History: The Problem of the Development of Style in Later Art*. English translation, New York: Dover, 1950.

Index

Index

Action: propositions of, 14, 44, 45, 46, 128;
  beginning of, 25; classical theory of, 52;
  and gullibility maxim, 70; in *Arden of
  Feversham*, 97
Acts, division in, 142 n18
Aeschylus, 29
Agamemnon, 96
Alliance, 52, 66; maxims of, 52; in *King
  Lear*, 105-6, 113-14
Anna Karenina, 8
Anthony and Cleopatra, 127
Antigone, 95
Arabian Nights, The, 132
Arden of Feversham, 8, 40, 64, 92-98, 121,
  123; notes on, 147-48
Aristotle, 56
Asides, 71-72
Athalie, 3
Attributive elements, 56, 62, 142 n24
Author, and grammar of plot, 84, 126
Auxiliary, 18, 19, 32, 99, 106; in *Auxiliary*-
  leading, 32; in comedy, 33, 126; in
  Auxiliary-oriented plots, 124-25
Axiology: in axiological propositions, 45,
  128; and conflict, 61; and counter-
  normative maxims, 69; in *Tamburlaine II*,
  62; in *The Jew of Malta*, 69-70; in
  Edward the Second, 82-83

Bal, Mieke, 14, 35
Baldwin, T. W., 142
Baroque. *See* Style
Barthes, R., 8, 133, 141 n10, 142 n13
Battenhouse, R. W., 143 nn30 and 32, 144
  nn 37-38, 40, and 42
Baudelaire, C., 7
Bevington, D. M., 144 n36, 145 n52, 146
  nn61 and 64
Biesterfeld, P. W., 147
Boas, F. S., 144 n34, 145 n49, 146 n59
Boccaccio, 26
Bowers, F., 147 n65
Bradbrook, M. C., 146 n62
Bradley, A. C., 10, 148 nn79 and 83
Brady, P., 149 n92
Brecht, B., 95
Bremond, C., 13, 14, 17, 20, 22, 27, 44,
  133, 141 n10
Brockbank, J. P., 146
Brooke-Rose, Christine, 127
Brooks, C., 10, 146 n57
Brooks, P., 40
Büchner, G., 8
Bucker, A., 117
Burckhardt, S., 8

Canon, 3

Categories: narrative, 14, 16, 17, 122-26, 133, 149; poetic and stylistic, 116, 117, 118, 122; grammatical, and their labels, 133, 149
Cavell, S., 148 n84
Cervantes, Miguel de, 9
Characters, 8, 14; actants and roles, 14; main and secondary, 44; in folktales and tragedy, 97; good and evil, in *King Lear*, 106, 110; groups of, 106, 143
Chatman, S., 141 n10
Chats, Les, 7
Chomsky, N., 16, 30, 131, 133, 140 n2, 141 n8
Chronology. *See* Order; Transformations
Cid, Le, 14, 15
Classic style, 117
Clemen, W., 146 n62
Colby, B. N., 149-50 n97
Cole, D., 143 n25
Comedy, 33; and *Auxiliary* plots, 126
Competence, literary, 5, 140 n1
Conflict, 28, 79
Consecrating test, 36
Constituent trees, 18, 131, 132-33; generalized, 131; narrative, 18
Conventions, 46; the Calumniator Credited, 110, 145 n54, 148 n79
Courtés, J., 41
Crane, R. S., 148 n79
Criticism: logical construction of, 91; textual, and plot analysis, 74
Crossman, I., 141 n4
Culler, Jonathan, 140 n1, 141 nn4 and 7
Cupchik, G. C., 149 n87
Cyzarz, H., 149 n88

Deception, 66
Denouement: fallacious, 79; syntactic, 107; general, 107
Description: requirements for, 3; structural, 4-5, 115; and interpretation, 9-10
Disguise, in *King Lear*, 106, 110
Doctor Faustus, 72-78, 93, 94, 121, 126, 127, 146 n57
Doležel, Lubomir, 13, 14, 43, 45, 46
Domains. *See* Narrative domains
Dominance: relation of, 30, 132, 142, n19, 149 n96; narrative interpretation of, 132, 135
Don Quixote, 9

Doran, M., 143 n25
Dorfman, E., 133, 142 n13
Dundes, A., 133

Edward the Second, 78-84, 95, 119, 121, 125, 126, 146 nn61 and 62
Edwards, P., 147 n68
Elements, attributive. *See* Attributive elements
Eliade, M., 149 n85
Eliot, T. S., 8, 125, 145 n44
Ellis-Fermor, U., 143 n31, 145 n50
Elton, W. R., 148 n82
Embedding: of *Moves*, 30; of stories, 131-32
Empson, W., 8, 118, 147 n71
Enjambment, 10
Episodes: unattached, 58; in *Doctor Faustus*, 72-75; structure and textual deformation, 74; iterative, 74-75; epistemic function of, 88, 90; weak integration of, 119, 144 n37; and *De Casibus* tragedies, 143 n25; in morality plays, 144 n36
Epistemic center, 60
Epistemic closeness and secrecy, 90-91, 95, 112
Epistemic conflict, 112
Epistemic medium in tragedy, 96
Epistemic openness, 48, 109-10
Epistemic partition, 48, 49
Epistemic perspective, 71, 91
Epistemic point of view, 68
Epistemic propositions: in *Tamburlaine I*, 48; in *Tamburlaine II*, 59-60; in *The Jew of Malta*, 66-68; in *Edward the Second*, 82; in *The Spanish Tragedy*, 90; in *King Lear*, 109-10
Epistemic structure, 110-11
Epistemic suspense, 67-68
Ermatinger, E., 149 n88
Evaluation, types of, 3
Events: essential vs. nonessential, 32; and chronology, 34-35
Everyman, 57
Exemplary structure, 76
Exemplum, 50, 76, 119, 121
Explanation and understanding, 7
Expression, laws of, in *King Lear*, 111-12
Expressionism, German, 8

Farnham, W., 143 n25

Fergusson, F., 148 n79
Fillmore, C., 131, 133, 141 n8
Fish, S., 141 n5
Folktales: grammars of, 11-12; and *King Lear*, 99-100
Fotino, S., 11, 12
Freeman, A., 147 n70
Frost, W., 148 n83
Frye, N., 149 n85
Frye, R. M., 72, 148 n82
Functions, Proppian, 54-55, 116

Games, language. *See* Language games
Genette, G., 14, 15, 35
Gillet, L., 147 n75
Goethe, J. W., 72
Grammar: formal, 5; generative, 5-6, 11-12, 13; context-free, 11, 16; of narrative and plot, 11, 12, 13, 16, 21, 115-16, 131; literary, 12; dependency, 14, 42, 149 n96; intuition and, 15, 16, 115; regular, 16; of plot and author, 84, 126; and style, 126
— transformational-generative, 16, 131-35; recursivity, 131-32; base component, 131
Greimas, A. J., 13, 14, 34, 41, 42, 43, 133, 141 n10, 142 nn16 and 21

Halliday, F. E., 141 n6
Hamlet, 12, 37, 74, 95, 127
Hamon, P., 127
Harbage, A., 149 n85
Hatzfeld, H., 9
Hays, D., 149 n96
Hendricks, W. O., 14, 43, 143 n27
Heyl, B., 117, 149 n93
Holinshed, 147, 148 n78
Homer, 22
Hübscher, A., 149 n88

Ihwe, J., 140 n1, 141 n9
Index: *Move*-numbering, 28-30, 133; time, 35; character, 43-44, 133-34
Interpretation, 9, 47; and description, 9-10
Intuitions, and grammar, 15, 16, 115
Itkonen, E., 140 n2

Jackendoff, R., 141 n11
Jakobson, R., 4, 7, 9, 140 n3
Jew of Malta, The, 62-72, 85, 91, 119, 121, 126, 144-46 nn43-55

Jewkes, W. T., 142 n18
Jones, L. G., 4

Kafka, Franz, 127
King Lear, 17-20, 38, 99-114, 119, 121-22, 124, 125, 127, 148-49 nn79-85
Kintsch, W., 141 n10
Knoll, R. E., 142 n24
Knowledge: tacit, 6-7, 10-11, 12; emergent, 7, 11-12; narrative, 12
Kocher, P. H., 144 n35
Köngäs, E., 18, 141 n10
Kyd, Thomas, 85-92, 94, 97

Labov, W., 141 n10
Lack, 40
Lakoff, G., 141 n10, 142 n15
Lamb, Charles, 99
Language games, 6
Leech, C., 144 n33
Levin, H., 72, 142 n23, 143 n33, 144 nn37 and 43, 145 nn 44, 46, and 48, 147 n65
Levin, R., 118, 148 n80
Lévi-Strauss, C., 4, 7, 34, 142 n16
Literary properties, 8
Literature, as rule-governed institution, 5, 9
Lounsbury, T. R., 148 n79
Love, maxims of, 83-84
Lubbock, P., 85

Macbeth, 37, 127
Machiavellism, 69-70, 113
Mack, M., 148 n79
Madness, narrative function in *King Lear*, 110
Main test, 36
Maranda, P., 17-18, 133, 141 n10
Marcus, S., 11-12
Marlowe, Christopher, 24-84, 85, 92, 94, 97, 125, 126
Maxims. *See* Alliance; Love; Power; Propositions
Meehan, V. M., 143 n31
Miller, G. A., 131
Morality plays, 56, 77
Moulton, R., 148 n79
Move: definition, 17, 18, 19; numbering of, 28-30; embedding, 30-33; major, 94; final, 102; formal definition, 131. *See also* Plot
Move-structure, 36, 38; as a syntactic object,

41; core segments, 74; soft segments, 74
Movement, and stagnation in plot, 107, 108
Mueller, J., 117
Murray, P. B., 147 n69
Myth, and language, 4
Mythocentrism, 50
Mythologiques, 4

Narrative: embedding, 13; possibility, 13; program, 13; semantics, 14, 24, 42, 47, 126-27; trees, 15, 18, 23-24, 31, 42; syntax, 15, 26, 41-42; propositions, 23-24, 43; flexibility, 26; plot-significant semantic elements, 50; semantics and plot-structure in *Doctor Faustus*, 75. *See also* Grammar; Plot
Narrative domains, 13, 15, 44; syntactic, 44-45; semantic, 44-45, 50-51; semantically homogeneous, 45; semantically partitioned, 45; logical properties of semantic, 46; book of, 50-51; semantic openness of, 51; plot-relevance of, 51; semantic focus of, 51; passive, 94
Narrative impact: direct, 27, 142; contingent, 27, 142
Narrative modalities, 45; and anthropological notions, 46-47; and logical modalities, 46-47
Narrative unity, 56; and complexity, 118-22
Narratology, 14-15
New Criticism, 10
Nontectonic form. *See* Tectonic form

Oedipus Rex, 8, 22, 23
Ontology, 45; propositions of, 45; and homogeneity, 47; center and periphery of, 77; medieval, 77; the natural and supernatural, 77, 88, 127; and realism, 127
— in plays: *Tamburlaine I*, 47; in *Tamburlaine II*, 59; in *The Spanish Tragedy*, 88; in *King Lear*, 108
Order: abstract, of events, 22, 28; textual, 22, 33, 35; logical, 28; chronological, 28, 33-35, 37, 135, 142; of constituents in a tree, 33-35; of episodes, 36
Oresteia, 29, 40
Ornamental devices, 50

Pavel, S., 132
Pavel, T., 14, 15, 29, 47, 116, 141 n10, 142, nn15 and 16, 143 n26

Perspective: and ambiguity of plot, 76, 135; local and dominant, 135
Petöfi, J., 141 n9
Pfandl, L., 149 n88
Plot: and game theory, 14; as language, 15; simple, 26; internally motivated, 48; as sequence of functions and as hierarchy, 55, 116, 134; ambiguity and perspective, 76, 135; plot-types and their use by Marlowe, 80-82; its understanding, 85; and character, 90; secondary, 99, 104-5, 119-22; stagnation in, and movement, 107, 108; definition of, 118; overplot, 147. *See also* Grammar; *Move*; Narrative
Plot-analysis, and criticism, 74
Polanyi, M., 6
Polemical configurations, 29, 30, 55, 57, 66, 78, 81, 99, 100, 102, 103, 125, 134; their *vendetta* structure, 57; absence of, 94; in *King Lear*, 125-26
Power, maxims of, 48-49; reasonable vs. demonic, 49; diagnosis and overestimation of adversaries, 49, 95; in *Tamburlaine I*, 51-52; in *Tamburlaine II*, 60-61, 62; in *Edward the Second*, 83; in *King Lear*, 100, 113
Precedence: relation of, 33-36; abstract narrative, 34
Prince, G., 13, 14, 141 n4, 142 n15
Problem, 17, 18, 119
Problem-creating situation, 40
Problem-leading, 32
Propositions, as general regularities, 46, 47
Propp, V., 17, 54, 116, 133, 141 n10, 142 n21, 148 n79
Proppian functions. *See* Functions, Proppian
Providence, as narrative agent, 48
Pseudo-plot, 118-22; clown subplots, 119-22; lateral developments, 122; exampla, 119-22

Qualifying test, 36

Racine, J., 3, 8, 22
Rapoport, A., 145 n47
Reader: average, 7, 8; ideal, 141
Recursivity, in transformational-generative grammar, 131-32
Regularities. *See* Propositions; Structural regularities
Remak, H. H. H., 149 n149

Repetition, 93. *See also* Episodes; *Solution*

Revenge, 69, 88, 99, 103; unrestrained, 86; simple vs. generalized, 89-90; and *Solution*-plots, 124, 126

Revenger's Tragedy, The, 40, 124, 125, 126

Rhythm, 9-10; and meter, 9-10; dramatic, 37, 71. *See also* Tempo

Ribner, H., 148 n81

Rieser, H., 141 n9

Riffaterre, M., 7

Robinson, J. J., 149 n96

Rothstein, E., 145 nn45 and 53

Rousset, J., 149 n88

Rules, 6-7; normative, 6, 7, 11; abstract, 10, 11, 12, 15; context-free, 16, 21; transformation, 16, 21, 22; of *Move*-grammar, 21

Rummelhart, D. E., 14, 141 n10, 142 n17

Ryan, M.-L., 13, 14, 43, 45

Sacks, H., 141 n10

Sandor Viteaz, 11-12

Schmidt, S., 141 n9

Scholes, R., 141 n10

Semantics. *See* Narrative domains

Seven against Thebes, 95

Shakespeare, William, 8, 9, 10, 15, 64, 71, 99-114, 118, 126, 127, 148 n79

Shank, R., 141 n10

Simplicity, structural, 64

Solution, 17, 18, 19, 20, 31; Bremond-stages, 20, 22, 27, 44; *Pro-* and *Counter-* 21, 94; *Principle of Postponement*, 31, 142; elements that lead to it, 31, 32; *Solution*-generalization transformation, 78-79; *Hubris-Solution*, 80; provisory, 93; and denouement, 107; repetitive, 122; cumulative, 122-23; algorithmic, 123-24; *Solution*-oriented plots, 122-24

Sophocles, 34

Space, 71; in *King Lear*, 108-9

Spanish Tragedy, The, 8, 48, 85-92, 119, 121, 124, 127, 147 nn65-78 *passim*

Spitzer, Leo, 9

Steane, J. B., 143 n32, 144 n35, 145 n52, 146 n60

Steinmann, M., Jr., 148 n79

Stoll, E. E., 46, 110, 145 n54, 147 n77, 148 79

Strategy: group, in *King Lear*, 106

Structural regularities, 3, 9, 118; and analysis of stories, 13

Structuralism, linguistic, 4

Style, 116; classic, 117; baroque; 117-18, 122; and grammar, 126

Suleiman, S., 141 n4

Summers, C. J., 142 n23, 143 n29, 145 n51

Suspense, narrative and epistemic, 67-68, 145 n47

Syntax. *See* Grammar; Narrative; Narrative domains

Sypher, W., 149 n93

Task, 32; in tragedy, 33

Tamburlaine I, 65, 80, 85, 113, 119, 121, 122, 126, 127, 135, 142-43 nn17-26 *passim*

Tamburlaine II, 54-62, 64, 65, 143-44 nn17-26 *passim*

Tectonic form, 118, 119, 122

Tempo: narrative, 65, 71; scenic, 66

Tesnière, L., 42, 149 n96

Text, 12; and *Move*-structure, 37; plot-reinforcing and counter-plot emphasis on, 38

Todorov, T., 13, 14, 23, 41, 43, 46, 133, 141 n10, 142 n14

Tourneur, Cyril, 124

Tragedy, 33; and susceptibility, 95; as epistemic medium, 96; and *Tribulations*, 100

Tragic flaw, 80; dumbness as, 95

Transformations: *Episode-Attachment*, 22, 88; *Solution*-generalization, 22, 78, 79; *In Medias Res*, 22, 23; chronological, 34; terminological problems, 142 n14

Trees. *See* Constituent trees; Narrative

Tribulations, 100, 121; and suffering on stage, 100, 103

Unamuno, Miguel de, 9

Understanding and explanation, 7

Valetzky, J., 141 n10

Van Dijk, T., 13, 141 nn9 and 10; 142 n20

Venesoen, C., 8

Violation, 40, 57-58; explicit, 57; involuntary, 57-58; fuzzy, 58

Voltaire, 3

Von Wright, G., 46, 140 n2

Waith, E. M., 144 n38

Walzel, O., 118, 119, 149 n93

Warnke, F., 149 n88
Webster, J., 64, 124
Wellek, René, 117
Welsford, Enid, 148 n81
White Devil, The, 124
Wiatt, W. H., 147 n66

Wilson, F. P., 146 n63
Wine, M., L., 147 nn72 and 73
Wittgenstein, L., 6
Wölfflin, H., 117, 149 nn86 and 87

Zeitgeist, 118, 122

A native of Rumania, **Thomas Pavel** was educated at the University of Bucharest and at the Ecole des Hautes Etudes en Sciences Sociales in Paris, where he received a Ph.D. in 1971. He is now professor of literature at the Université du Québec à Montréal. Pavel is the author of *La syntaxe narrative des tragédies de Corneille, Hésitations de voix*, and a novel, *Le miroir persan*.

Wlad Godzich teaches comparative literature at the Université de Montréal and is co-editor, with Jochen Schulte-Sasse, of the series Theory and History of Literature.